THE PLANTAGENET CHRONICLES

THE PLANTAGENET CHRONICLES

1154–1485

DEREK WILSON

METRO BOOKS
NEW YORK

HENRY II

HENRICVS.
II,

The kings who ruled from 1154 to 1485 took their name from the heraldic device of Geoffrey of Anjou, the founder of the line – a sprig of yellow broom, known in Latin as *planta genista*. The earlier rulers of the dynasty were also known as Angevins (from Anjou). Geoffrey never actually ruled England. He had extensive territories in what is now France but only held England in the name of his wife, Matilda.

The complex family rivalries that form the background of Henry's accession began with the death without a male heir of his grandfather, Henry I. It was the late king's wish that his daughter, Matilda, should inherit the crown, and by marrying her to Geoffrey he created an extensive bloc of territories extending from the Scottish border to the Pyrenees, and his intention was that the son of Matilda and Geoffrey, christened Henry, should ultimately enjoy undisputed control of this extensive empire.

Unfortunately, several of England's powerful barons were not prepared to accept the rule of a woman, and they offered the crown to Stephen (who had been brought up at Henry's court), the only available legitimate grandson of William the Conqueror. The result was almost two decades of internal chaos. Rival baronial armies fought for Stephen and Matilda, and the Scots and Welsh took advantage of England's weakness to invade. Monastic chroniclers lamented the appalling state of the country and, because their prayers seemed to avail nothing, they called this a period when 'Christ and his

LEFT **Geoffrey of Anjou**, *the father of Henry II, gave his name to the Angevin line of English kings. This portrait plaque, a rare artefact of enamel on copper, is from Geoffrey's tomb and is contemporaneous with his death (1151).*

OPPOSITE **Matilda** *was married as a child to the Emperor Henry V and, after his death in 1125, to Geoffrey of Anjou. She was a benefactress of St Albans Abbey and, in this miniature of 1380, is shown holding an abbey charter.*

PREVIOUS PAGES **The seal** *of Henry II (1133–89) and* **portrait of Henry II** *from a 17th-century oil painting.*

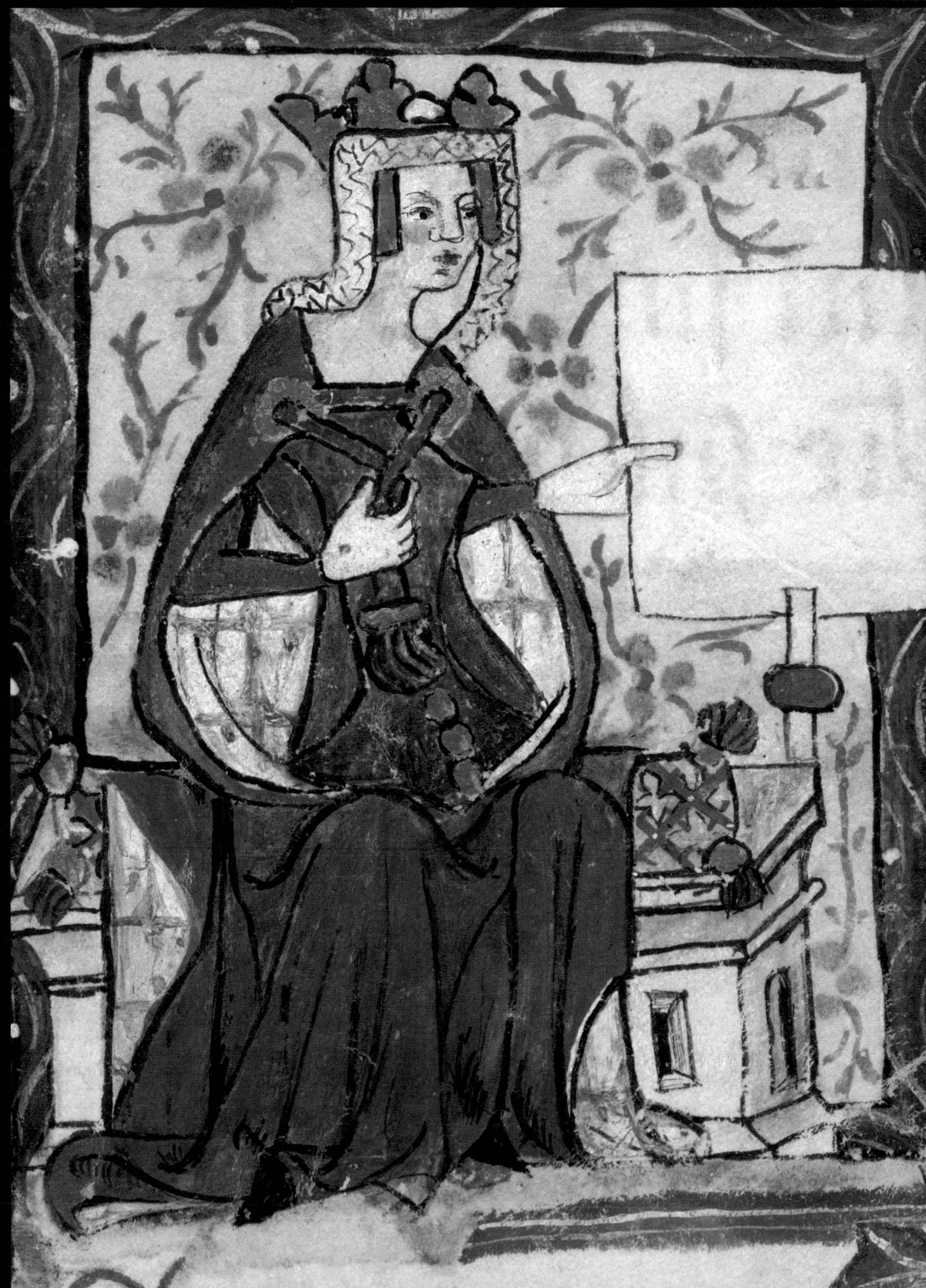

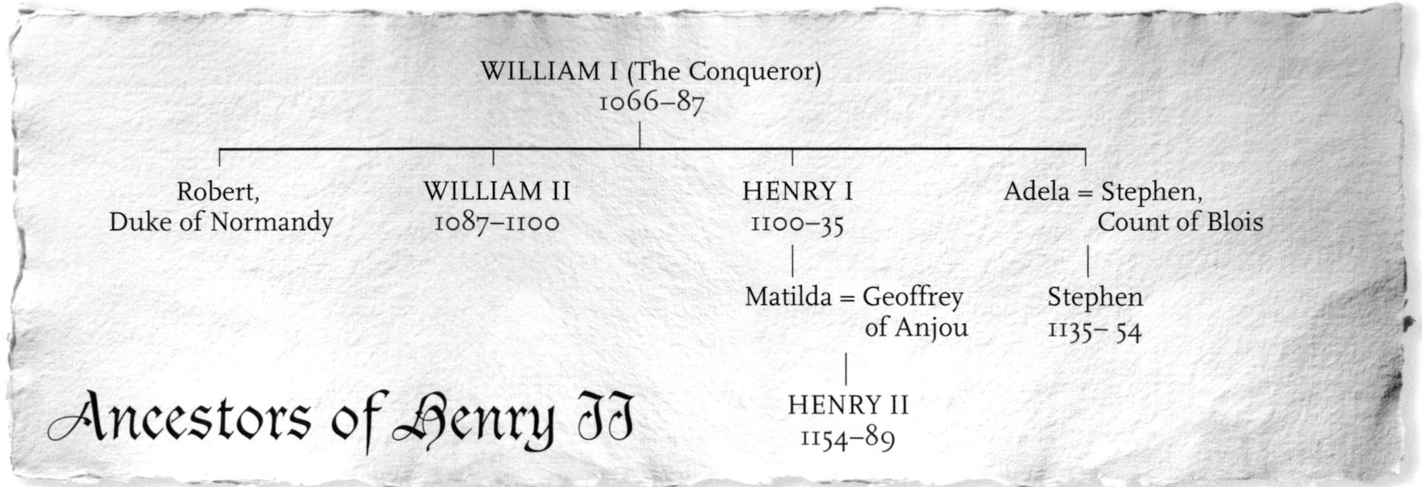

Ancestors of Henry II

Know that I have granted to my citizens of Winchester all the privileges which they had in the time of Henry my grandfather. And I order that they have and hold all their purchases and pledges and their tenements according to the custom of the city, as freely, quietly and honourably as ever they did in the time of King Henry. And if other customs have unjustly arisen in the war let them be suppressed.

WINCHESTER CHARTER, *c.*1156

saints slept'. In 1153, after another exhausting military campaign, Stephen and Henry reached an accord in the Treaty of Wallingford. Henry was acknowledged as king of England but Stephen would be regent for his lifetime. Stephen died the following year. Henry had already entered into his continental inheritance on the death of his father (1151), and he was, at last, able to assume the rule of the considerable territory his grandfather had planned that he should have. His first task was to restore peace and good order to his English domains.

1154–8

AT THE AGE OF 21 Henry was a vigorous, ambitious, no-nonsense young king, who enjoyed military campaigns and had little interest in the pomp and ceremony of kingship. He was energetic and impulsive, but, when necessary, he exhibited great mental stamina, worked long hours and needed little sleep.

Henry hastened to pay homage to Louis VII, his nominal feudal overlord, before crossing the Channel to deal with his troublesome English subjects, and his decisive action took most of his opponents by surprise. He expelled the Flemish mercenaries on whom Stephen had had to rely and forced barons to dismantle the castles they had built without royal licence. By the end of 1155 he had restored a semblance of order and sound administration to much of the country, but he then had to return to sort out problems in his French possessions. The need to maintain personal control of lands separated by 20 miles of sea was a basic problem with which Henry had to contend throughout his reign. In 1157 he was back to root out the last vestiges of opposition and obliged King Malcolm IV of Scotland to restore lands that he had recently claimed. The chronicler William of Newburgh laconically remarked: 'The king of England had the better of the argument by reason of his greater power.'[1]

The Welsh princes posed a more difficult problem. English barons who controlled the Marches (the borderlands) were perennially locked in territorial competition with the Welsh rulers who, at the same time, were trying to extend their boundaries eastwards. During the previous reign Owain, prince of Gwynedd, in north Wales, had expanded his territory and expelled many English settlers.

Contrary Henry

If the king has said *he will remain in a place for a day – and particularly if he has announced his intention publicly by the mouth of a herald – he is sure to upset all the arrangements by departing early in the morning. And you then see men dashing around as if they were mad, beating packhorses, running carts into one another – in short, giving a lively imitation of Hell. If, on the other hand, the king orders an early start, he is sure to change his mind, and you can take it for granted that he will sleep until midday. Then you will see the packhorses loaded and waiting, the carts prepared, the courtiers dozing, traders fretting and everyone grumbling.*

LETTER OF PETER OF BLOIS, *c.*1177, *PATROLOGIA LATINA*, 1844–55, CCVII, P. 48

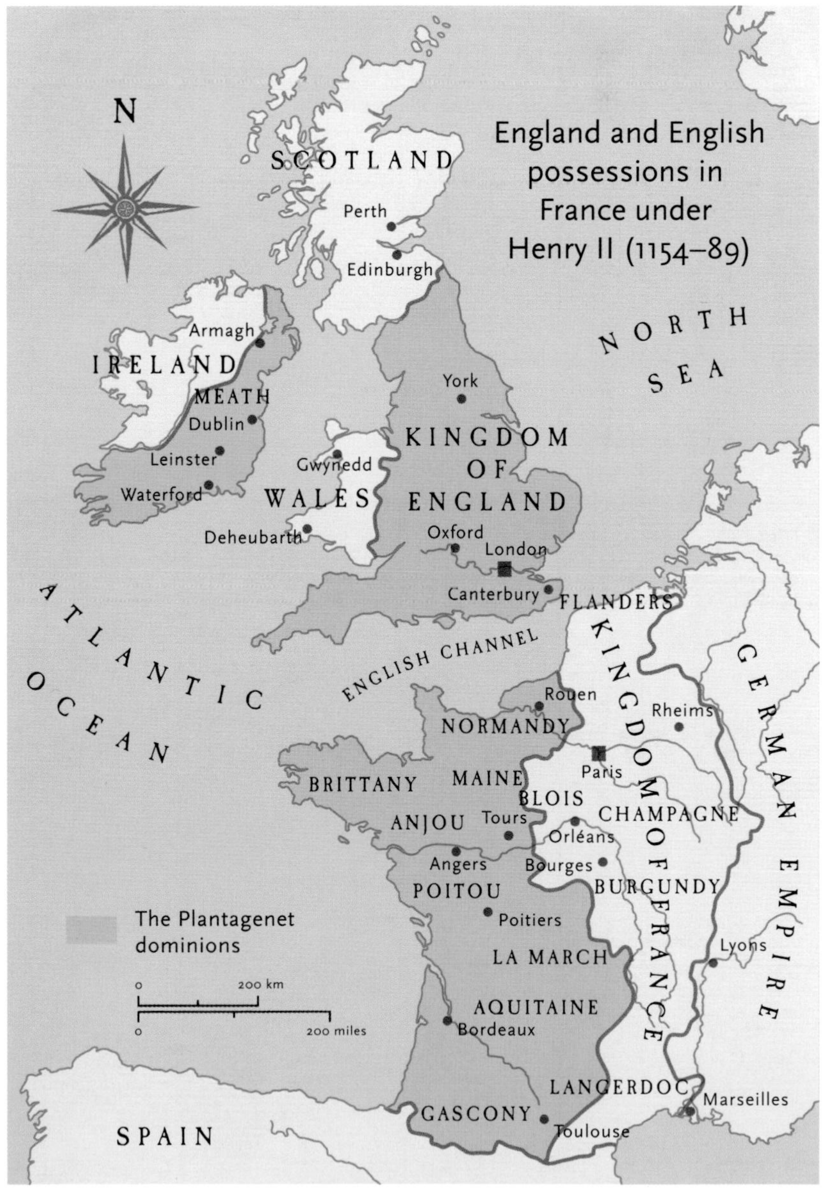

RIGHT **At the height of his power Henry II** *ruled an empire that stretched from Hadrian's Wall to the Pyrenees. But he and his successors were constantly under pressure from two directions. The kings of France repeatedly attempted to bring parts of this empire under their direct control and regional rulers struggled for independence from their Plantagenet overlords (often with help from Paris).*

1159–69

HENRY WAS DETERMINED to reinforce the power of the crown permanently. This meant securing all his frontiers and asserting royal justice over the law courts, which were operated by the barons and the church. But he was not content simply to consolidate and rule effectively his inherited lands. He saw himself as the most powerful ruler of western Christendom. His mother, Matilda, had by her first marriage, been empress of the Holy Roman Empire and had been much involved by her husband in the administration of his vast territory. Henry, eager to show himself more than the equal of King Louis of France and the Emperor Frederick, was always on the lookout for ways of extending his own boundaries. Half of his considerable estates in western France had come to him on his marriage to Eleanor of Aquitaine in 1152. She had a claim to the county of Toulouse, which extended from Aquitaine to the Mediterranean coast and which controlled some of the most vital trade routes in Europe.

In 1159, when Count Raymond V of Toulouse declined to recognize Henry's overlordship, Henry gathered an enormous army to enforce his will. He levied taxes to pay for foreign mercenaries, and he obliged all his feudal barons to attend him with their own armed retainers. These included King Malcolm of Scotland and one of the Welsh princes. Henry's great army successfully fought its way southwards to the very gates of Toulouse. But there it stopped. Early in 1160 Louis VII arrived in Toulouse to support Raymond (who was married to his daughter). Henry was stymied; according to the feudal code anyone taking arms against his overlord was guilty of rebellion, and Henry was obliged to call off the siege. By the terms of the truce reached in May 1160 he lost much of his recently conquered territory. This marked the limit of Henry's territorial expansion, but it nevertheless established him as the most influential ruler in Europe, and he often acted as arbiter in the disputes that sprang up between rival monarchs.

Henceforth, Henry concentrated on strengthening control of his own lands and modernizing their administration. He knew that effective kingship depended on both personal contact with his people and a trusted network of officials to carry out his will, and he travelled constantly throughout his extensive dominions.

OPPOSITE **The marriage of Eleanor of Aquitaine to Louis VII of France** *and Louis' departure on the Second Crusade. Illustration from the 14th-century* Chroniques de France ou de St Denis (1375-1400). *Eleanor was about 15 when she was married to the French king who was of a similar age (1137). She performed her queenly duties faithfully, gave birth to two daughters and accompanied her husband on crusade in 1146. She enjoyed the adventure of travel and warfare, especially the company of lusty knights. Louis alleged his wife's adultery as cause for the dissolution of the marriage in 1152. It was Eleanor's subsequent marriage to Henry of Normandy and Anjou (the future Henry II of England) that lay at the root of the long conflict between the two monarchs. Louis had annexed his wife's duchy of Aquitaine to the French crown but now it passed to his rival.*

du Roy dangleterre a mortemer en hors

De la venue saint thomas de cantorbie en france au pape alixandre xiiij

En ce meismes an saint thomas de cantorbire senfouy exilles dangleterre et vint en france Et en lan mil C lxiiij fut il sa

1170–74

IN MAY 1170 the 37-year-old king made his biggest mistake, setting in train events that ended in tragedy and blackened his name for posterity. He had his eldest son, Henry, crowned by the Archbishop of York. This reinforced his promise to divide his inheritance, but it was also a deliberate sign of defiance to Becket and Louis. It angered Becket because to preside at coronations was the prerogative of the Archbishop of Canterbury. It annoyed Louis because his daughter, Margaret, who was the wife of the young Henry, was excluded from the ceremony. Henry II was making it clear that any reconciliation would be on his terms. Becket protested vigorously at his treatment and was backed by the pope, who threatened to excommunicate Henry.

On 22 July 1170, Becket and the king met at Fréteval, on the road between Tours and Chartres, and some kind of reconciliation took place, but the personal animosity between the two men remained as strong as ever. Henry was in no hurry to let the archbishop return, and it was 30 November before Becket, on his own initiative, crossed the Channel. His attempt to restore his authority led to fresh conflicts with bishops and secular lords, and these were reported back to Henry at his Normandy manor near Bayeux. He gave vent to his anger in the presence of several of his retainers, though it is doubtful that he uttered the words, 'Will no one rid me of this turbulent priest?' Be that as it may, four of Henry's household knights took it upon themselves to be the king's avenging angels. They hurried back to England and, on 20 December 1170, murdered Becket in his own cathedral.

News of the outrage shocked Europe, and no one was more upset than Henry, who realized the negative effect it would have on his standing inside and outside his own dominions. It handed Pope Alexander III a propaganda initiative, and in order to recover the church's goodwill Henry was obliged to negotiate. By the Compromise of Avranches (May 1172) he had to relax some of the Constitutions of Clarendon relating to the power of the bishops and their courts. In August he did public penance for Becket's death and received absolution.

It seemed to many of Henry's subjects that the overmighty king, who had for years been increasing royal power at the expense of the barons and bishops, had,

OPPOSITE **Thomas Becket meets Pope Alexander III.** *A painting on vellum from* Le Speculum Historiale *by Vincent de Beauvais (c.1190–1264). Vincent was a Dominican monk and a scholar who had a truly prodigious literary output. The* Speculum Historiale, *just one of his works, was a catalogue of all human history known in France at that time. It ran to 1,400 double-column pages. The story of Becket was obviously considered an important part of human history. During Becket's self-imposed exile he appealed to Alexander III (1159–81), a hard-line pope who agreed with the archbishop's stance regarding the independence of the church. However, Alexander had to consider very carefully the political relations of the papacy with European monarchs. Vincent's picture suggests that Becket knew the power of money in eliciting papal support.*

Becket's murder

A letter of William, Archbishop of Sens, to Pope Alexander III about the murder of Becket:

'The king of the English, that enemy to the angels and the whole body of Christ, has wrought his spite on that holy one. Arise thou man of God, and put on the strength of the successors of Peter; smite thou son of smiters ... For of all the crimes we have ever read or heard of, this easily takes first place – exceeding all the wickedness of Nero, the perfidy of Julian, and even the sacrilegious treachery of Judas.'

ROGER OF HOWDEN, *GESTA REGIS HENRICI SECUNDI*, ED. W. STUBBS, 1867, I, PP. 15–26

at last, overreached himself and been humbled. This was not Henry's view of things. In fact, he spent the autumn and winter of 1171–2 extending his empire still further. In September he assembled an army of 4,000 troops on the Welsh coast for an invasion of Ireland, a project he had been planning for a long time. In 1166 he had taken under his protection the deposed king of Leinster, Diarmait Mac Murchadha. This native ruler died in May 1171, and thc man who took his place as self-appointed leader was his son-in-law, Richard de Clare, known to his followers as Strongbow, an immigrant knight from Wales.

It was to prevent de Clare becoming the powerful head of a potentially rival state that Henry now decided to act. So impressive was Henry's show of force that all the native and immigrant leaders of eastern and southern Ireland did homage to him without a battle being fought. Strongbow was forced to acknowledge Henry as his liege lord and received from the king's hands fresh grants of the lands he already held. Henry strengthened the existing fortifications, arranged for the building of new castles and installed Hugh de Lacy at Dublin as his viceroy. He also established a colony of Bristol merchants in the city and thus set in train its rise to the status of an important and prosperous commercial centre.

In the spring of 1172 Henry returned to the continent to make his peace with the pope, but the church was not his only problem. By now his enemies were multiplying. They included his own family. The coronation of young Henry had been a means of keeping control of England while the king was elsewhere, and the boy had only been given

LEFT **Pope Alexander III**. *An illuminated capital from the Charter of Marchiennes, (1157). Alexander, the pope to whom Becket turned for support, was born Rolando Bardinelli and became pope in 1159. Like Becket he knew what it was to be a religious exile, having been forced to flee Rome twice because of conflict with the Emperor Frederick Barbarossa.*

OPPOSITE **The murder of Becket**. *The archbishop's death caused a long-lasting storm of controversy throughout Europe. This illustration is from the French* Playfair Book of Hours, *(late 15th century).*

minimum power and resources. Now aged 18, he decided that he wanted to be king in reality, and discontented barons and churchmen were only too ready to make him a figurehead for a revolt against the 'tyrant' Henry II. When, early the next year, the king angrily refused, his son fled for support to the court of Louis VII. He was joined by his brothers, Richard and Geoffrey. Their mother, Queen Eleanor, tried to follow, disguised as a man, but Henry's officers discovered her and returned her to her husband, who had her placed under close – and permanent – guard. Henceforth, wherever she lived she was virtually a prisoner.

The years 1173 and 1174 were those of the 'great war'. Henry's realms were convulsed by conflict because all his enemies sensed that the time was right to make a concerted strike against a king who had, as they believed, taken too much power into his own hands. The opposition was led by Louis VII, and he was supported by Henry's sons, the counts of Blois, Flanders and Boulogne, the king of Scotland and numerous English barons, of whom the most prominent was Robert de Beaumont, Earl of Leicester. With armed revolt occurring simultaneously in several parts of his dominions it was extremely difficult for the king to organize effective military response. That he did so is proof of his clear thinking and of his forceful character. His brilliant campaign tactics included a forced march right across Normandy in two days, which took the rebels of Brittany completely by surprise. With his continental enemies in confusion Henry offered talks with his sons, but they remained obdurate, knowing as they did that Henry's resources were stretched to the uttermost. This meant that he was unable to cross the Channel to attend personally to the situation in England.

There his deputy, Richard de Lucy, was confronted by a north–south divide. The area to the north of a diagonal line from Felixstowe to Chester was controlled by disaffected barons. He invested the principal rebel stronghold of Leicester but was unable to take the castle because he had to break off the siege in July in order to cope with the Scots. King William, known as the 'Lion', had succeeded his brother, Malcolm, in 1165 and it did not take him long to fall out with Henry. In 1168 he formed an alliance with Louis VII – the first example of the 'Auld Alliance' of Scotland and France against England. He now raided Northumberland. De Lucy forced him back across the border and would have inflicted considerable damage on the Lowlands had he not been forced to return southwards to face a new

OPPOSITE **The temporizing Bishop of Durham. Hugh de Puiset** *(c.1125–95) was Henry's representative in the north but as a bishop he also had loyalty to the pope. He was careful not to take sides over the Becket controversy but when the king's sons rebelled in 1173 he made no attempt to prevent William the Lion, King of the Scots, from invading. When the rebellion collapsed Hugh hurried to the royal court to make his peace with Henry. This detail from an illumination in* Chroniques de France ou de St Denis *shows Hugh cosying up to the king and, outside, plotting. Meanwhile, culprits are being hanged.*

Eleanor of Aquitaine

Eleanor was one of the more remarkable women of the Middle Ages. She was born about 1122, the eldest daughter and heiress of William X, Duke of Aquitaine.

In 1137 her father died, having already betrothed Eleanor to Louis VII. Between 1146 and 1149 she accompanied her husband on crusade to the Holy Land, and the couple's estrangement seems to have begun at this time, perhaps as a result of Eleanor's liaisons with one or more lovers. Louis was also disappointed that his queen had given birth to only two surviving children, both daughters, and had failed to provide him with an heir. In March 1152 the marriage was dissolved.

Eleanor's ambitions

As a princess with considerable lands of her own, she was now a tempting matrimonial prize, but before any potential suitor could waylay her she fled to her castle at Poitiers. Popular legend credits her with several adventures as she eluded amorous pursuers, but she had already determined to marry Henry, Count of Anjou, Duke of Normandy and soon to be king of England. He was 11 years her junior but an attractive and energetic young man with a promising future. Eleanor wrote to Henry, in effect proposing to him, and the couple were married within weeks. In the first 15 years of their marriage they had eight children – five boys and three girls.

As time passed, with her husband continually on the move around his wide dominions, it was natural

that Eleanor's life became more bound up with her children, for whom she was ambitious. She supported (and, perhaps, egged on) Henry when he proposed to crown his eldest son as king of England. In the same year she persuaded him to invest their second son, Richard, with the Duchy of Aquitaine (1170). She hoped that she would be able to rule her hereditary lands as regent in Richard's name, but, as with England, the king had no intention of relinquishing any of his own power. Richard was as much a cipher as his brother. It was resentment that caused Eleanor to throw in her lot with her sons when they rebelled in 1173.

The failure of her escape bid to join the royal princes in Paris condemned her to 16 years' captivity. She was housed in honourable confinement in various palaces, but she and her husband seldom met. Henry referred to her as his 'hated queen', and there was occasional talk of divorce. Henry had taken up with his mistress, Rosamund Clifford (known as the 'Fair Rosamund'), but whether this was before 1173 (and therefore a cause of Eleanor's desertion) is not known. Henry kept Eleanor at his beck and call, ordering her to appear with him for ceremonial occasions. Her restrictions were somewhat eased after 1184, when Henry and his sons were partially reconciled, but she did not regain her independence until Henry's death in 1189.

An influential matriarch

In the remaining years of her long life Eleanor became the influential matriarch she had long aspired to be, easily dominating her characterless sons. In preparation for Richard's coronation she toured England to secure the allegiance of the leading lords and churchmen. She intervened to prevent her youngest son, John, stirring up trouble against his brother. When Richard was taken prisoner in 1192 on his way back from the crusade it was Eleanor who held the government together and organized the payment of his ransom. And on Richard's death in 1199, the aged dowager even took to the field in person to help crush a revolt in Anjou against King John. To the end of her days Eleanor was active in international diplomacy, spending all her energies in the interests of her dynasty. Her children were, by marriage, related to several of the leading princely houses of Europe. She died in 1204, one of the few medieval women who can be said to have exercised real political influence over much of the continent.

ABOVE **Queen Eleanor in captivity**. *This fresco in the chapel of St Radegonde appears to show Eleanor with her daughter, Joanna, being conveyed under close guard to a place of confinement after her complicity in the rebellion of Henry II's sons in 1173. It is a near contemporary representation at Chinon, where once Henry had one of his most spacious and secure castles and is the earliest representation of Eleanor of Aquitaine still in existence.*

1174–82

HENRY LOATHED CIVIL WAR. He remembered only too well the devastation it had caused in Stephen's reign. War was expensive, it took a large toll in human lives and it made good government impossible. For these reasons and also because he wanted to be reconciled to his sons, he behaved leniently towards the rebels. He laboured hard and long to bring about a cessation of hostilities.

On 8 September Louis and young Henry agreed terms with the king, but Richard continued his resistance. Only when Henry appeared with an army before the gates of Poitiers, Richard's headquarters, did the recalcitrant son submit to the inevitable. By the terms of the settlement, sealed at Falaise in October, prisoners were released, properties restored and few punishments exacted. Hugh Bigod and Robert de Beaumont were deprived of their castles and not immediately restored in blood. William the Lion had to pay handsomely for his liberty. In December, by the Treaty of Falaise, he was obliged to do homage publicly to Henry at York and to surrender five of his Scottish castles. Only Eleanor did not share in Henry's well-calculated forgiveness; she remained her husband's virtual prisoner until the end of his reign.

Henry now dealt energetically with the inevitable lawlessness that had broken out during the war. In January 1176 he issued the Assize of Northampton, which was basically a reaffirmation of the Assize of Clarendon. 'This assize,' it was declared, 'shall hold good for all the time since the assize was made at Clarendon down to the present and henceforth during the lord king's pleasure, with regard to murder, treason and arson and with regard to all offences ... except minor thefts and robberies which were committed in time of war, as of horses, oxen and lesser things.' Henry believed that strengthening royal justice, limiting the

Our lord the king and all his liegemen and barons are to receive possession of all their lands and castles which they held 15 days before his sons withdrew from him; and in like manner his liegemen and barons who withdrew from him and followed his sons are to receive possession of their lands which they held 15 days before they withdrew from him.

RALPH OF DICETO, *RADULFI DI DICETO DECANI LUNDONIENSIS OPERA HISTORICA*, ED. W. STUBBS, 1876, I, PP. 394–5

OPPOSITE **The Assize of Northampton, 1176.** *An assize, from the Old French 'assise', meaning 'a sitting', describes the gathering of a consultative body and also the document setting out the results of a consultation. The assizes Henry II held with representatives of his barons were of fundamental importance in defining the rights and responsibilities of the king and his subjects. The resulting documents are vital to the development of the English constitution. Many were copied by monastic chroniclers and it is from such transcripts that we know the agreements that were reached at these assizes. This is part of the transcript made by Roger of Howden in his* Annals *written late in the 12th century. The Assize of Northampton issued early in 1176 confirmed and clarified the Assize of Clarendon (1166).*

Iudicium curie sue de eis habere uoluerit sicut de contemptoribus precepti sui. Item.

Iusticie inquirant de excaetis. de ecclesiis. de terris. de feminis. que sint de donatione domini regis. Item.

Ballivi domini regis respondeant ad scaccarium tam de assiso redditu quam de omnibus perquisitionibus suis que faciunt in bailliis suis exceptis illis que pertinent ad uicecomitatum. Item.

Iusticie inquirant de custodiis castellorum. et qui et quantum et ubi eas debeant. et postea mandent domino regi. Item.

Latro ex quo capitur uicecomiti tradatur ad custodiendum. et si uicecomes absens fuerit: ducatur ad proximum castellanum. et ipse illum custodiat donec illum liberet uicecomiti. Item.

Iusticie faciant querere per consuetudinem terre illos qui a regno recesserunt. et nisi redire uoluerint infra terminum nominatum et stare ad rectum in curia domini regis: postea uthlagentur. et nomina utlagorum afferant ad pascha et ad festum sancti michaelis ad scaccarium et exinde mittantur domino regi.

Ad predictum uero concilium apud Northamtun celebratum: uenit Willelmus rex scottorum per mandatum domini regis ad duces secum Ricardum episcopum sancti Andree. et Jocelinum episcopum de Glascou. et Ricardum episcopum de Dunkelden. et Christianum episcopum de candida casa. et Andream episcopum de Catenesse. et Symonem de Touni episcopum de Mureuia. et abbates et priores regni sui. Qui cum coram domino rege anglie conuenissent: precepit eis dominus rex per fidem quam ei debebant et per sacramentum fidelitatis quod ei fecerant: quod eandem subiectionem facerent anglicane ecclesie quam facere debebant et solebant tempore regum anglie predecessorum suorum. Cui responderunt quod ipsi numquam subiectionem fecerant anglicane ecclesie nec facere debent. Ad hoc autem respondit Rogerus eboracensis archiepiscopus affirmans quod Glascuenses episcopi et episcopi de candida casa subiecti fuerant eboracensi ecclesie tempore archiepiscoporum predecessorum suorum. et super hoc priuilegia romanorum pontificum sufficienter instructa: premonstrauit. Ad quod Jocelinus glascuensis episcopus respondit. Glascuensis ecclesia specialis filia est romane ecclesie et ab omni subiectione archiepiscoporum siue episcoporum exempta. et si eboracensis ecclesia aliquo tempore do

LEFT **A jousting victory**. *An illuminated illustration from a four-volume prose work by Regnault de Montauban made for Philip the Good Duke of Burgundy (1396–1467), but based on a poem by the 13th-century troubadour, Huon de Villeneuve (fl. c.1200). Tournaments became popular in the 12th century. They were seen as essential preparations for war and as expressions of the myth of chivalry. The most spectacular of the tiltyard sports was the joust, single combat with lances by two armoured knights. In later developments battle axes, maces and swords were also used. The objectives were to break a lance against the opponent's shield or to unhorse him. Successful jousters were the sporting celebrities of their day, admired by ladies and often accumulating large sums of money by performing at jousting 'circuits'.*

politics was a matter of terrorism and bloodshed. Geoffrey's death had further complicated international affairs because Philip Augustus of France demanded the guardianship of his infant son. Discord between the two kings was put on hold in October 1187 when, in response to an appeal from Pope Urban III, they agreed jointly to mount a crusade. All Christendom had been shocked by the news that the Christian kingdom of Jerusalem had been conquered by the Muslim leader, Saladin. Advance contingents were mustered and despatched to the Holy Land while Henry and Philip Augustus imposed a new tax, the Saladin tithe, to pay for a full-scale expedition. This was bitterly resented, and Henry faced the prospect, after many years of internal peace, that his English barons might, once more, rise against him. Meanwhile, the peril of Jerusalem failed to push into the background the three-way conflict of Henry, Philip Augustus and Richard.

After months of alternate fighting and negotiation the three met at Bonmoulins in November 1188. Gervase of Canterbury tells us that: 'On the first day they were sufficiently restrained and discussed calmly. On the following day they began little by little to bandy words. On the third day, however, they started to quarrel and so sharply countered threats with threats that the knights standing about were reaching for their swords.'[7] Richard demanded assurances that he would succeed to Henry's throne, but the king refused. Perhaps he feared to contemplate his own demise. Perhaps he genuinely could not decide what was best for his empire. Perhaps, as Richard suspected, his father intended to replace him as heir with his favourite son, John. Whatever the truth, the end result was that Richard publicly transferred his allegiance from Henry to Philip Augustus.

Desultory fighting continued until the following summer, when Richard and his ally besieged Henry in Le Mans, his birthplace. Henry and a small retinue escaped, leaving behind a burning town. By July he was at Chinon in the Loire valley. Near there, sick in body and depressed in mind, he met his adversaries. The French king presented a humiliating list of demands. Listlessly Henry assented. He returned to Chinon and there received a list of all the great men who had defected to Richard. At the head of the list was that of his other son, John. That was, for him, the last straw. He stopped fighting the fever that was raging through his body and, on 6 July 1189, he died.

OPPOSITE **Philip II's victory at Le Mans, 12 June 1189.** *Richard and his ally Philip II attacked the city where Henry II had taken refuge. The defenders were taken by surprise and set fire to the suburbs in order to impede the attackers but the wind carried sparks into the city and set light to its wood and thatch buildings. Henry and his guard withdrew through one gate as his enemies entered through another, which is the scene depicted here. In fact, this triumph did not prove decisive, for Richard, pursuing his father, was almost killed in an ambush. It was only Henry's death on 6 July that enabled Richard to become king.*

RICHARD I AND JOHN

JOHANNES REX

During the reigns of Henry II's two turbulent sons England became an offshore kingdom, increasingly separated from the rest of the Angevin empire. Richard reigned for ten years (1189–99) but spent no more than six months in England during all that time. His brother John was given lands on both sides of the Channel but had no share in the government of the country, which he resented. He tried to oust Richard's officials from power, but it was not until Richard lay dying that he nominated John as his heir.

The dukes of the continental Angevin lands refused to recognize him, and his 17-year reign (1199–1216) saw him lose his grip on these territories. By the time of his death the continental possessions owned by Henry II had been lost to the king of France, and the failure of Henry's sons to keep their inheritance intact led to the emergence of England as a separate nation state.

1189–91

'ENGLAND IS COLD and always raining.' That was Richard's opinion of the island that formed part of his inheritance. He had no interest in it, save as a source of revenue. His two passions were Anjou and crusading. By the time of his accession Richard had vowed to go on a crusade to the Holy Land, and his chief concern was to gather an army to recover Jerusalem from the Saracen conqueror Saladin, who had taken the city in 1187. He raised taxes, granted charters, sold offices of state and even demanded huge payments from those already in office to retain their positions. For 10,000 marks he released King William of Scotland from his oath of fealty. By these and other measures Richard was able to raise an army of 8,000 mounted and foot soldiers and a hundred ships.

Richard's coronation was marred by one of the worst atrocities of the age. Henry II had encouraged Jews to settle in several cities, and they performed a valuable service as money-lenders – there were, of course, no banks at this time – but the Jews were never popular. People resented being financially dependent on them, hated their exclusivity and considered them as enemies of the Christian faith. They were not allowed to attend the coronation (a holy Christian rite), but two prominent Jews did attend in order to present gifts to the new king and assure him of the loyalty of their community. They were thrown out. A rumour spread that Richard (a devout Christian champion about to fight the enemies of the faith in the Holy Land) had ordered a massacre. Mobs went on the rampage through London's streets, killing any Jews they could lay their hands on, burning their houses and ransacking their property. The violence spread to other towns and cities, but the worst outrages occurred in York.

In March 1190 the leader of the Jewish community, fearing for the safety of his friends and neighbours, obtained permission from the warden of the castle to move the Jews into the

Raising Money

Richard, by the Grace of God, *King of England, Duke of Normandy and Aquitaine and Count of Anjou, To all Archbishops, Bishops, Abbots, Earls, Barons, Justices, Sheriffs, Ministers and all faithful subjects in France and throughout all England, health. Know ye that we grant to our citizens of Hereford in Wales the town of Hereford to hold in perpetuity upon their rendering forty pounds sterling per annum, and also they shall afford their assistance in fortifying that town. And for this grant they shall give to us forty marks in silver. Therefore we command that they hold the said town in perpetuity by the aforesaid rent of forty pounds per annum, with all its free liberties and free customs and all things thereto belonging. So that no sheriff of ours shall intrude in any wise upon them concerning any plea, quarrel or other thing relating to the aforesaid town. Witnesses: H. Bishop of Durham; W. de St. Johanne Dated from Westminster the first year of our reign the ninth of October under the hands of W. De Longo Campo our Chancellor-elect of Ely.*

THE MANUSCRIPTS OF RYE AND HEREFORD CORPORATIONS: 13TH REPORT, APP. PART IV, 1892, P.284

OPPOSITE **Statue of King John** *at Lichfield Cathedral. The west front of the cathedral is 'alive' with numerous statues of kings, queens and saints. The originals have decayed and the present images were installed by the architect, Sir George Gilbert Scott, in the late 19th century. They represent the interpretation of a later age. King John is shown holding a quill pen, as a reference to the creation of Magna Carta. In fact, the king could not write. He only set his seal to the document – and that very unwillingly. To see him as the man responsible for this foundation document of English liberties is far from accurate. Part of Lichfield Cathedral was built during John's reign. Work began in 1195 and the choir had been completed by the time of his death.*

PREVIOUS PAGES **The seals** *of King Richard I (1189–99) and King John (1199–1216).* **A portrait of King John** *by an unknown artist, painted c.1620.*

castle, and they were allowed to find refuge in a wooden tower that formed part of the fortifications. There they were besieged by an angry mob, aided by the county militia. The victims were urged to save themselves by converting to Christianity, but their religious leader, Rabbi Yomtov of Joigney, told them to kill themselves rather than deny their faith. In response, parents killed their children, their wives and then each other. Several died when the tower caught fire, and many others were cut down trying to escape the flames. At least 150 men, women and children died in this tragedy. Richard and his deputies denounced the massacre, and some ringleaders were arrested and punished, but government action was far from thorough, and most offenders escaped.

Richard could hardly wait to embark on his next military adventure. Before the end of 1189 he had left England and would not return for more than four years, but the arrangements he made for the government of the country in his

absence constituted a recipe for disaster. There was no place in the administration for his remaining brother, John, who was ordered to remain outside England for three years. Richard nominated as his heir, in the event of his dying childless, his nephew Arthur (son of his late brother, Geoffrey). He compensated John generously – and rashly – with a large grant of land. The 22-year-old prince retained Ireland and was now granted the counties of Nottinghamshire, Derby, Dorset, Somerset, Devon and Cornwall, as well as castles and lands in other parts of the country. John's position was, however, subordinate to Richard's justiciars, the men who acted as regents in the king's absence. These were Hugh de Puiset, Bishop of Durham, who controlled all the country north of the Humber, and William Longchamps, the chancellor and Bishop of Ely. Not only was John jealous of his brother's officials but also they were at odds with each other.

Longchamps was ambitious, arrogant and grasping, and in 1190 he had little difficulty in shouldering his colleague aside. Furthermore, he had the pope appoint him as legate (the pope's personal representative) so that he became the supreme authority in both church and state. He was of humble Norman origin and had worked his way up the ladder of preferment by cleverly changing sides during the wars between Henry II and his sons. He spoke no English and openly held the people of the country in contempt. He travelled around with a train of 1,000 men-at-arms, who had to be fed and housed wherever he went. He took every opportunity to extract money from Richard's subjects in order to support his own extravagant lifestyle and to raise yet more funds for the cash-strapped king. In all this Longchamps was an effective representative of Richard, and he continued to enjoy royal favour. He strengthened the Tower of London with new walls and ditches and made it his impregnable base. His behaviour provoked enormous resentment. The chronicler William of Newburgh commented: 'The laity found him more than a king, the clergy more than a pope, and both an intolerable tyrant.'[1]

John, meanwhile, enjoyed similarly royal power and status. He was released from his ban and returned to England early in 1191. His power base in the west and the Midlands enabled him to maintain an impressive court and a military entourage that rivalled the justiciar's. Many of the barons transferred their allegiance to John and encouraged him to undermine Longchamps's authority.

LEFT **Persecution of Jews**. *There was always a strong undercurrent of anti-semitism in most European cities. It erupted in London during the coronation of Richard when a group of Jews tried to attend the sacred Christian ceremony to offer their allegiance to the new king. Angry mobs attacked Jewish homes and business premises and the ugly mood soon spread to other towns, culminating in the appalling massacre at York (March 1190). This detail from the* Chronica Roffense *produced at Rochester in the early 14th century shows a London lout attacking three elderly Jews with a club.*

PREVIOUS PAGES **Coronation procession of Richard I**. *This Netherlandish painting from the* Chroniques d'Angleterre *dates from the late 15th century but is based on the words of the contemporary chronicler, Roger of Howden, who gave a long description of the procession: '... then came four barons bearing four candlesticks of gold ... next came six earls and six barons, carrying on their shoulders a very large [coffer] in which were placed the royal arms and robes; and after them William de Mandeville, Earl of Aumarle, carrying a great and massive crown of gold, decorated on every side with precious stones. Next came Richard, Duke of Normandy, Hugh, Bishop of Durham walking at his right hand, and Reginald, Bishop of Bath, at his left and four barons holding over them a canopy of silk ...'*

Crusades

One reason for the massacre of English Jews was 'crusade fever'. Palestine was the geographical homeland of Christianity and Judaism and was of considerable importance to Islam. In the 7th century the land was conquered by Muslim Arabs, and 400 years later another Muslim horde, the Seljuks, overran Asia Minor and threatened Byzantium, the eastern bastion of Christianity.

In 1095 Pope Urban II called for the leaders of Christian Europe to 'take up the cross', halt the Muslim advance and free the Holy Land from the rule of 'unbelievers'. The result was the First Crusade, which set up the Christian Kingdom of Jerusalem and brought part of Palestine under the control of European princely dynasties. Another crusade in 1147–9 petered out in quarrels among the various European contingents. It was the rise of the great warrior-sultan, Saladin, that prompted Pope Gregory VIII to launch the Third Crusade, the only one in which an English king took part. Saladin had called for a holy war (jihad) against the Christians, and in 1187 he recaptured Jerusalem.

The knight's calling

Henry II agreed to lead the crusade with the Emperor Frederick I, Barbarossa, and Philip II of France. After Henry's death Richard vowed to take his place. He and Philip raised money in their respective kingdoms by a special levy called the Saladin tithe. This was extremely unpopular, and Philip actually had to abandon it. In England several barons, caught up in enthusiasm for the cause and believing the pope's assurance that they would win heavenly reward, readily enlisted.

LEFT **Massacre of Muslim prisoners at Acre.** *The biggest stain on the image of Richard as the chivalric Christian knight is his massacre of 2,700 Muslim prisoners after the siege of Acre in 1191. This image from a manuscript by Sebastien Mamerot (1490) captures the event in horrifying detail.*

They regarded warfare as the knight's calling, and it was glorified by court poets and wandering troubadours.

Maces and swords, coloured helmets,
The useless shields hacked through
We'll see when fighting begins,
Many liegemen together striking
Some lost in the bewilderment of battle,
And horses galloping, riders wounded or slain.
Once fighting's started make every nobleman
Think only of destruction of arms and legs.
A dead man's worth more than alive and beaten.[2]

So wrote the knight and poet Bertran de Born, who fought alongside Richard during the latter's conflict with his father.

The reality was usually far less glorious. Leaders often fell out among themselves and differed over matters of strategy. The journey to the Levant was long and hazardous, and more soldiers died of disease and shipwreck than in battle. With armies to feed and pay the crusading heroes sometimes degenerated into mercenaries, hiring themselves out to rulers through whose lands they passed. Looting and pillage frequently marred the image of the holy crusade.

'Taking up the cross' remained a romantic ideal until well into the 14th century, but it was stronger in Spain and Portugal and lands actually under threat from the Muslim advance. Enthusiasm in England waned after the Third Crusade.

In April a council of leading nobles and churchmen patched up a truce between the parties and recognized John as heir to the throne. But three months later another meeting shifted power back towards Longchamps. Richard had sent his own agent, Walter of Coutances, Bishop of Rouen, to restore order, support his justiciar and check the pretensions of his brother. He summoned both parties to meet him at Winchester and tried to lower the political temperature, but neither rival was interested in a peaceful compromise. In another move to try to maintain a balance Richard had Henry II's illegitimate son, Geoffrey, appointed as Archbishop of York. The justiciar saw this as a threat to his position and sent men to arrest Geoffrey when he arrived at Dover. Longchamps's soldiers dragged the archbishop from the altar of the nearby priory. This shocking event was far too reminiscent of the Becket episode to be tolerated, and it played into John's hands. He and Walter of Coutances summoned Longchamps to appear before a council near Reading, at which it was clear he would be dismissed from office. The justiciar declined to attend. Instead he set off for London and shut himself up in the Tower. After a three-day siege he surrendered on 10 October, and at the end of the month he left England in the hands of John and Walter of Coutances, who now assumed the office of justiciar. The barons acknowledged John as heir to the throne and, thus, jumped from the frying pan into the fire.

1192–9

RICHARD LEFT THE HOLY LAND but was shipwrecked and captured (see p. 65). This played into the hands of Philip II of France. He had left the Holy Land ahead of his comrade-in-arms with the object of benefiting from Richard's absence to nibble away at his continental lands. He knew that John's nobles were divided in their allegiance, some preferring Arthur as heir to the throne, and that John was locked in a struggle with the justiciar as he tried to extend his authority. Philip offered to do deals with John and with Emperor Henry VI. He promised to back John in a bid for power and tried to persuade the emperor either to hand Richard over or keep him a prisoner indefinitely.

OPPOSITE **Richard I doing homage to Philip II**. *Before embarking on the crusade Richard, as he was bound to do by feudal law, paid homage to his overlord, the king of France, for his dukedom of Normandy. However, there was no love lost between these brothers-in-arms. In return for his submission Richard had the right to expect the support and protection of his feudal overlord. However, Philip was set on extending direct control over Angevin lands. He left Palestine early and took advantage of Richard's continuing absence to intrigue with his brother, John, in order to extend the area directly controlled by the French crown. This image is from* Chroniques de France ou de St Denis.

Prince yalast personelment en la compaignie dautrui
chascuns des dits chevaliers seront tenu de aler personne
lment et di demorer continuelment tant comme le
dit Prince y demorra salue se aucune expresse et appa
rant necessite ne le contredeist.

The Lionheart myth

Richard I, a king who disliked England, spent little time there, exploited it shamelessly and made no sound provision for its good government, has become, in popular legend, Richard Coeur-de-Lion (Richard the Lionheart), one of the great English heroes. There are only a few elements of truth mixed up in the myth.

Richard's appearance and bearing were impressive. He was over 6 feet tall and had a handsome face beneath a shock of red-gold hair. He was athletic, a fine horseman and skilled in the military arts. As he never expected to succeed his father, he concentrated on becoming a warrior prince. He was a brave and skilful leader in battle, adored by his men and respected by his enemies. He was also immersed in the ideals of chivalry as exalted by the poets and singers who attended the court of his mother, Eleanor of Aquitaine. Richard was, himself, a minor poet. But there was another side to his character: he was cruel, short-tempered and ruthless. Though theoretically committed to the ideal of courtly love, it is quite likely that he was homosexual.

The Third Crusade

Richard set out on the Third Crusade in company with King Philip of France in July 1190. Travelling through Italy, Richard had a near-fatal encounter thanks to his bullying behaviour. He tried to steal a hawk, was caught and severely thrashed by its angry owner. He and his men wintered in Sicily, where Richard unceremoniously evicted monks from a monastery in order to provide his men with accommodation. His next port of call was Cyprus, where he conquered the island and delivered it from the hands of the brutal mercenary invader, Isaac Comnenus, who had amassed a considerable treasure by appropriating the property of the unfortunate inhabitants. Much of this now went to replenish Richard's military chest.

The siege of Acre

The king arrived in the Holy Land in June 1191 and found a crusader army engaged in a long and, so far, unsuccessful siege of the Muslim fortress of Acre. The walls of the fortress were thick and impregnable, but Richard solved the problem by offering his men a generous reward for every stone they excavated. After little more than a month Acre capitulated. Richard and Philip imposed severe terms on Saladin: the Muslims in the town were to be ransomed for 200,000 gold crowns, some being kept as hostages until full payment was made. On 20 August Richard, apparently believing that the terms of the agreement were not being met, brought 2,700 hostages out of the town and had them slaughtered in full sight of Saladin's army.

By this act, shocking to all – Christian and Muslim alike – who followed the chivalric code, Richard made sure that Acre could not serve as a rallying point for his enemies. He pushed on to Jerusalem. At Arsuf he confronted Saladin's host in pitched battle, and a Muslim observer described the charge of Richard and his knights that won the day: 'They grasped their lances, shouted their shout of battle like one man, the infantry opened out, and through they rushed in one great charge in all directions – some on our centre, till all was broken.'[3] On this defeat of the mighty Saladin hung Richard's future reputation. But it was not followed up by the retaking of Jerusalem. Within sight of the city the king halted and turned back towards the coast, for he knew that the taking of the Holy City made no sense strategically. From afar, Jerusalem was a glittering prize; close to it was an isolated city in enemy-controlled territory that could not long remain in Christian hands. News also reached the king of John's misdeeds at home, and in September 1192 Richard signed a peace treaty with Saladin and set off on the journey back to England.

He was shipwrecked on the Adriatic coast near Dubrovnik and attempted to make his way home overland. But he had made too many enemies. He

OPPOSITE **Setting out for the crusade.** *This manuscript illustration from the* Ordre du Saint Esprit *indicates both the organization necessary for a crusading expedition and the chivalric splendour associated with it. Baggage and horses are loaded onto a ship and the resplendent heraldic devices of the knights are displayed.*

ABOVE **The capture of Acre, 1191.** *In this illumination from* Chroniques de France ou de St Denis *Philip II is shown entering the besieged city while a Muslim defender kneels in surrender and another seems about to be struck with a sword.*

was captured and in January 1193 delivered into the hands of the Emperor Henry VI, who grasped the opportunity to take political and pecuniary advantage of this piece of good fortune. It was Richard's secure but comfortable imprisonment that give rise to one of the most romantic legends about him. The story was told of the troubadour Blondel, who toured the castles of eastern Europe seeking his royal master by singing outside the walls and hoping for a response. At last he came to Dürrenstein, and when he performed his song a strong voice from within one of the towers joined in. Richard had been found! This was a fantasy based on the slender foundation of two facts: Richard was held in Dürrenstein Castle, and there was a nobleman-poet called Jean Blondel. The rest is fiction.

Such stories originated a century or more after the exploits they purport to celebrate. From the mere fact that Richard was the only English king to take up the cross there grew the image of him as the perfect Christian knight – Richard the Lionheart.

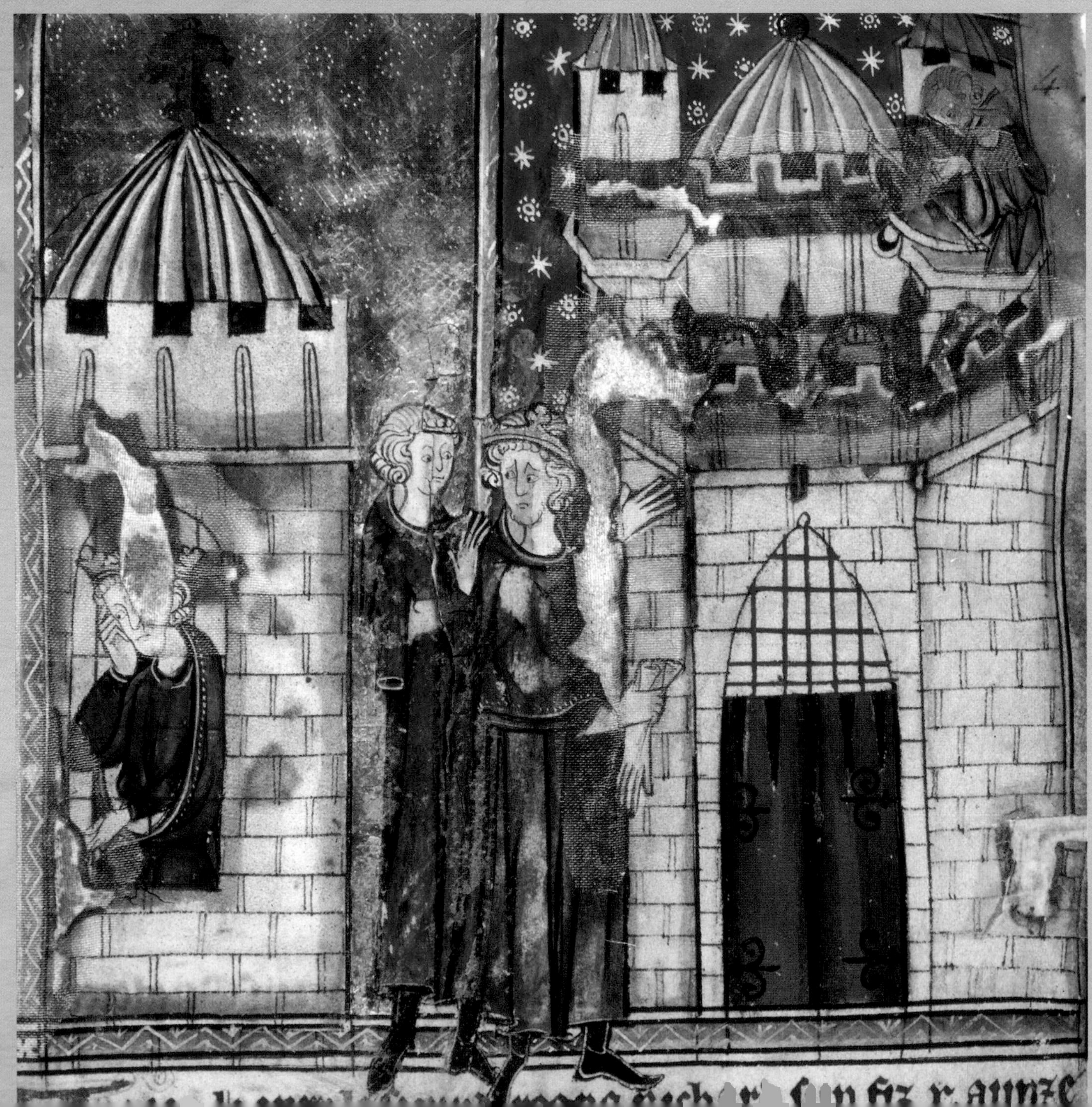

In this situation the dowager queen, Eleanor, once more entered the limelight. She had all the barons renew their oath of loyalty to Richard, restrained John, organized the defence of England's southern coast to guard against a surprise attack by Philip and zealously set about gathering a ransom for the king. It was largely thanks to his mother's efforts that Richard was persuaded to overlook his brother's disloyalty. It was Eleanor, now in her seventies, who travelled to the emperor's court and made the final arrangements for Richard's release. The king returned to his English realm in March 1194. Having firmly re-established his authority, he left after two months, never to return.

Richard's remaining years were spent in warfare with Philip, something welcomed by the troubadour, Bertran de Born:

Now the warm season has arrived
When English ships with come to
French ports
And the bold, worthy king will land.
King Richard. The like there never was.
Then we'll see gold and silver in plenty.
Siege weapons constructed,
Loaded for bombardment.
We'll see great towers shiver and collapse
And enemies captured and imprisoned.[4]

John thought it wise now to make a great show of supporting his brother, who rewarded him by restoring many of his lands and nominating him as his heir to the throne. It was in April 1199 that Richard, the hero of chivalric romance, died in a rather unchivalric and unromantic way. While engaged in the siege of Châlus he was involved in a petty feud with someone who fired a crossbow bolt at him. Though the projectile was extracted, the wound turned septic, and he died in pain after several days.

Eleanor Writes

Eleanor of Aquitaine *writes to Pope Celestine III to complain about Richard's imprisonment:*

'The kings of the earth have set themselves and all the rulers have agreed to set themselves against my son, the Lord's Anointed. One tortures him in chains, another destroys his lands with a cruel enmity, or to use common phrase, "One shears, another plunders, one holds the fort, another skins it." The supreme Pontiff sees all this, yet keeps the sword of Peter sheathed, and thus gives the sinner added boldness, his silence being presumed to indicate consent.'

Eleanor, by the wrath of God, queen of England

T. Rymer, *Foedera*, 1704-35, I, p.72

OPPOSITE **Richard I imprisoned** *by the Emperor Henry VI. On his way back from the Holy Land in 1192, King Richard was forced to land on the Adriatic coast and make his way overland in disguise. Unfortunately, he found himself in the territory of Leopold V of Austria who had a score to settle. After the siege of Acre his banner was displayed on the walls beside those of Richard and Philip but Richard had ordered it to be taken down. In revenge Leopold arrested Richard on 21 December and held him hostage. On 7 January 1193 Leopold handed his prisoner over to the Emperor Henry VI for such a huge sum that he was able to refortify the walls of Vienna and two other cities with the proceeds. Henry, in his turn, demanded 150,000 marks (about three tons of silver) for Richard's return. The picture shows Richard being ushered into his prison, staring despondently from a window and singing songs on the battlements.*

1199–1213

JOHN, THE LAST OF THE TURBULENT sons of Henry II known collectively as the Devil's Brood, was 31 when he came to the throne. He possessed few of Richard's virtues and most of his vices. 'No one may ever trust him, for his heart is soft and cowardly' was the verdict of one troubadour.[5] The condemnation is not wholly fair, for John could display moments of courage and commitment. What he lacked was consistency. Episodes of energetic, even brilliant, activity were interspersed with long periods of inactivity. All too often he was thrown off course by blinding rage or debilitating passivity. Where Richard was unusually tall and sinewy, John was short and rather stout. Where Richard was essentially a man of action, John was a thinker. Where Richard was content with a soldier's simple life, John hankered after luxury, display and self-indulgence. What both brothers shared was the

Plantagenet tendency to violence, cruelty and hasty temper. Richard's character has been distorted by legend into the personification of the perfect, Christian knight. By the same process John has been demonized as the archetypal 'bad king'.

In fact, he was a hard worker who took the responsibilities of government seriously and, like his father, cared about justice. Though he had been nominated by Richard, he had to fight for his crown. England and Normandy recognized John as king. Aquitaine remained loyal to Eleanor. Brittany, Anjou and Maine looked to 12-year-old Arthur. John was, therefore, immediately plunged into the old, complex task of keeping the Angevin empire together. Things began well. By the Treaty of Le Goulet (May 1200) Philip recognized John's title to Normandy and England, and Arthur did homage to John for Brittany and his other territories. But the rift was far from being completely closed.

John had a genius for making enemies, and he soon added fresh names to the list of those who did not respect or trust him. In an attempt to strengthen his hold over his continental possessions he unceremoniously divorced his wife in order to pursue a more prestigious and politically useful marriage. First, he began negotiations with the king of Portugal for the hand of his daughter. Then he changed his mind and pursued a marriage alliance with the Count of Angoulême. It mattered not that Isabella of Angoulême, whom he planned to marry, was already engaged to the son of the Count of La Marche. This led to an unnecessary war, which Philip was only too ready to join. By the summer of 1202 John faced a formidable array of foes. Philip

LEFT **The Battle of Gisors**. *During the bitter conflict between Richard I and Philip Augustus the two armies engaged in a skirmish at Gisors in Picardy. Richard won the battle and Philip in his ensuing flight was almost drowned in Gisors's moat while trying to get into the city.*

(as John's feudal overlord) summoned the contending parties to his court to discuss a settlement, and when John refused to attend he stripped him of his continental lands and transferred his support to Arthur, giving the duke his daughter in marriage.

To wage war successfully John needed money, men and weapons. He hired mercenaries and taxed his subjects, both lay and ecclesiastical, to pay for them. His demands were extortionate, but he did create an impressive fighting force. Particularly, he built the best navy England had seen up to that time and established Portsmouth as its permanent base. Diplomatically, he prepared for war by reaching new agreements with the Welsh princes and the Scottish king.

The military initiative, however, remained with John's enemies – until the king was roused to fury by Arthur's latest stratagem. The young duke laid siege to the aged Eleanor of Aquitaine in her castle of Mirebeau (August 1202), and John immediately rushed to his mother's assistance. His uncharacteristic haste took Arthur and his army completely by surprise, and the teenage duke was thrown into prison at Rouen. He was never seen again.

There were several accounts of how young Arthur met his end, most of them written by monastic chroniclers who disliked John and deliberately spread stories to discredit him. The commander of Rouen Castle asserted that John had sent

ABOVE **The Treaty of Le Goulet, May 1200.** *In this illustration from the* Grandes Chroniques de France *(c.1370) John and Philip II embrace, having reached an agreement over the division of Richard's territory. John had to cede Evreux and the Norman Vexin to Philip in return for recognition as his brother's heir.*

OPPOSITE **John Lacklands.** *In his* Verses on the Kings of England, *from which this illustration comes, John Lydgate (c.1370–1451) wrote of John: 'He lost Anjou and Normandy anon, This land interdicted by misgovernance, And as it is put in rememberance, XVIII years King of this region, And lyeth at Worcester dead of poison'. None of the chroniclers ever had a good word to say for John.*

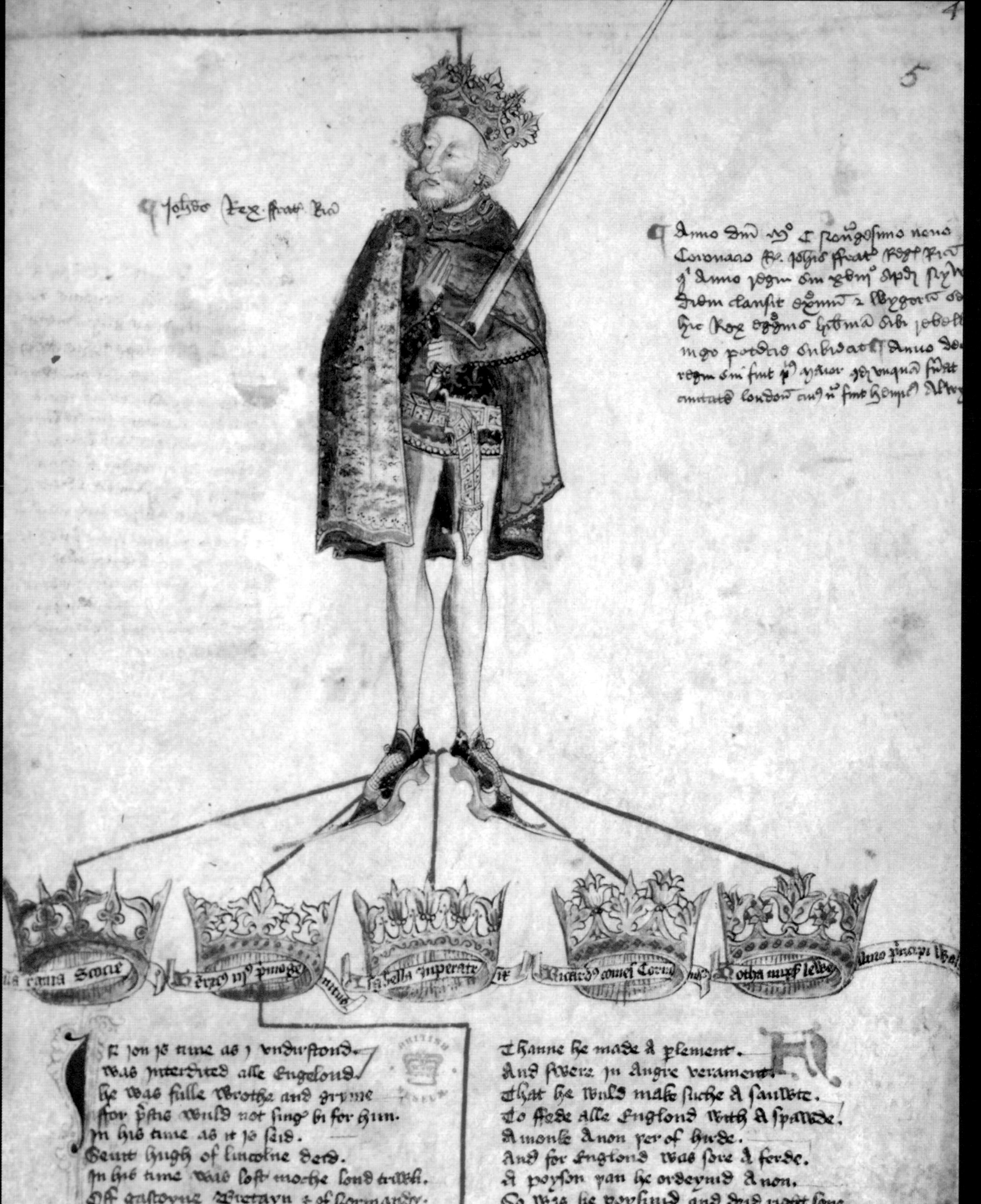

It Jon is time as I vnderstond.
Was interdited alle Engelond.
he was fulle Wrothe and gryme
ffor prestis wuld not sing bi for him.
In his time as it is seid.
Seint hugh of lincolne deid.
In his time was lost mo-the lond trewli.
Off gastoyne Bretayn & of Normandy.
In his time was grete du-the.
xij pens an halfe pany lofe was worth.

Thanne he made a plement.
And swere in angre verament.
That he wuld make suche a sawte.
To ffede alle Englond with a spawde.
A monk anon yer of herde.
And for Englond was sore a ferde.
A poyson yan he ordeynid anon.
So was he poysinid and deid right sone.
he regnid here xix yere.
And to Wurcetre men him bere.

country on a war footing, either to face the threat of invasion or to recover the lost provinces. In January 1205 John summoned a council that set up a nationwide organization of constables in every community who were to be responsible for training and mustering all males over 12 years of age. The king imposed fresh taxes on the barons and the church, including the first ever income tax. In the summer John proposed to gather his largest army and convey it to France in a huge fleet. But most of the barons simply refused to support the venture and it had to be aborted.

John became more defiant. Isolated and angry, he hit out against churches and monasteries. Over the next two years he filched over £100,000 from the clergy.

National unity was further undermined by a conflict between the king and the pope. In July 1205 the Archbishop of Canterbury, Hubert Walter, died. John tried to replace him with one of his close supporters, but this was resisted by the cathedral chapter, who put forward their own candidate. Pope Innocent III now intervened, rejecting both nominees and summoning the parties concerned to Rome. Proceedings continued until the end of 1206, when Innocent made his own appointment, Stephen Langton. John refused to allow Langton to enter the country, and he remained on the continent for the next six years. The king retaliated by throwing out the Canterbury monks and seizing the cathedral revenues.

At about the same time, Geoffrey, Archbishop of York, fell out with the king (his half-brother) over the issue of taxation and refused to allow his clergy to pay John's latest levy. Then, in the summer of 1207, he too fled abroad. Several other bishops followed suit, and Innocent placed England under interdict, which meant that the clergy were forbidden to take services. John's subjects could not be married in church or buried in consecrated ground. The pope further threatened John with excommunication if he refused to come to terms. John responded by confiscating more church property, and Innocent carried out the threatened excommunication in November 1209. Instead of submitting, John became even more defiant. Isolated and angry, he hit out against churches and monasteries. Over the next two years he filched over £100,000 from the clergy. Because the only chroniclers of these years were monks, who exaggerated or even invented stories about John's bad behaviour, his reputation has permanently suffered.

As well as amassing considerable wealth and putting England in a state of military preparedness, the king used diplomacy to create alliances that would help him regain his continental possessions. By 1212 he had formed a league against Philip that included the Emperor Otto IV, the Count of Flanders and various northern European dukes. But before he could cross the Channel with all his men of war John had to watch his back. In 1211 he led an army to Ireland to ensure the loyalty of the barons there. He marched through eastern Ireland and forced into exile his two most troublesome vassals, Hugh de Lacy and William de Braose, and

Papal Bull, 1213. *A bull was a kind of charter or directive issued by the pope and authenticated with a lead seal (bulla). In this bull Innocent III ordered all the leaders of church and state in Ireland to maintain their loyalty to John. This was in return for John declaring himself a vassal of the pope.*

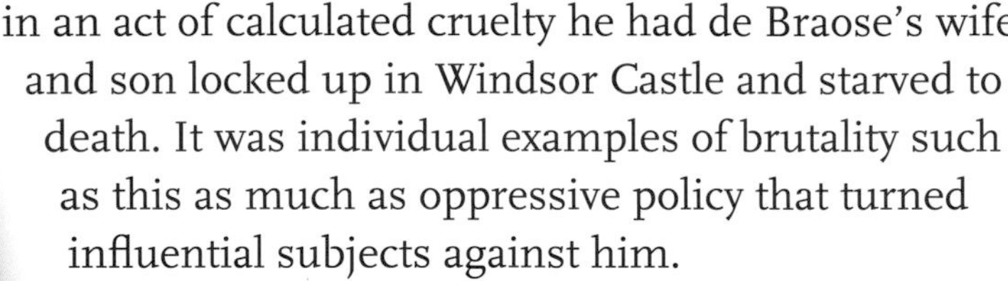

in an act of calculated cruelty he had de Braose's wife and son locked up in Windsor Castle and starved to death. It was individual examples of brutality such as this as much as oppressive policy that turned influential subjects against him.

In 1212 John prepared for a major invasion of France, but plans for the campaign had to be abandoned when Philip successfully intrigued with Llewelyn-ap-Iorwerth, prince of Gwynedd, who had made himself master of much of Wales. The rebels destroyed the castle at Aberystwyth and captured the castles of Rhuddlan and Degannwy. John led his army to the border and had his fleet brought round to Chester in order to bring the Welsh to submission. Then he abandoned the enterprise and disbanded his force. The reason? Rumours of conspiracy among his own followers. Egged on by the pope, Eustace de Vesci and Robert Fitzwalter planned to murder the king or abandon him to his enemies in the forthcoming campaign. John's mounting unpopularity made him increasingly suspicious, and his suspicion made him increasingly tyrannical.

By now it was clear to John that he would have to make his peace with the church. In November 1212 he sent an embassy to Rome offering his submission. Matters became more urgent when news arrived the following spring that Philip was planning an invasion of England. The terms of John's humiliating surrender were finally confirmed by papal bull in October 1213. John agreed to allow Stephen Langton to take up his post and to make full restitution of everything he had confiscated from the church. More importantly, he surrendered his kingdom to the pope and received it back as a papal vassal for an annual tribute of 1,000 marks.

ABOVE **Pope Innocent III**. *Illumination (c.1208–16) from Peter of Poitiers's* Compendium Historiae in genealogia Christi. *Innocent, who ruled from 1198 to 1216, was born Lotario de Conti di Segni of noble Italian descent and was one of the strongest of the medieval popes. It was John's misfortune to pick a quarrel with this particular head of the Catholic church, a man who stopped at nothing in defence of the rights and privileges of the clergy, who organized savage purges of heretics and who enthusiastically promoted crusades. Innocent had emerged triumphant from conflicts with the rulers of France, Aragon, Denmark, Poland and Portugal. The battle of wills between king and pope lasted from 1207–12 and the brunt of it fell upon the English people who were deprived of all the ministrations of the clergy, while the clergy suffered reprisals from John's officers. John's climb-down in 1213 was a total humiliation. The pope, henceforth, owned England while John and his successors were obliged to pay 1,000 marks a year for the privilege of acting as the pope's agent.*

1213–16

THE FINAL YEARS of John's reign began well. Philip assembled a large fleet at Gravelines to conquer England and place his son, Louis, on the throne, and he confidently expected to receive the support of many of John's vassals against their excommunicated king. John's submission to Pope Innocent was a blow, but the French king continued with his plan. John, meanwhile, had not been idle. He had assembled in the southeast his own force augmented by that of his ally, the Count of Flanders. On 28 May 1213 his fleet of 500 ships crossed to Damme, the port of Bruges, to which Philip had moved his ships. The Anglo-Flemish force fell upon 1,700 vessels, which were unprotected because Philip's troops were engaged in the siege of Ghent. They plundered and burned at will and put a stop to Philip's invasion plans.

John now intended a quick counter-strike, and this would have been the ideal moment for a successful campaign. Unfortunately, his barons declined to support him. By now they identified themselves as 'English' and had little interest in risking life and limb to help the king recover his foreign lands. In fury John marched northwards to deal with his recalcitrant barons. The newly arrived Stephen Langton hurried after him and, with difficulty, dissuaded him from vengeful action (November), but John was committed to his allies and determined to recover his territory, and he pressed on with the strategy agreed with his continental comrades. While Otto and his contingent advanced from the Low Countries, John landed at La Rochelle (February 1214) and struck northwards, crossing the Loire between Nantes and Angers. All was going well until he learned that Prince Louis was coming to meet him. Without waiting to do battle, John fled in disorder (July), claiming that retreat was forced on him by the disloyalty of his Poitevin vassals. Meanwhile, Philip faced Otto at the Battle of Bouvines, where he was victorious. This battle was one of the turning points in European history: it ended the imperial reign of Otto IV; it established Philip as the most powerful monarch in Europe; and it marked the end of the Angevin empire.

John arrived home to a realm on the brink of rebellion. Taxed beyond endurance in order to finance what they now regarded as a lost cause, many of the barons were determined to assert their rights against the crown. And they were not alone. The senior clergy still smarted over the exactions

Fealty to John

The king, however, *wishing to take precautions against the future, caused all the nobles throughout England to swear fealty to him alone against all men, and to renew their homage to him; and the better to take care of himself, he, on the day of St Mary's purification, assumed the cross of our Lord, being induced to this more by fear than devotion.*

ROGER OF WENDOVER, *FLOWERS OF HISTORY*, ED. J.A. GILES, 1849, P.308

The Battle of Bouvines, *27 July 1214, depicted in an illustration from* Chroniques de France ou de St Denis. *It was one of the great decisive battles in English history, although no English army took part. John formed an alliance with the Emperor Otto IV and Ferrand, Count of Flanders again Philip II of France. The plan was that he would engage Philip in battle in mid-France while his allies marched on Paris. The plan fell apart because, after brief engagements, John withdrew his forces southwards and Otto was slow in organizing his advance which gave Philip time to prepare for battle and choose the ground. He confronted his enemies at Bouvines, between Lille and Tournai. The battle was a rare contest between groups of armoured knights and, after several hours, the imperial cavalry fled the field, having lost 170 knights and thousands of foot soldiers. There was nothing now to prevent Philip claiming the mainland territories of John Lackland.*

they had suffered during the interdict, and burghers of several towns felt that the king had trampled on their ancient liberties. John met a delegation of the discontented barons in London in January 1215, listened to their demands and managed to persuade them to take no further action till Easter. In the interval, both sides sent to Rome for the support of Innocent, their liege lord.

John now indicated his intention of going on crusade. Whether this was a serious vow or one designed to win the approval of the church and defer indefinitely having to meet his discontented subjects is not clear. What is clear is that it did not impress the barons. Robert Fitzwalter summoned 40 malcontents to meet him at Northampton in May, and they marched on London. The rebels also knew how to cloak their actions with piety – they called their host the

ABOVE **King John** *hunting the stag is shown in this English 14th-century illumination. Hunting was regarded as the sport of kings and was the main source of relaxation for kings and barons. Large tracts of country, known as 'forests', were kept exclusively for this purpose and other people were prohibited from snaring, tracking or hunting animals and birds in them (a source of great discontent). For the nobility, hunting combined several important features: obtaining food and hides, exercise, developing horsemanship for use in battle and socializing. For kings it served the purpose of uniting the crown with leading royal vassals.*

OPPOSITE **A charter of King John**. *Dated 9 May 1215, this document, affixed with the king's impressive seal, granted the people of London the right to choose their own mayor, so long as he was 'faithful, discreet and fit to govern the city'. This was an important concession. Earlier kings had sometimes controlled the government of the capital, which was always overawed by the royal fortress of the Tower.*

King John, when he saw that he was deserted by almost all, so that out of his regal superabundance of followers he scarcely retained seven knights, was much alarmed lest the barons would attack his castles and reduce them without difficulty ... deceitfully pretended to make peace for a time with the aforesaid barons ... he also sent word to the barons ... to appoint a fitting day and place to meet. ROGER OF WENDOVER, OP. CIT., P.327

'Army of God' – but rebels they were. They had renounced their obedience to John and sent to Philip II for aid. For his part, John brought in foreign mercenaries. Fitzwalter's men made a valuable coup when the gates of London were thrown open to them by dissident citizens. Exeter and Lincoln also sided with the rebels.

John now knew that he would have to discuss the barons' grievances or, at least, make a show of so doing. The king was at Windsor, and the rebels had pitched their camp at Staines, so a midway location was decided on, a Thameside meadow at Runnymede. There both parties met on 15 June 1215. John set his seal to a draft agreement called the Articles of the Barons and, on the 19th of the month, after four days of haggling and transcribing, Magna Carta was ready to receive endorsement with the great seal.

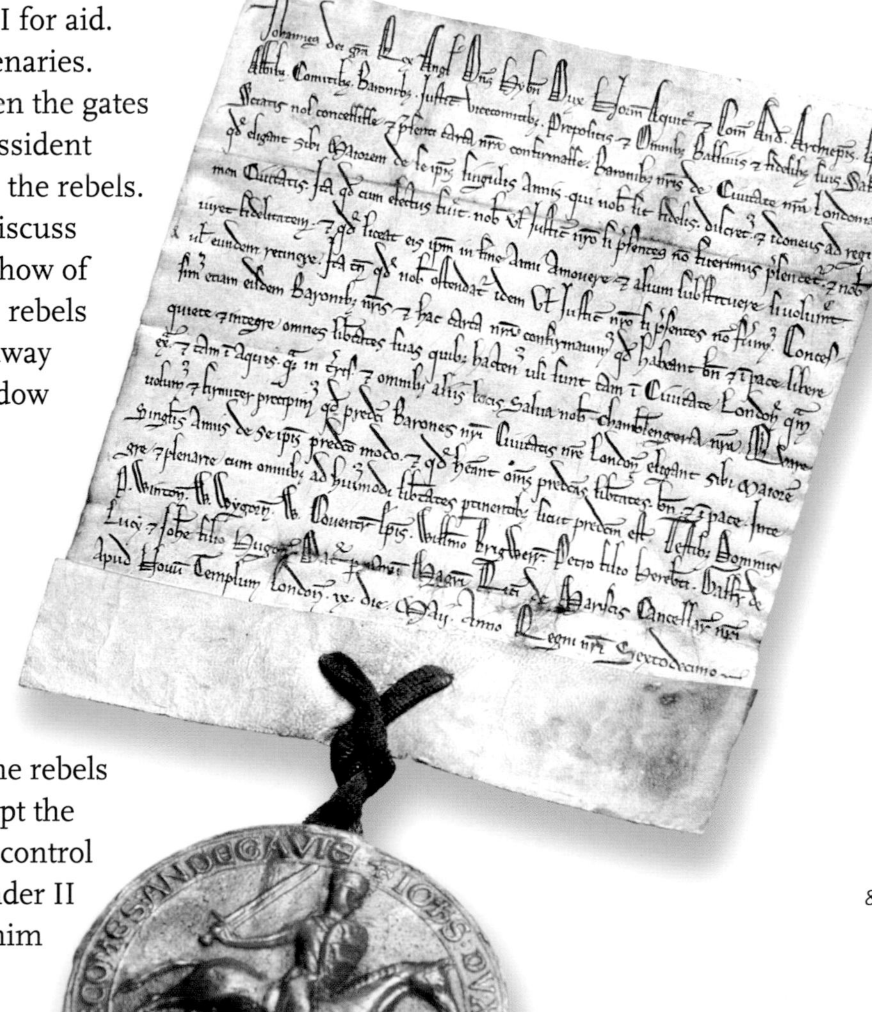

Now civil war broke out in earnest, and all John's enemies made common cause. The rebels invited Louis to come from France and accept the crown. Llewelyn-ap-Iorwerth re-established control of most of Wales. The barons invited Alexander II to come down from Scotland and invested him with considerable lands in the far north of England. But John, faced with the real prospect of losing England as well as

Magna Carta

The Great Charter, now considered to be the foundation stone of English constitutional rights, did not have that significance at the time. As a document guaranteeing the liberties of John's subjects, it failed because John simply ignored it. But it was a unique and novel definition of the relationship between king and people, and, once that definition had been made, it could not be unmade.

Magna Carta was a list of demands under 63 headings, and the points covered did not only relate to the concerns of the great magnates. Archbishop Stephen Langton was the principal drafter of the document, and he ensured that the interests of the church and other subjects were covered. Most of the clauses dealt with specific issues relating to the king's financial exactions, rights of inheritance and the conduct of royal officials. The right of the church to elect its own bishops and other senior clergy without royal interference was guaranteed. The ancient privileges of the city of London were to be upheld, and merchants were assured of free movement to ply their trade, except in times of war, when foreign merchants were to be detained 'until we or our justiciar know how the merchants of our land are treated in the enemy country'.

Magna Carta denounced

The rebels tried to give the charter administrative teeth by inserting a clause permitting the barons to appoint 25 of their number to ensure the king's compliance, 'so that if we or any of our servants offend in any way ... then those 25 barons together with the community of the whole land shall distrain and distress us in every way they can, namely by seizing castles, lands and possessions ... until in their judgement amends have been made'.

The drafters of the charter claimed to be doing no more than holding the king to his coronation oath and setting out in more detail what that oath implied. In fact, Magna Carta was a denial of the king's sovereignty, and John could scarcely have been expected to abide by its provisions. He soon had the backing of Innocent III in rejecting it. The pope denounced Magna Carta as, 'Not only shameful and base but also illegal and unjust ... Under threat of excommunication we order that the king should not dare to observe and the barons and their associates should not insist on it being observed. The charter with all its undertakings and guarantees we declare to be null and void of all validity for ever.' [6] The pope, who had appointed Stephen Langton to his office in the face of firm opposition from John, now suspended the archbishop for not backing the king against his barons.

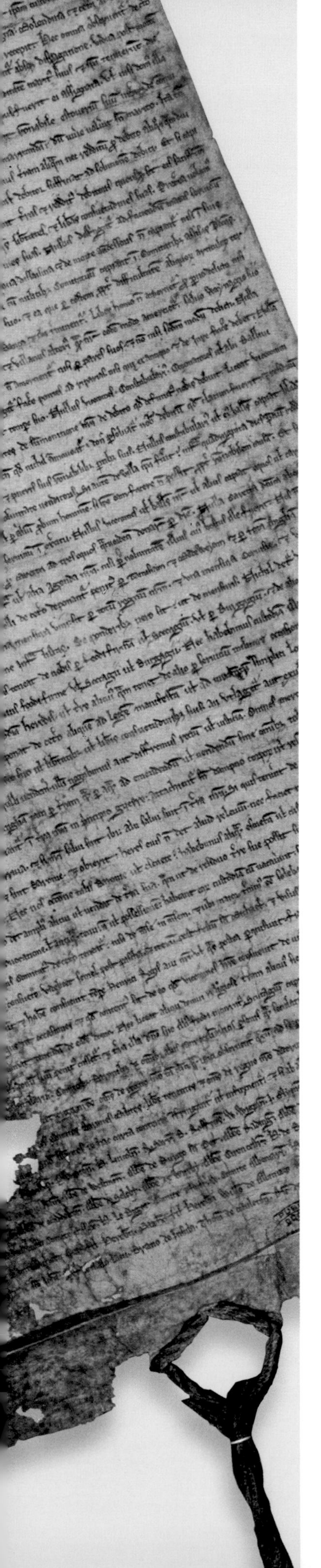

his continental possessions, fought like a tiger. He captured Rochester Castle after a determined seven-week siege, then marched northwards at the head of his mercenaries. His object was to terrify his subjects into submission.

John advanced into Scotland, harried the Lowlands and burned Berwick to the ground (January 1216). Within two months he was in East Anglia, laying siege to Colchester. In May Louis crossed the Channel and marched to London, where he was warmly welcomed. Alexander II came south in person to pay homage to the French prince. All seemed lost, but John refused to give in. In September he was in Lincolnshire. In October he was victorious in a skirmish at King's Lynn. Days later he was on his way northwards again. As he crossed the estuary of the River Welland his baggage train foundered in quicksand with the loss of his household goods and treasure. His spirit was not bowed by the procession of disasters, but his body was failing. He fell prey to dysentery. By 18 November he had reached Newark. There, during the following night, he died.

LEFT **Magna Carta**. *Of the many original copies of this important document only four have survived more or less intact. This example dates from 1225 and is housed in the archive of the Department of the Environment. Later versions, such as this, were made as additions and amendments were made to the original as a result of repeated negotiations between the king and his parliaments.*

RIGHT **Effigy of King John**. *The recumbent image of the king was placed upon his tomb in Worcester Cathedral. It was made some 20 years after his death but may well be a reasonable likeness. John is shown as 5 feet 9 inches tall, considerably shorter than his brothers. Shortly before his death in distant Newark John asked to be buried in the church of the Blessed Virgin and St Wulfstan (his patron saint) at Worcester and his wishes were scrupulously followed.*

HENRY III

Henry III was nine years old when he succeeded his father John, and he reigned for 56 years, longer than any other medieval king. In fact, his record stood for almost 600 years – until the reign of George III (1760–1820). This should suggest that under his rule England enjoyed a long period of stability and peace, something that was greatly needed after the conflicts between crown and barons that had disturbed his father's reign.

No longer did the king have to divide his time between possessions on both sides of the English Channel, and the basis of sound and just government had been laid down in Magna Carta. Unfortunately, things did not work out like that. Henry inherited a bankrupt treasury and was obliged to rely on unpopular taxes. He also showed himself to be insensitive and incompetent. As a result the later years of his reign saw a return to civil war.

1216–27

THESE WERE THE YEARS of Henry's minority. The affairs of the kingdom were put in the hands of a group of regents who had been involved in John's government and who enjoyed the respect of most of the barons. Prominent among them were William Marshal, Earl of Pembroke, and

ABOVE **Tomb effigy of William Marshal c.1146–1219.** *This time-worn effigy in the Temple Church, London is the only close representation of one of the age's more remarkable men. He has been called 'the greatest knight who ever lived' and his fame spread throughout Europe. He served all the Angevin kings from Henry II to Henry III and was one of the few barons to remain loyal to John. On John's death there was no one better qualified to act as regent for the young Henry III, a post he filled with efficiency and dignity despite his great age.*

PREVIOUS PAGES **The seal** *of Henry III (1216–72).* **A portrait of Henry III.** *Oil on panel, c.1620 and not, necessarily, accurate.*

the justiciar, Hubert de Burgh. Much of the baronial opposition faded with the death of John, but Louis of France still controlled much of southeast England and was supported by some of Henry's barons. The priority faced by the government was to expel the French invaders. On 20 May 1217 William Marshal defeated Louis' army at Lincoln, but this was not the end of the war. Louis expected considerable reinforcements, organized by his formidable wife, Blanche of Castile. She assembled a fleet of 80 ships in Calais, ten carrying over a hundred knights with their troops and the remainder loaded with vital military supplies. The leader of the expedition was Robert de Courtenai, the French queen's uncle. However, the most experienced naval commander in the fleet was Eustace the Monk, an ex-Benedictine turned mercenary pirate, who, from his base in the Channel Islands, had carried out raids on the French and English coasts.

> The English began to throw finely pulverized lime in great pots upon the deck, so that a great cloud arose. Then the French could no longer defend themselves for their eyes were full of powder.
>
> Li Romans de Witasse le Moine, I, eds. W. Foerster and J.Trost, halle, 1891, II, p.2289

Hubert de Burgh hastened to gather a naval force to confront the French and was able to put to sea some 40 or so vessels. The French set out on 24 August, a fine day when they could clearly see the cliffs of Dover. De Burgh's ships sailed to meet them, and thus began one of the more remarkable engagements in English naval history.

The two fleets met off Sandwich. De Burgh made as if to engage the enemy, then slipped past them. Eustace the Monk advised the admiral to make for the Thames estuary with all speed, but Robert de Courtenai, confident of defeating the enemy with his larger force, turned to fight. Now de Burgh's stratagem was revealed. He came upon the French downwind, assailing them first with crossbow bolts, then, at closer range, with pots of quicklime, which smashed on the enemy decks throwing up a blinding dust. In the confusion the English were able to board, capture several knights for ransom and massacre many of the soldiers and sailors. Only 15 French ships were able to escape. Eustace tried to escape by hiding below decks, but he was found and dragged out. He offered a 10,000 mark ransom, but his captors were more interested in revenging themselves on the treacherous pirate who had caused such havoc over the years. Eustace was summarily decapitated and his body was paraded through the streets of Dover and Canterbury. De Burgh's clever tactics (the first recorded instance of such a manoeuvre in English naval history) resulted in a valuable haul of ships and military equipment. Some of the booty was sold, and St Bartholomew's Hospital was set up near Sandwich as a thanksgiving for the victory. More importantly, it deprived Louis of the reinforcements he needed to continue his conquest of England, and he was forced to enter into peace talks with William Marshal.

Rex a filio e h audiss; att econe adsi uiuit W. marecallus. eidem imo. Irex. n g timeo de filio meo. Vn W. mareschall

nob & nris i urbe omniu u titulum gna. q e si habundarent in ciuitate u bene un illa emamus. Vo ecca uob significo qd n habeo facultate resistendi. n ab anglia recedendi n in puideatis potiue in subsidio militari. Cumq; ad prem de filio & ad uxorem de marito talia puenissent; doluerunt ualde illu i tali articulo fuisse constitutum. Et cum rex timuit filio excommunicato q semper notat fuit de prodicone.

Ric cicestr q iuadia... cpat sua ... ut pacaret ...

Petrus eps Wint. Ric Sar. Jos Bathoniensis. Hugo cicestr. cancell.

W. mar escal lus

Com Hereford.
Com Sarer.
Com Warenn.
Com Albamarl.

Absolucio pro liberacione anglie morituros.

...in omni cu processione solle... solemnibus festiuis occurrebant cum hymnis ... miracula a ...

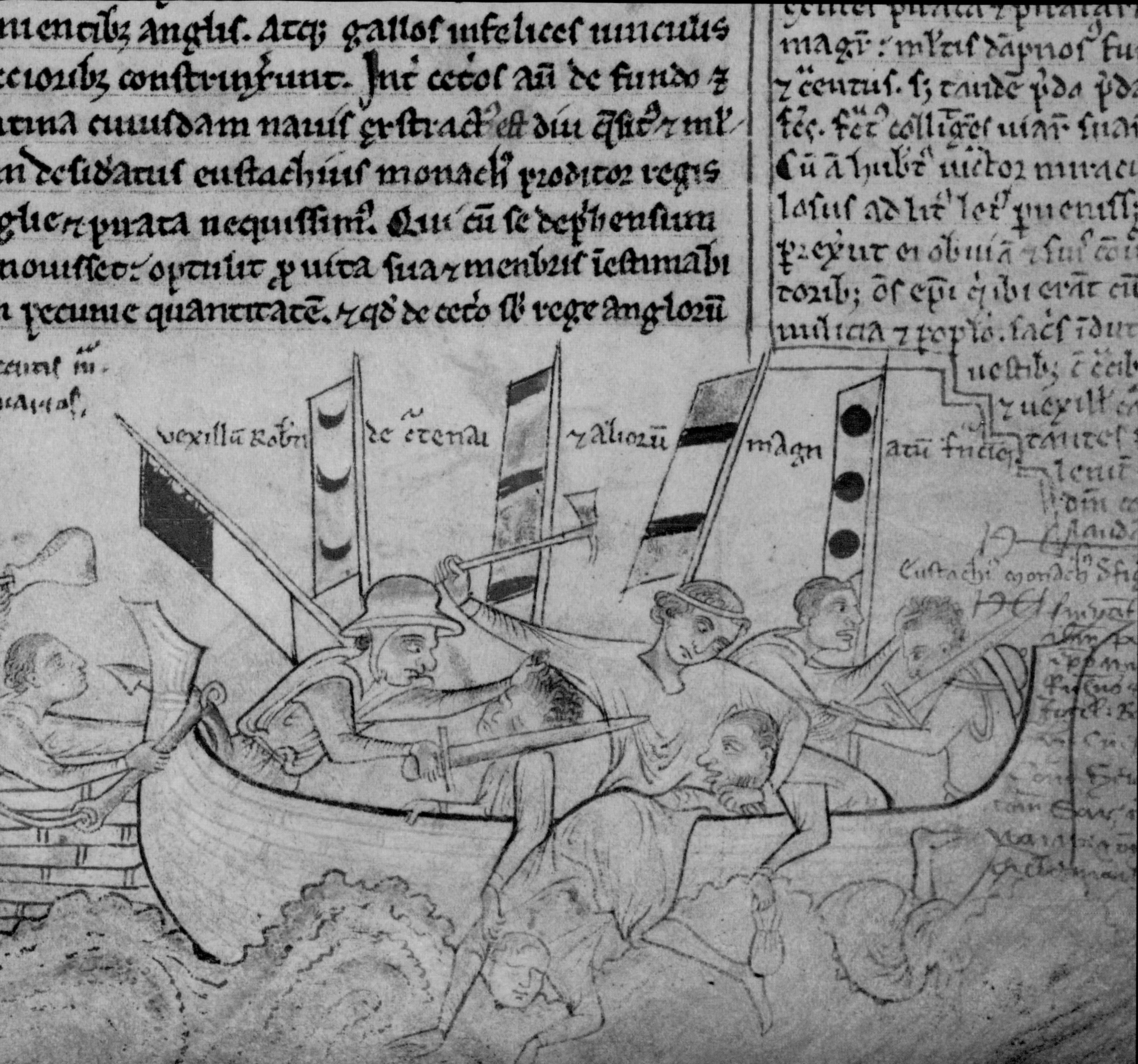

Death of Eustace the Monk, 1217. *This freebooting pirate – symbolic of the seaborne lawlessness of the age – met his end at the Battle of Sandwich. Having switched allegiance between England and France, he was eventually forced to do battle off the Kent coast on 24 August 1217. This illustration from the Chronicle of Matthew Paris shows bishops blessing the English fleet, sailors grappling Eustace's ship, firing pots of powdered lime and Eustace being beheaded.*

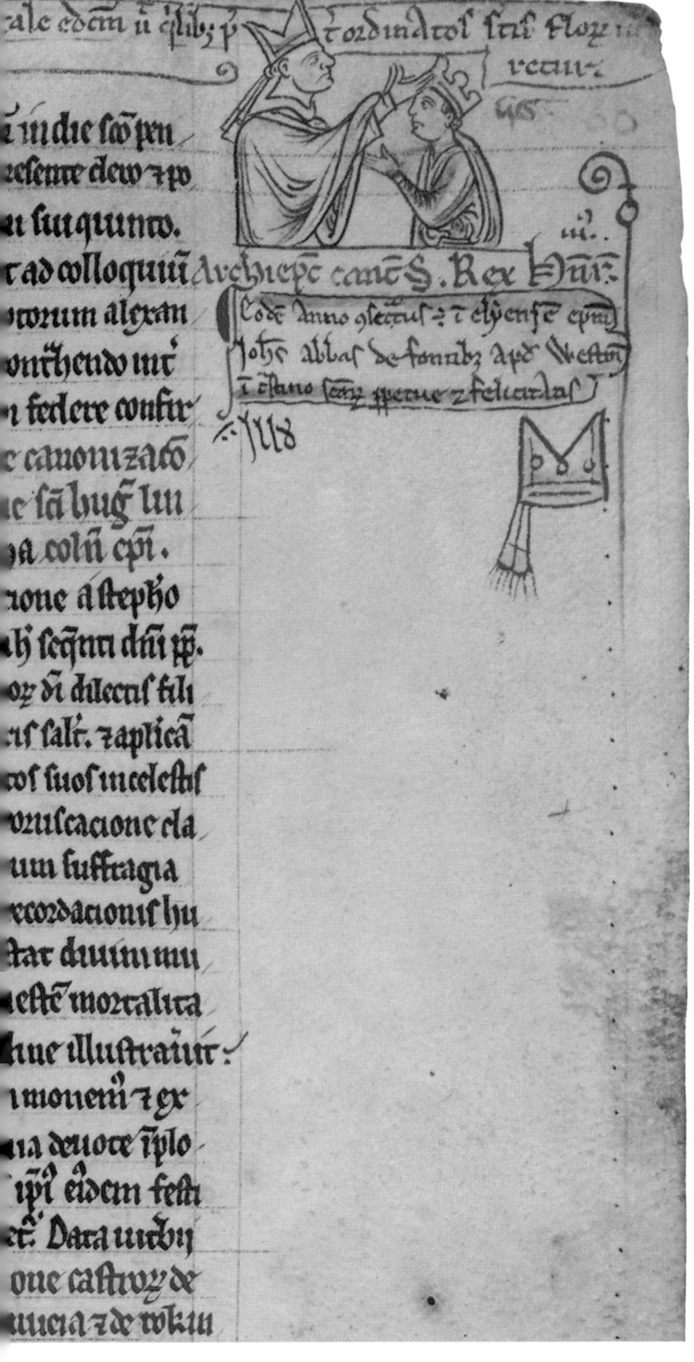

By a treaty agreed at Kingston in September, Louis recognized Henry as king of England, acknowledged his right to the Channel Islands, promised to help him recover his father's continental possessions and agreed never to aid Henry's rebellious subjects. In return, William Marshal agreed to pay Louis £7,000. Some barons were angry with the aged regent for paying off the French king and not pressing home his military advantage, but William was concerned to put a rapid end to all the fighting and rivalries that were unsettling the young king's realm. William Marshal died in May 1219 after a long life of faithful service to the crown.

A year later Henry had a full coronation at Westminster. The ceremony carried out immediately after John's death had been a hurried affair, but now the young king did obeisance to the pope for his lands and also confirmed Magna Carta. Under the tutelage of de Burgh and his other councillors Henry gradually assumed more and more executive authority. In 1223, when he was 16, his mentors allowed him limited use of the royal seal.

By the time he reached manhood Henry was well built, of stately demeanour and fair of face. His only blemish seems to have been a drooping eyelid. He was a man of many – often conflicting – parts. The chronicler Matthew Paris, who knew him well, referred often to his 'simplicity', by which he meant a childlike enthusiasm and exuberance. Henry was impulsive and readily gave his trust and affection. Yet he could also fall prey to suspicion and insecurity. He was an aesthete who spared no expense to surround himself with beautiful things. He was inquisitive and loved to marvel at unusual objects – such as the exotic animals he collected in his menagerie – and he adored elaborate ritual, especially that connected

ABOVE **The second coronation of Henry III**. *When Henry was crowned at the age of nine in 1216 the ceremony was a very low-key affair. The 'crown' used was a small circlet of gold because of Henry's age and also because most of the royal regalia had been lost when John's baggage train foundered while crossing the estuary of the River Ouse. Pope Honorius III, Henry's overlord, decreed that the rite had not been carried out according to prescribed church rules. He ordered a repeat performance and, on 17 May 1220, Henry's second coronation was a full-dress affair presided over by Archbishop Stephen Langton.*

OPPOSITE **Louis IX and Queen Blanche** *appear in this illustration from the* Moralised Bible *(c.1320). Blanche of Castile, a granddaughter of Henry II and Eleanor of Aquitaine, had much of her grandmother's strength of personality. Her husband, Louis VIII, claimed the English crown through Blanche's descent and she vigorously supported the French invasion of 1216. On Louis' death in 1226 Blanche became regent for her 12-year-old son, Louis IX. It was Blanche who, by a mix of warlike preparation and skilful diplomacy, held the kingdom together. This illustration shows Blanche and her young son together with a scribe receiving dictation, probably from a court official.*

The coronation of Louis VIII and Blanche of Castile. *The couple were married in 1200 when they were both minors and came to the throne as king and queen on the death of Philip II in 1223; the coronation took place at Rheims on 6 August. Louis, however, died in 1226. The illumination from* Chroniques de France ou de St Denis *shows the 'doubling' of church and state leaders in the ceremony – i.e., the Duke of Burgundy carries the crown and the Archbishop of Rheims crowns the king; the Count of Flanders the royal sword and the Bishop of Beauvais carries the royal mantle.*

Falkes de Breauté

Conflicts between baronial houses and between baronial factions and the government form a constant background to the reign of Henry III. The career of Falkes de Breauté provides an example of the turbulence that made England so difficult to govern.

De Breauté was a Norman adventurer who won favour with King John and served him effectively in his war with the barons in 1215–16. In a series of ruthless campaigns he sacked and pillaged Worcester, Ely and St Albans. According to Matthew Paris, the fearless soldier was troubled with a dream after the sacking of St Albans Abbey, went to the abbot and begged forgiveness. He bared his back to receive a scourging from the monks, but when the question was raised of returning the silver he had extorted, he told the abbot: 'My wife has made me do this because of a dream but if you want me to restore what I took from you I will not listen.'[1] Five years later de Breauté announced his intention of going on crusade, but in this venture too his religious resolve seems to have been quickly dissipated.

De Breauté's bravery

On the accession of Henry III, de Breauté became one of the more effective military leaders in the war against Louis. His bravery was most conspicuously demonstrated at the siege of Lincoln. When the well-fortified city held out against the royal army he led a

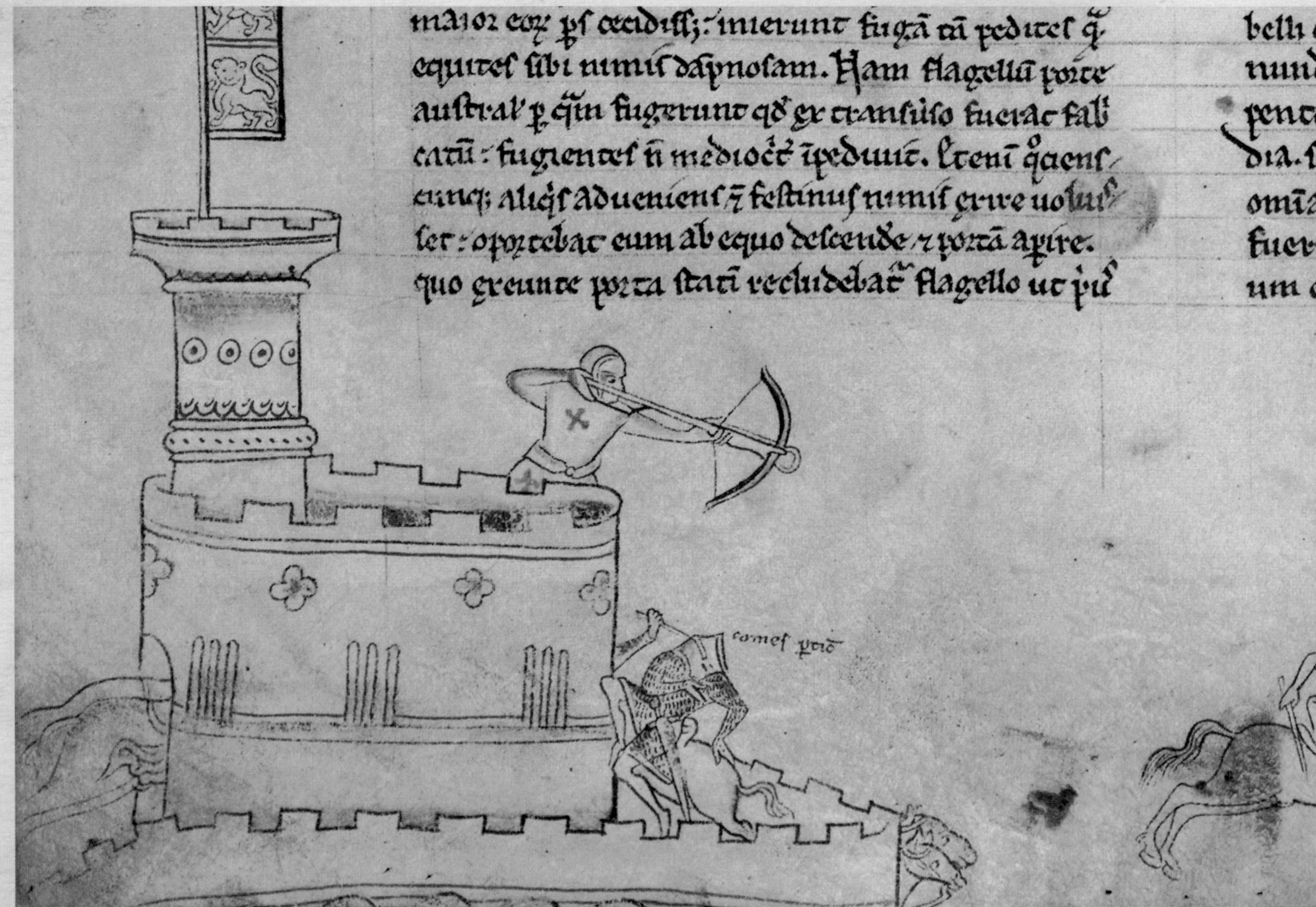

small force that scaled one of the walls and created havoc among the defenders by attacking them from the rooftops. When the main army broke in, de Breauté took part in the fearful slaughter of the inhabitants. By this time he had become probably the most powerful man in the kingdom. He was in possession of several royal castles, held large personal estates and was sheriff of six counties. After the war against Louis, the government demanded the surrender of royal castles that John had bestowed upon his foreign supporters, but de Breauté refused to comply.

He was now a potential threat to the king and a rival of the justiciar, Hubert de Burgh. He emerged as a leader of opposition to de Burgh and drew around him a faction that included such men as Ranulf, Earl of Chester, and Peter des Roches, Bishop of Winchester. In November 1223 the anti-de Burgh party tried to seize the Tower of London, and civil war was averted only by the intervention of Stephen Langton, Archbishop of Canterbury, who threatened the rebels with excommunication. De Breauté made his submission to the king and was forced to give up several castles and some of his offices, but resentment continued to fester.

Bedford Castle

Matters came to a head in the summer of 1224. De Breauté refused to relinquish Bedford Castle, where his brother, William, was constable. William seized one of the royal justices and refused the king's demand to release him. The brothers defied Henry in the belief that they could hold Bedford until the Earl of Chester and their other friends came to their aid. Henry and the justiciar now mounted a determined siege. They ordered a whole wood to be felled to provide the timber for a battery of siege engines with which they bombarded the castle for eight weeks. Heavy losses did not deter the royal leaders, nor did the excommunication pronounced by Langton against the defenders to persuade them to surrender. On 14 August Bedford Castle was overwhelmed. William and more than 80 members of the military garrison were hanged.

Falkes had escaped, but his attempt to continue defiance was balked by the desertion of his allies, and on 19 August he submitted to the king. But he could not face a trial – he had made too many enemies among the barons. He preferred to go into exile, and he travelled to Rome, where, forsaken by his fellow rebels and even by his wife, de Breauté died from eating poisoned fish. This troublesome, brave military leader was no more cruel, arrogant, greedy and selfish than many other members of his class, some of whom prospered and founded long-lasting dynasties, while others fatally miscalculated their power. These were the sort of men England's kings had to deal with.

LEFT **The Battle of Lincoln, 1217,** *from the Chronicle of Matthew Paris. When the English barons were divided in their loyalty to Henry III and Louis VIII, the city of Lincoln was taken by the French king, but Lincoln Castle remained in Henry's hands. William Marshal brought up an army and laid siege to the city while, within its walls, Louis' forces were besieging the castle. The French were scattered and because of the great quantity of booty acquired by Marshal's men, the battle was known as 'Lincoln Fair'.*

Hubert de Burgh seeking sanctuary, 1232. *The well-established custom of sanctuary provided a means for a fugitive to avoid rough or over-hasty justice by entering and remaining in a church. Shelter was afforded, usually for 30 or 40 days. His lands and goods might be forfeit and he might opt for voluntary exile but his person was safe. The fate of Hubert de Burgh, Henry III's justiciar, illustrates the problems inherent in the system. Having incurred the hatred of many barons and bishops Hubert was charged with numerous murders, extortions and embezzlement. He took sanctuary in Merton Priory. His balked enemies raised an army of 20,000 to seize him but Henry forbade them to violate sanctuary. Hubert moved to a chapel at Brentwood. This time he was taken thence by force. The Bishop of London forced his captors to return him on pain of excommunication. A similar sequence of events occurred when Hubert later took sanctuary in Devizes Church. Only in 1234 were Hubert and the king reconciled. According to Matthew Paris, de Burgh 'bore all the assaults of fortune with calm patience'.*

with religious devotion. He tried to impress his subjects with lavish and expensive displays of kingliness, but his fine judgement in matters artistic did not extend to people. He made favourites of unworthy men and ignored the advice of those who deserved his trust. He had the fiery, quick temper of his Angevin forebears but lacked their military ardour. He had been brought up to expect deference rather than to earn it and, largely for this reason, he was unable to establish close and constructive working relations with the leading men of the realm. Henry's reign was littered with the ruins of grand projects, which he began but failed to bring to fulfilment. There is no doubt that he had the good of his subjects at heart, but he ended up taxing them beyond endurance, losing the respect of his barons and provoking another period of civil war. Ironically, it was Henry's shortcomings and his long reign that permitted the further limitation of royal power and the development of constitutional change.

King Philip of France died in 1223 and was succeeded by his son as Louis VIII. Henry immediately demanded that Louis, as promised, should restore his French lands to him, but Louis refused, and an expedition sent from England failed to regain possession of Normandy and other territories. Louis died in 1226, leaving the crown to his 12-year-old son, Louis IX, and Henry tried to achieve by intrigue what he had not achieved by force. He took advantage of France's internal discord and sought an alliance with nobles rebelling against the crown, but this too came to nothing. In the meantime, in January 1227, Henry declared himself to be of age and assumed full kingly authority.

1227–34

IN FACT, THE YOUNG KING continued to be dependent on his justiciar, Hubert de Burgh, who, by now accustomed to wielding virtually absolute authority, continued to frame policy, sometimes acting in secrecy. This created tension between king and justiciar and encouraged the opposition of a baronial faction jealous of de Burgh's power. In 1230, after a long and difficult period of preparation, Henry crossed the Channel at the head of an army for the recovery of his Angevin inheritance. But this campaign, the last real attempt to recover Normandy for the English crown, was carried out in a half-hearted fashion and came to nothing.

When, in 1231, Peter des Roches, Bishop of Winchester, returned from crusade to great acclaim he became the leader of the court faction opposed to the justiciar. Henry havered in his support for first one, then the other of his advisers, but in July 1232 he had a fierce argument with de Burgh, dismissed him as justiciar and gave the job to des Roches. But the bishop was no more capable of uniting the baronage behind the throne than his predecessor had been. The new Archbishop of Canterbury, Edmund Rich, accused the regime of corruption and maladministration and threatened the king with excommunication if he did not get rid of des Roches. In May 1234 Henry weakly gave in and ordered the bishop to retire to his diocese. The office of justiciar lapsed. Only now did Henry III's personal rule truly begin.

Henry's marriage

There were assembled *at the king's nuptial festivities such a host of nobles of both sexes, such numbers of religious men, such crowds of the populace, and such a variety of actors, that London, with its capacious bosom, could scarcely contain them. The whole city was ornamented with flags and banners, chaplets and hangings, candles and lamps, and with wonderful devices and extraordinary representations, and all the roads were cleansed from mud and dirt, sticks and everything offensive. The citizens, too, went out to meet the king and queen, dressed out in their ornaments, and vied with each other in trying the speed of their horses ... The ceremony was splendid, with the gay dresses of the clergy and knights who were present. The abbot of Westminster sprinkled the holy water, and the treasurer acting the part of sub-dean, carried the paten. Why should I describe all those persons who reverently ministered in the church to God as was their duty? Why describe the abundance of meats and dishes on the table? The quantity of venison, the variety of fish, the joyous sounds of the glee-men, and the gaiety of the Waiters? Whatever the world could afford to create pleasure and magnificence was there brought together from every quarter.*

MATTHEW PARIS'S ENGLISH HISTORY, TR. J.A. GILES, 1852–4, I, P.8

1235–41

ENGLAND NOW ENTERED on a period of peace and relative stability. Henry could not afford a foreign war, and the old faction leaders were either soon dead or had made their peace with each other and the king. Henry concentrated on diplomacy in his foreign affairs. He married his sister, Isabella, to the Emperor Frederick II in 1235 and began in earnest to seek a wife for himself. He eventually chose Eleanor, the 11-year-old daughter of the Count of Provence. Eleanor's sister was married to Louis IX, which made the English and French kings brothers-in-law. Henry was now connected by marriage to the leading figures in European affairs. In 1236 he and Louis agreed a four-year truce. Moreover, Eleanor was connected on her mother's side to the influential counts of Savoy, whose lands were strategically placed to control the Alpine passes into Italy. The wedding took place in January 1236, and Henry made sure that the lavish ceremonial would set new standards of royal magnificence.

The marriage was a success. Despite the difference in their ages, Henry and Eleanor not only developed a great affection for each other, but the young queen exercised considerable influence. She was intelligent and soon developed a keen sense of political realities. She brought with her several of her Savoyard relatives, which proved to be both an advantage and a disadvantage to Henry. The establishment of more foreigners at court led, in time, to a build-up of resentment, but some of Eleanor's relatives were men of real ability who gave good advice.

Foremost among them was the Bishop of Valence, William of Savoy, and when Henry reorganized his council he put William in charge. The new body carried out important economic and administrative reforms that placed the royal finances on a more secure footing. It also instituted a survey of English law, which culminated in the Statute of Merton (1236). The council meeting in Merton Abbey was augmented by the leading judges, among whom was the brilliant legist William Ralegh. The document that emerged sought to apply in detail the general principles enunciated in Magna Carta: it defined the rights of vulnerable members of society such as widows and minors; it protected from exploitation children who had inherited property on the death of their parents; it tidied up the law relating to the enclosure of common land by powerful magnates; and it brought Irish law into line with English law.

In January 1238 Henry's sister, Eleanor, was married in clandestine circumstances. She had previously been the wife of William Marshal, Earl of Pembroke (son of the regent), and on his death in 1231 she had taken a vow of permanent

ABOVE **The seal of Richard of Cornwall.** *Richard (1209–72) was the second son of King John and one of the most influential men in 12th-century Europe. In 1231 he married Isabel, the rich widow of the Earl of Gloucester, and, after her death, he married in 1243 Sanchia, Henry III's sister-in-law. In 1257 he was elected king of Germany but seldom visited his territory. Richard was immensely wealthy and lent large sums to his spendthrift brother. He gained considerable international kudos from his participation in a successful crusade (1240–42) and was a highly respected English envoy in various diplomatic negotiations. Several of the barons looked to Richard as leader of the party in opposition to Henry III. The earl frequently took Henry to task for his poor administration but, apart from a period early in Henry's reign (c.1227–33) when he sided with opponents of the regime, he remained loyal to his brother.*

The Tower of London

Henry III made enormous changes over many years to the simple Norman fortress that had been built by William the Conqueror. He enlarged, strengthened and beautified it, turning it into a palace/fortress complex reflecting the splendour of monarchy and providing a refuge for himself and his court in times of crisis.

He had a moat dug around three sides, which was fed by the Thames on the other side. A bridge connected the Tower to the mainland and was overlooked by an imposing gateway. In 1240 this gate collapsed (followed by another section of the wall a year later). Matthew Paris moralized on this event by describing how a London priest dreamed that the fall of the walls was the work of Thomas Becket: 'an Archbishop, dressed in all his finery, and brandishing a cross in his hand, appeared at the wall which the King had recently built ... His face shining with anger, he struck the wall hard with the cross in his right hand and cried out, "Tell me for what purpose you are now being rebuilt." Suddenly the walls came tumbling down, though newly built, as if they had been struck by an earthquake ... The priest was informed, This is the Blessed Martyr Thomas, a Londoner by birth, who has seen all these things now being done to harm the people of his city: he has therefore destroyed them irreparably ... these works were made not for the defence of the kingdom, but to harm innocent citizens.'[2]

Paris's verdict was, apparently, confirmed when Henry caused the central keep to be lime-washed. It now stood out starkly as an imposing statement of royal power. (It is still called the White Tower.)

ABOVE **The White Tower.** *The central keep of the Tower of London is an imposing edifice but it was much more so when Henry III ordered that it was to be completely lime-washed. His intention was to overawe the citizens of the capital. London was the economic hub of the kingdom and its wealthy merchants and their guilds were very jealous of the independence granted to them in their charters. If the city sided with rebels and opened the gates to baronial armies the threat to the crown was very real. Small wonder, then, that Henry spent vast sums on strengthening its defences and confronted Londoners with the dazzling display of the White Tower whenever they turned their gaze eastwards.*

OPPOSITE **The death of Gruffydd-ap-Llewelyn, 1244.** *This Welsh prince was held in the Tower as a hostage at the instigation of his own brother, Dafydd, who was on good terms with King Henry and feared that Gruffydd would stir up a revolt. Accordingly, Gruffydd was lodged in the royal apartments of the Tower in September 1241. On 1 March 1244, Gruffydd, despairing of ever being released, made an escape bid. With a rope of knotted sheets he let himself down from one of the walls. Unfortunately, the rope broke and Gruffydd plunged headfirst to the ground. According to Matthew Paris, who drew this picture, 'his head and neck were crushed between his shoulders'.*

Turris London

12h

136

Griffinus

Henry had a new great hall and other lodgings built and lavishly decorated as a fitting palace for his court. By enlarging the Tower he had incorporated one of the local churches, and this was now dedicated to St Peter ad Vincula (St Peter in Chains), much beautified and provided with a peal of bells.

The royal menagerie

In 1251 the Sheriff of London was ordered to pay 4 pence a day for the upkeep of the king's polar bear and to provide it with a muzzle and chain. This is the first extant documentary evidence for the royal menagerie – London's first zoo. Henry, ever interested in curios, kept at the Tower a variety of exotic animals, most of which were presents from other kings: the polar bear was sent by the king of Norway, King Louis IX presented Henry with an elephant and three leopards came as a wedding gift from the Emperor Frederick III. The king's beasts, one of the sights of London, were housed in the outer ward to which citizens and visitors had access.

But for many the Tower evoked foreboding rather than admiration. When Henry summoned parliament to meet there members declined to be lured within the stout walls.

BELOW **Henry's elephant.** *This image from the Bestiary of Matthew Paris shows the beast given to Henry by Louis IX in 1255. Such a creature had not been seen in England since Roman times. It was a great curiosity and, thus, added to the king's prestige. It was housed in the Tower, though exactly where is not known, and, if the writer is to be believed, was fed on beef and wine. If that is, even partially, true it is not surprising that the poor animal died after a couple of years. About this time the 'elephant and castle' became a heraldic device. Pictures of these beasts carrying howdahs were misinterpreted as showing elephants with crenellated stone towers on their backs.*

chastity. But she had been only 16 at the time, and her resolve weakened when she met a young Frenchman who had arrived in England to claim his inheritance as Earl of Leicester. This was Simon de Montfort, a vigorous young knight who had proved himself in military service to the French king. The couple formed a liaison (Henry would later claim that Eleanor had been seduced) and, to avoid scandal, Henry had them secretly married. This caused a furore. The king's brother, Richard of Cornwall, felt personally affronted, the leading barons insisted that they should have been consulted, and the Archbishop of Canterbury complained that Eleanor had broken her sacred vow. Richard and his supporters flew to arms, and Henry retreated to the Tower of London. Thanks to the intervention of William of Savoy peace was achieved by a payment of 16,000 marks to Richard to enable him to go on crusade. The next year Simon was invested with the Earldom of Leicester. He and Eleanor went to live in France but were reconciled to the king in 1240, shortly before Simon went on crusade.

In June 1239 Henry and his subjects were able to rejoice in the birth of an heir – the baby was named Edward, in honour of Henry's favourite saint – but at the end of the year the news was brought to Henry that William of Savoy had died in Italy, and the king was distraught. Matthew Paris recorded that he had torn off his clothes and thrown them into the fire. Despite this, 1239 and the following few years were the happiest of the king's reign. In 1240 his wife gave birth to a daughter, and Henry engaged in a successful campaign against Gruffydd-ap-Llewelyn of Wales. Meanwhile, more and more of the queen's Savoyard relatives were arriving in England and receiving lands and offices from the king. In 1241 Boniface of Savoy, another of Eleanor's uncles, was appointed to the important position of Archbishop of Canterbury (though he was not confirmed in office by the pope until 1243).

1242–52

STILL DETERMINED to recover his family's possessions on the continent, Henry led an expedition to Poitou in the spring of 1242. His army was too small for the task, and he was seriously short of money to equip his soldiers or to buy mercenaries. The result of this rash enterprise was a humiliating and costly failure, and the king also lost the respect of seasoned campaigners, such as Richard of Cornwall and Simon de Montfort. Simon was heard to blurt out that Henry was so incompetent that his subjects ought to lock him away. It was October 1243 before the king was able to renew his truce with Louis and return to England. As for his brother Richard, Henry bought him off with large gifts, the weak response he frequently made to win the support of potential opponents.

In 1244 Henry, needing more taxes, summoned a parliament. The magnates refused to give him any money unless he appointed a justiciar and a chancellor to exercise some control over royal policy and finances, but Henry refused this restriction of the royal power. The birth of a second son, Edmund, softened the attitude of the barons, and a compromise was worked out and a modest financial grant agreed. To augment this grant Henry imposed a tax on the Jews (always an easy target). What particularly galled him was that, while he found it difficult to extract money from his own subjects, the pope made frequent financial demands on the clergy, which they met. Henry was not the only one who resented money being drained out of the country in this way. The papal nuncio (representative) went in fear of his life and appealed to the king: 'For the love of God and the reverence of my lord the pope, grant me a safe conduct.' Henry retorted: 'May the devil give you a safe conduct to hell and all through it.' At a great council in 1246 king and magnates drafted a protest to Rome about these exactions and refused to allow the English church to pay, but the papacy held all the European churches in a stranglehold and, as Bishop Grosseteste of Lincoln pointed out, Henry's clergy had no choice but to pay.

'May the devil give you a safe conduct to hell and all through it.'

Meanwhile, in 1245, perhaps to placate the pope and to exhibit his own piety, Henry embarked on a grandiose reconstruction of the abbey church at Westminster. In 1245, Henry launched an expedition against Dafydd of Wales, but the Welsh refused direct engagement. For months Henry's troops, underemployed and underpaid, carried out savage raids throughout north Wales, impoverishing the country and creating a famine in the land. Eventually the death of Dafydd without an heir enabled Henry to establish his overlordship. This was another costly and unnecessary military expedition.

Later in the year Henry staged a spectacular ceremony that was both a genuine expression of piety and a bid for popularity. He had acquired from the Holy Land a phial supposedly containing some of the blood of Christ. He went personally to St Paul's Cathedral to receive the relic, having spent the previous night in a vigil and a bread-and-water fast. Determined to gain maximum publicity, he ordered Matthew Paris to record the event in detail, which the chronicler duly did:

OPPOSITE **Henry carrying the phial of holy blood, 1245.** *This illustration in Matthew Paris's* Chronica Majora *accompanies his long description of the installing of a supposed phial of Christ's blood at Westminster. It depicts the king carrying the precious relic under a canopy and delivering it to the archbishop. Medieval worshippers set enormous store by physical objects believed to have real connection with holy people. Just as, today, autographs, clothing and other personal objects associated with celebrities command high prices, so medieval people were overawed by objects which gave them a physical connection with spiritual heroes and heroines. An important difference is that saintly relics were believed to possess miraculous power. This explains why pilgrims would travel long distances to gaze upon or touch the splendid reliquaries in which such objects were housed. The offerings of such pilgrims provided a major source of income for the churches where relics were displayed.*

ut spectatur: ut pro ipso orantes: missa solempnit omnes monachi cantarent. cuius prima collecta foret de sancto Albano: secunda autem pro infirmo. scilicet Omnipotens sempiterne deus salus eterna credentium etc. Et per dei gratiam puero sanitas est restituta. Hic recreo dictum ipsius murmur populi dicentis. Ecce laici orant dominum et exaudiuntur. et ipse non orat sed facit per eam sua immo vera et universalis ecclesie orare, immo rapinis inhiat pecunie indefessus. dictumque est et affirmatum, quod non sine lachrimis scribi debet vel quomodolibet recitari plus confidit in pecunie thesauris quam fidelium precibus vel elemosinis. Magnates Alemannie elegerunt

In crastino vero Willelmum comitem Hoilandie in sancti Michaelis magnum regem suum et ei homagium tres Alemannie ad quos ius electionis ligium fecerunt. Comes spectat pro maiori parte: elegerunt sibi ultimo in regem alemannie Willelmum comitem Hoilandie adolescentem. habentem in etate circiter xx. annos. iuvenem elegantem et probum atque genere suo. Cui et fecerunt homagium. Dux tamen Saxonie et quidam alii magnates huic electioni non consenserunt. Unde maior cisma surrepsit in imperio dicente. Ecce militia quasi sacerdotium per superbia. Ecce sacerdotium eadem contra militiam.

Circa idem tempus scripsit dominus rex de sanguine Christi omnibus regni sui magnatibus allato loco. ut in festo sancti Edwardi videlicet translatione que celebratur in quindena sancti Michaelis: iubens ut omnes ibidem convenirent: ut iocundissimos eundem sancti beneficium celitus Anglie nuper collati exaudisset. Et preterea ut tam gloriosi regis et martiris translationem venerarentur. Tercio: ut Willelmi de Valentia fratris sui uterini quem ipse rex ea die baltheo cincturum

Recepit igitur dominus rex ut omnis presbiteris clero sancto consonanter festive vestiti superpelliciis et capis sancti ac pis cum suis clericis decenter vestitis cum vexillis crucibus et cereis accensis die crastina videlicet translationis S. Edwardi summo mane ordinate et reverenter convenirent apud sanctum Paulum. Quo et ipse rex venit. Et cum summo honore et reverentia ac timore accipiens illud vasculum cum thesauro memorato: tulit illud ferens in prato super faciem suam. iens pedes. habens humilem habitum. scilicet pauperem capam sine capucio precedentibus vestitis predictis. sine pausatione. usque ad ecclesiam Westmonasterii. que distat ab ecclesia sancti Pauli circiter uno miliari. Nec pretermittendum quod ambabus manibus illud deferebat: cum per strata salebrosa et inequalem pergeret: sed vultum in celum vel in ipsum vas lumina tenebat defixa. Supportabatur autem palla per iiii. hastas. Supportabantque duo coadiutores brachia sua ne in tanto forte labore deficeret. Conventus autem Westmonasterii cum omnibus qui conveniant episcopis abbatibus et monachis qui plus quam centum estimabantur. cantantes et exultantes in spiritu sancto et lacrimis: occurrebant eidem domino regi sic advenienti usque ad portam curie episcopi Dunelmensis. Tunc autem reversi sicut iverant videlicet processionaliter ad ecclesiam Westmonasterii: viri in ea pre copiosa turbe multitudine continebantur. Nec adhuc cessabat dominus rex quin indefessus ferens illud vas ut prius circuiret ecclesiam. Regiam et thalamos suos. Demum illud quasi donum inestimabile et quod totam Angliam ditando illustraverat: donavit et optulit deo et ecclesie sancti Petri Westmonasterii et caro suo Edwardo et sacro conventui qui ibidem deo et sanctis suis ministrant.

Rex Henricus
Sanguis Christi.
Episcopi anglie [illegible] ... plati
Sequela tur conventus Westmonasterii cum abbatibus et monachis quasi longum esset enumerare festive vestitis. et canentibus et classicis magno pulsato

Early Gothic architecture

Henry III was an extremely devout king. He customarily heard mass several times a day, and the schedule of government business was often upset by his stopping to attend worship. In this way royal journeys sometimes took hours or even days longer than was necessary. Henry's piety was shown in the large number of church buildings that he directly sponsored or encouraged to be constructed, and his reign coincided with the establishment in England of the Gothic style of church architecture.

The Gothic style is conventionally divided into three phases: Early English (*c.*1180–1275), Decorated (*c.*1275–1380) and Perpendicular. The earlier Gothic churches and cathedrals were similar in design to those being built in northern continental Europe, but gradually there evolved a uniquely English style of architecture.

Power and strength

The fundamental difference between Early English Gothic and the Norman (or Romanesque) style that preceded it was the pointed arch (lancet). Hitherto the roofs and upper structures of churches had been borne on round arches, which conveyed the weight to massive pillars and thick walls. Lancets were discovered to be both more elegant and stronger. The pillars could be replaced by slender columns, which became decorative features in themselves – shafts of polished stone arranged in clusters around a central column of relatively small circumference. The overall impression was one of greater height, with soaring arches pointing heavenwards. The outer walls could also be used for decoration as well as support.

By using flying buttresses – external half-arches braced against the walls to provide extra strength – the builders were able to devote more wall space to windows. Narrow lancet windows pierced the walls, carrying stained glass, which glowed with multi-

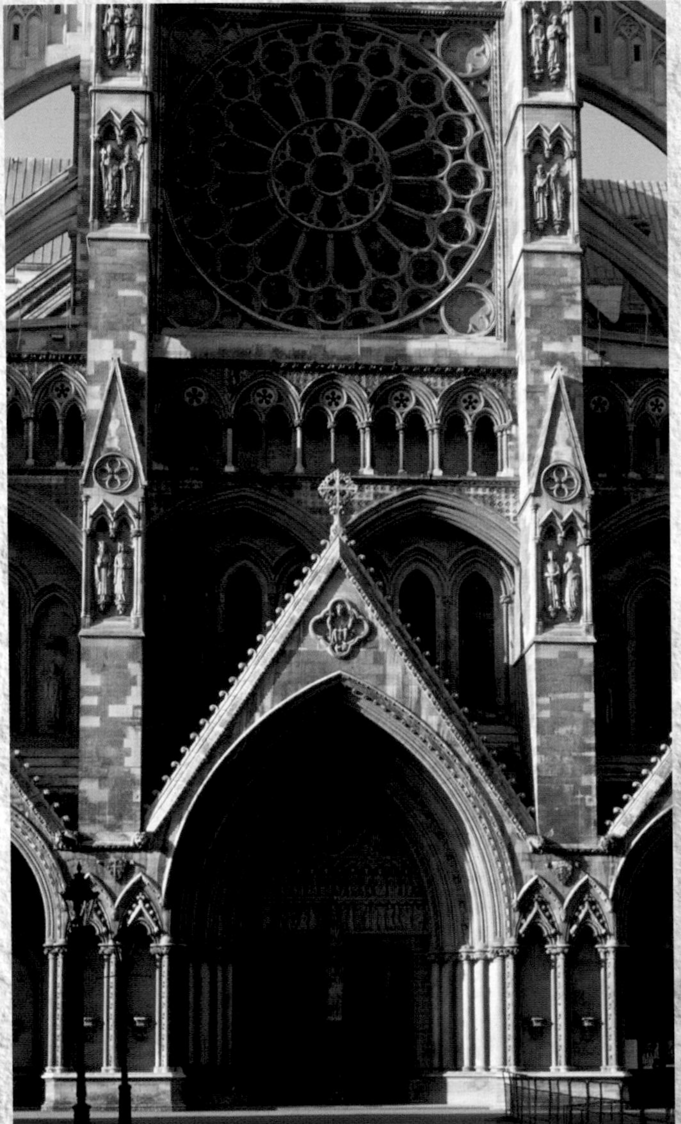

ABOVE **The north front of Westminster Abbey** *was Henry III's chief legacy to English architecture. Building continued throughout the second half of the reign and was not finished when the king died in 1272. One feature of early Gothic style copied from continental church design was the rose window, a feature of the north transept at Westminster.*

OPPOSITE **The nave vault at Westminster Abbey.** *In 1245 Henry had the eastern part of the Norman abbey pulled down so that work could be begun on a choir in the latest style. Because money ran out this choir remained 'tacked on' to the old nave. However, when work was resumed a century later the designs of Henry's master mason, Henry de Reyns, were closely followed.*

coloured light when the sun shone through. The 'rose window' also made its appearance at this time. This was a large, circular window, divided internally by stone tracery into panels that were filled with coloured glass. The total effect was one of awe-inspiring spaciousness, which could not but have a psychological effect on worshippers. The concepts of power and strength that many earlier churches had conveyed was replaced by those of gracefulness, radiance and intricacy. Glaziers could use the windows to illustrate stories from the Bible and the lives of the saints.

Westminster Abbey

Stonemasons were given more space to perfect their art. They provided columns with elaborate capitals and introduced carved roof bosses representing animals, heraldic devices and biblical figures. Church buildings came to have an educative value – it was said that stained glass windows, carved images and wall paintings were sermons in themselves.

Henry III's most impressive architectural project was the rebuilding of Westminster Abbey. The king visited France in 1243 and was immensely impressed by the building projects of Louis IX, who was creating churches and cathedrals in the new style in Paris and Rheims. Determined to outdo his rival monarch, Henry immediately set in hand a transformation of the abbey church at Westminster. This had been built 200 years earlier by the English king and saint, Edward the Confessor. St Edward was Henry's favourite saint, and the king wanted to create a more impressive building to house his remains. Part of the Confessor's church was pulled down so that building could commence in 1245. At a time when he was taxing his subjects heavily Henry lavished £45,000 on his pet project. The church was unfinished at the time of Henry's death and later benefactors made their contributions in currently prevailing styles, but the famous church as it stands today is largely as Henry III's architects conceived it.

The transition from massive monumentality to ethereal refinement reflected something of Henry III's own personality in the church building.

ABOVE **St Edward the Confessor (*c.*1003–66).** *Edward, who built the original abbey church at Westminster, was the patron saint of English kings and Henry III's aim in rebuilding the church was to provide a more impressive shrine as a resting place for the saint's bones and an important centre of pilgrimage. This illumination is from the* Westminster Abbey Psalter *of the late 12th century.*

OPPOSITE **Edward the Confessor's Chapel in Westminster Abbey**. *The first part of Henry III's abbey to be built was designed as an impressive space for the 'theatre' of coronations and other royal events and also as a burial place for Henry and his descendants. Originally the stonework and roof bosses were polychromed and gilded. Spaces between windows carried colourful frescoes.*

Henry III and the English church

Henry's attitude to the church was ambivalent: his natural piety gave him a deep respect for it, but his need for money obliged him to exploit to the full his rights in such matters as taxation and insinuating his own candidates into important ecclesiastical posts.

In accordance with Magna Carta, Henry was pledged to defend the church, and this included defending it from the exorbitant demands of Rome, but he was more interested in staying in the pope's good books.

During his reign there was a spiritual and intellectual revival in the Western church, which invigorated it and made it less susceptible to royal direction. This movement was largely due to the astonishing spread of Franciscan friars. The Franciscan order, founded by St Francis (d. 1226), was a body of men committed to poverty and the renunciation of worldly wealth, power and pomp. They wore only a simple habit, went barefoot and begged for their sustenance, devoting themselves to preaching and teaching. Several Englishmen had been attracted to the order before the death of the founder and, in 1224, they began a mission to the British Isles. By 1240 they had established communities in London and at least a dozen other major centres. Oxford was a particularly important location, and the Franciscans played a leading role in establishing the university there. Among the prominent men associated with the order in these years were the scholars Roger Bacon (*c.*1214–2) and Robert Grosseteste (*c.*1170–1253).

Robert Grosseteste

Grosseteste was an intellectual giant, whose studies and numerous writings embraced natural science, astronomy, theology, poetry and classical translations. He even rendered from the French a book on the tending of trees and vines. About 1225 he became a lecturer at Oxford, and in 1231 he took the post of lector (teacher) to the local Franciscan community. The Franciscan ideal of poverty appealed to him, and although he did not become a full member of the order he began to live a life of austere simplicity. In 1235 he was elected Bishop of Lincoln. At a time when many bishops were political appointees, more interested in their revenues than their duties, Grosseteste stood out as an indefatigable pastor and reformer of his diocesan flock. As he travelled the parishes of his large see he was accompanied by hand-picked friars, skilled as preachers, teachers and confessors, and he was uncompromising in the standards of behaviour and instruction he demanded of parish clergy and religious men and women within his jurisdiction. When it came to the church's relationship with the crown he was equally steadfast.

In 1236 at Merton a major issue came before the royal council: the relationship between the law of the king's courts and canon law, the law of the church. There were several points at which the two systems came into conflict – for example, the church accepted as legitimate children born out of wedlock whose parents subsequently married, while the common law regarded them as bastards, which had considerable importance where issues of inheritance were concerned. Grosseteste argued strongly for the church's position and demanded that the royal courts should be brought into line with the 'superior' customs of the church. The king's justices could not accept this, and the issue remained unresolved. Issues of great legal,

OPPOSITE **Robert Grosseteste**, *Bishop of Lincoln (d.1253). Matthew Paris described Grosseteste as courteous and charitable but fearless in standing up for what he considered to be right. 'At the table of bodily refreshment he was hospitable ... and affable. At the Spiritual table devout and ... contrite. In his episcopal office he was sedulous, venerable and indefatigable.'*

1259–63

THE BARONIAL COMMITTEE OF 24 worked assiduously to put more flesh on the Provisions of Oxford and, particularly, to define more precisely the relationship between central government and the various law courts. As well as baronial leaders and government officers, the best legal brains in the country were brought to bear on a complete overhaul of most aspects of the judicial system. Old laws were reinforced, and new ones were drafted that covered aspects of relationships between all classes in society – everything from taxation and inheritance to murder (differentiated for the first times from accidental death). Agreement was not arrived at without argument, but the new measures reached their final form in the Provisions of Westminster of October 1259. This was a major achievement, the greatest since Magna Carta.

Over the next four years, Henry had three major problems: the baronial revolt was a severe check to his authority; Llewelyn threatened the geographical integrity of his kingdom; and there were rumours that his eldest son, Edward, was plotting against him. The situation was confused and all parties – king, barons, Llewelyn's supporters, shire knights, town burgesses and the heir to the throne – were pursuing their own interests, and it was this that would eventually undermine the constitutional reform movement. For the time being, however, the initiative lay with Simon and his followers. While Henry spent long periods on the continent looking after his Gascon territories and seeking the support of the French king and the pope, Urban IV, the Earl of Leicester strove to hold his coalition together and to come to terms with Henry. His task was made easier by the behaviour of the young Edward (19 years old in 1258). The heir to the throne surrounded himself with an entourage of hired, foreign mercenaries and behaved with an arrogance that often tipped over into cruelty. When the prince's party stayed at Wallingford Priory they ate the monks out of house and home and beat them when they protested. Englishmen were outraged by such events and particularly resented their country's 'invasion' by German and French soldiers.

In May 1261 news arrived from Rome that Pope Alexander had absolved Henry from his oath to abide by the Provisions of Westminster. The king brought more mercenaries into the country and took up residence in the Tower of London. In August he announced his repudiation of the Provisions and his intention to take royal castles back into his possession and appoint his own advisers. In September he summoned representatives of the shires to meet at Windsor and not to attend the parliament at St Albans. He and Edward had reconciled their differences, and the king opened up fresh negotiations with Llewelyn.

The baronage was now divided between a majority who were appalled by Henry's behaviour and a minority who remained loyal to the king and his papal

ABOVE **Pope Urban IV** *(reigned 1261–4) was one of the few non-Italian popes. Born Jacques Pantéleon, he was the son of a French cobbler. But he became a prominent academic and it was his intellectual abilities that won him preferment. He proved himself a valuable papal diplomat and was appointed, by turns, Bishop of Verdun and Patriarch of Jerusalem. Much of Urban's brief pontificate was taken up with the long-running conflict between the papacy and the Holy Roman Empire. Unsurprisingly, he supported the claim of Charles I of Anjou (1226–85), son of Louis VIII of France, to the crown of Sicily. It was division into pro- and anti-French factions within the church hierarchy that eventually led to a long period of schism (the Avignon papacy, 1309–78). Pope Urban IV's only positive legacy was the authorizing of a liturgy for the festival of Corpus Christi, drawn up by the great Catholic theologian and philosopher, Thomas Aquinas (1225–74), shown in this painting by Tadeo di Bartolo (1363–1422).*

tunc adheserunt. Quod et totum factum est. Nam po
tenciores ciuitatis apud castrum de Windesore
carceri fuerant mancipati. qui postmodum pena pec
cuniaria ad summam non modicam multabantur.
libertas sunt ciuibus introducta. et terris lond' per tri
pertes et cathenas ciuitatis forcior fuit facta.

De castrum Douorie regi redditur.

Audientes quidam nobiles qui in castro
Douorie in carcere tenebantur quod domino
suo regi prospera contingebant. spiritu hausto for
titudinis turrim castri uiriliter occupabant

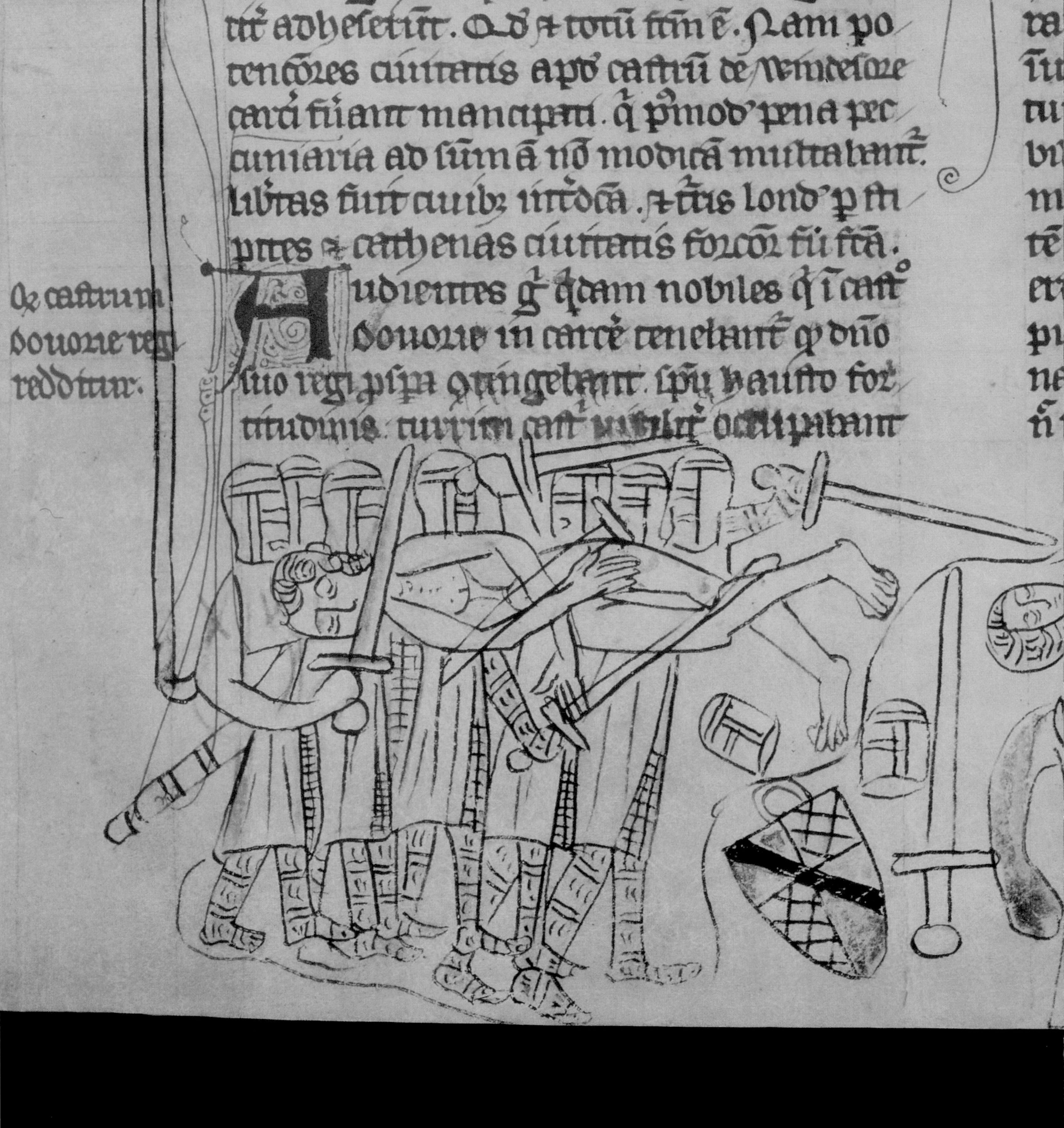

ABOVE **The Battle of Evesham, 1265.** *King Henry was wholly discredited by defaulting on the Provisions of Westminster and by being defeated at the Battle of Lewes. However, Prince Edward was beginning to emerge as an alternative to his father and support was leaching away to him from de Montfort. At Evesham on 4 August the*

Llewelyn-ap-Gruffydd

Sometimes known as 'Llewelyn the Last', this independent Welsh ruler came to control much of Wales and was a constant irritant to both Henry III and Edward I. Born about 1223, he was a grandson of Llewelyn the Great. As a result of family rivalries, his father, Gruffydd, was surrendered to Henry III and imprisoned in the Tower of London, and he had the dubious distinction of being the first prisoner to be killed while attempting to escape from that fortress in 1246. Llewelyn's uncle, Dafydd, ruler of Gwynedd in north Wales, died two years later, leaving him undisputed head of the family. Llewelyn spent the rest of his life contesting power in Wales with the king of England and the barons of the Marches.

A career of territorial expansion

His career of territorial expansion began in 1256 when he overran lands that had been given by Henry III to his eldest son, Edward. The following year he defeated a Marcher army sent against him. Other Welsh rulers now paid homage to Llewelyn, and by 1258 he held most of central and northern Wales and took the name Prince of Wales, an ancient title but seldom claimed. Preoccupied with his rebel barons, Henry was unable to challenge him, and a truce reached in 1258 was extended from year to year. After the Battle of Lewes Llewelyn made a deal with Simon de Montfort, who recognized his title and territorial claims in return for 30,000 marks (approximately £20,000).

On Simon's fall Llewelyn did not wait for Henry to recover his full strength, and a series of raids against his neighbours greatly increased his territorial base. This put him in the position of being able to make the favourable Treaty of Montgomery in 1267.

Edward I, who succeeded in 1272, was determined to bring Llewelyn to heel. The Prince of Wales was weakened by fresh family feuds

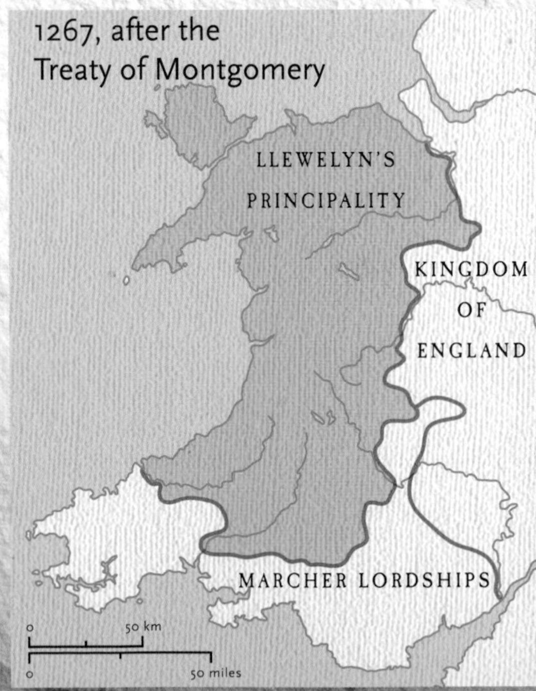

RIGHT **These maps necessarily give a simplified version of the rise and fall of Llewelyn**. *The area over which he gained control was contested not only by English kings but by marcher lords, Welsh clan leaders and members of Llewelyn's own family. It was by skilfully playing on the divided loyalties of landholders in the principality as much as by military action that Edward I was able to establish his feudal rule throughout most of Wales.*

and narrowly survived an assassination attempt in 1274. Edward detached several Welsh rulers from their allegiance to Llewelyn and in 1277 led a sizeable army across the border. By the Treaty of Aberconwy Llewelyn was stripped of most of his lands and reduced to his family domains in Gwynedd. In the same year Llewelyn married Eleanor, the daughter of Simon de Montfort and first cousin of King Edward. In 1282 Llewelyn reluctantly joined in a revolt of several Welsh rulers and was killed at the Battle of Orewin Bridge at Builth Wells. The title of Prince of Wales was, from this time, bestowed on the eldest son of the English king.

LEFT **The death of Llewelyn the Last, 1282.** *The Welsh leader and his followers were ill-prepared for their final battle against Edward I at Orewin Bridge near Builth Wells. Accounts of his death vary. Some say that he was encountered by a lone English soldier who cut him down. Others insist that he and his companions were pursued into a wood, where they made a last valiant stand. Either way, Llewelyn was decapitated on the spot. This is an early 14th-century English illumination.*

1266–72

THE ROYAL VICTORY AT EVESHAM was not the end of the civil war. Instead of ordering many of the rebels leaders to be executed, Henry satisfied himself with confiscating their lands or imposing financial burdens on them, which simply bred more resentment while allowing malcontents the freedom to create more trouble. A group of rebels, led by de Montfort's son, also called Simon, occupied de Montfort's castle at Kenilworth in Warwickshire, and when Henry sent a messenger to discuss terms with them they sent him back – minus his hands.

ABOVE **Mounted warriors, *c.*1225–50.** *The equipment and armour of knights developed steadily throughout these centuries. The basic protection for torso and limbs was chain mail. In the 13th century a long outer garment was added to this. The head was protected by a hood of mail (a coif). Such defensive gear was not altogether effective as is shown in this contemporary illustration for a French chanson about the exploits of Charlemagne. The shortcomings of chain mail led to the development of plate armour in the next century. An unusual feature of this illustration is the presence of a mounted archer.*

OPPOSITE **Effigy of Henry III.** *The magnificent gilt-bronze tomb effigy in Westminster Abbey was commissioned by his son, Edward I, about 1291. It was cast by William Torel and set upon a plinth of porphyry decorated with mosaics. Thus Henry III rests permanently in the cathedral he created.*

Throughout much of 1266 the king laid siege to Kenilworth, but the fortress proved impregnable, and only when the king offered lenient terms to the rebels, known as the Ban of Kenilworth, was it surrendered (December).

Resistance continued in the fenland around Ely, and in April 1267 a band of rebels briefly occupied the Tower of London. Not until August, when Henry negotiated a peace with Llewelyn and Edward mopped up the last of the rebels in East Anglia, did all the fighting cease. The rebellion had been put down at great cost but could not be regarded as a royal 'victory' because, at a parliament at Marlborough in November 1267, Henry conceded most of the demands made in the 'Mad Parliament' of 1258.

In October 1269 Westminster Abbey, though not completed, was ready to admit worshippers, and Henry took the opportunity to stage what would be the last gorgeous spectacle of his reign. He transferred the remains of Edward the Confessor to a resplendent new shrine in a ceremony attended by all the great men of church and state. In the following August Prince Edward departed on crusade, thus undertaking the holy enterprise that Henry himself had longed to embark upon but had never accomplished. Soon afterwards Henry was taken ill and begged Edward to return, but his health improved somewhat, and in August 1272 he was able to travel to Norwich to deal in person with a mini-rebellion. This, however, overtaxed his ageing frame, and, on 16 November, he died at the age of 65.

EDWARD I

WAR DVS: REX
IS
ETIA
DAN DI
EGI VM

Edward I's reign may be seen as a continuation of much that his great-grandfather, Henry II, had set in motion. The tumults of the previous three reigns subsided, leaving the king free to concentrate on legal reform, constitutional development and relations with Wales and Scotland. Edward clung stubbornly to his lands in Gascony, which involved continuing disputes with the kings of France, despite the reluctance on the part of his English magnates to involve themselves in the defence of foreign territory.

Edward was over 6 feet tall (hence his nickname Longshanks), and he was strong and athletic. A fine horseman and swordsman, he was a forceful leader of men in battle. He was firm but fair in his dealings with his parliaments, so that even those who opposed his policies knew where they stood with him. This was a relief after the vacillations of Henry III.

1272–7

EDWARD ENJOYED MILITARY SUCCESS in the Holy Land until an assassination attempt weakened him and news of his father's failing health obliged him to start for home. He did not, however, make great haste to return. Immediately after Henry's death, the barons had recognized Edward as the new king and sworn fealty to him. Edward believed that the government was in safe hands and that his absence would give time in which the wounds opened up by the civil war might heal. He spent a year (1273–4) in Gascony, trying unsuccessfully to suppress a revolt, and did not reach England until August 1274.

On 18 August he and his wife were crowned at Westminster. All who owed allegiance to the king, including Alexander III of Scotland, swore their loyalty

OPPOSITE **The coronation of Edward I, 18 August 1274** *from the* Flores Historiarum *of Matthew Paris. It was almost two years after the death of Henry III that Edward was crowned at Westminster. He was a man of impressive presence, partly because of his great height; he was over 6 feet tall and was known as 'Longshanks'. He had already been on crusade – something Henry had only promised to do. The contrast between Edward and his father could hardly have been stronger.*

PREVIOUS PAGES **The seal** *of Edward I.*
Edward I *from a portrait in Peterhouse, Cambridge. Peterhouse, the first Cambridge college to be founded, received its charter in 1284 from Edward I. This portrait, however, is much later in date.*

Anglia letatur Edwardus dum cathedratur.

cc°. lxxiiii°

Coronacio regis Edwardi

Anno gratie supradicto. In ecclesia
Westm. Edwardus in regem
et alienora soror regis hyspanie in re-
ginam a Roberto archiepiscopo Cantuar.
xiiii. kl. septemb. pariter coronantur.
huic coronationi interfuerunt rex scocie

mauuais fais et dementes

King Edward I was valiant, prudent, wise and bold and was adventurous and fortunate in all feats of war.

Froissart's Chronicles, ed. J. Jolliffe, 1967, pp. 4–5

but a notable absentee was Llewelyn-ap-Gruffydd, the Welsh leader. In November Edward travelled to Shrewsbury and summoned Llewelyn to meet him there, but not only did Llewelyn fail to turn up, he also declared his defiance by raiding English territory, building himself a castle that would govern the approach to central Wales along the Severn valley and declaring his intention to marry the sister of Simon de Montfort.

But before he could deal with Llewelyn, Edward had more pressing priorities. In October 1274 he had his new chancellor, Robert Burnell, organize a complete survey of the realm. This was an attempt to sort out the confusions over land tenure and infringements of royal rights that had grown up during his father's reign. The monumental task of Burnell and his agents was completed by April 1275, when Edward called a parliament to meet at Westminster. Following de Montfort's initiative in 1265, as well as barons and churchmen, two representatives from each shire and two from each city or town were summoned. This parliament produced 51 statutes, many clarifying aspects of Magna Carta, and made clear Edward's willingness to consult with his subjects on the promulgation of law. This parliament and another later in the same year laid the foundation of the king's finances. Edward borrowed from Italian bankers to provide for his regular needs, and these loans were guaranteed by export duties levied on English merchants. For extraordinary expenditure Edward relied on grants of taxation made by parliament from time to time.

In the autumn of 1277 Edward dealt with the Welsh problem. He advanced along the coast from Chester at the head of an army of some 15,000 men. He had ships brought round from Kent and Sussex to convey his host to Anglesey, where the king seized all the standing grain, thus depriving Llewelyn of his food supply. The Welsh leader realized that further resistance was impossible, and he hastened to make peace at the Treaty of Aberconwy.

PREVIOUS PAGES **Edward I's return from Gascony, 1274.** *One reason for the new king's delayed coronation was his need to establish his authority in Gascony. His father had given Edward responsibility for the duchy. Relations between England and Gascony remained close and Gascon soldiers served in Edward's wars with the Welsh and the Scots. Economically, Gascony was very important to the crown. Taxation, largely derived from the wine trade, was bringing in £18,000 a year by the end of Edward's reign. But the duchy was not only a region to be exploited – also Edward's government devoted considerable attention to economic development. For example, numerous charters were issued for the formation of* bastides, *which were administrative mini communities, often involving settlement by English developers aimed at bringing wasteland under cultivation and improving production in other ways.*

Edward I's parliaments

ABOVE **The court of Edward I.** *In this image, taken from a collection of miscellaneous chronicles produced c.1280–1300, we see the king, holding the royal sword as his symbol of authority, in consultation with bishops and nobles, while tonsured clerks report the proceedings.*

Parliament was essentially a meeting of the king's council to which other subjects, representing different interest groups, were occasionally invited. Kings normally summoned parliament for financial reasons: they declared their intention to impose taxes and sought the cooperation of their people in collecting the money. Edward called more parliaments than any of his predecessors – usually two a year – which was largely because he needed money for his various wars, but it did mean that the body began to develop its own identity. Parliament became a bargaining assembly at which the representatives sought concessions from the king in return for agreeing to his taxes. Edward I is sometimes called the 'Father of Parliament', although he did not have the intention of increasing the rights of his people or limiting the power of the crown.

One of the major tasks of legislation at this time was the maintenance of the feudal system of land tenure. All property was held from the king in return for service. The major landholders were tenants-in-chief, who were pledged to provide a stated number of armed men for the king when he went to war. The tenants-in-chief granted lands to their followers on a similar basis, requiring in return military service or a percentage of the produce of the land. The same arrangements continued right down the social scale to the simplest peasant landholders. Over the years, as men died, fell from royal favour or had no heirs to succeed them, legal problems arose over who held what lands and on what precise terms, and civil war caused the greatest upheaval within the system. It was for this reason that in 1274 Edward ordered the biggest 'stocktaking' since Domesday Book, and several parliaments in the years following made statutes defining and enforcing the results of this investigation.

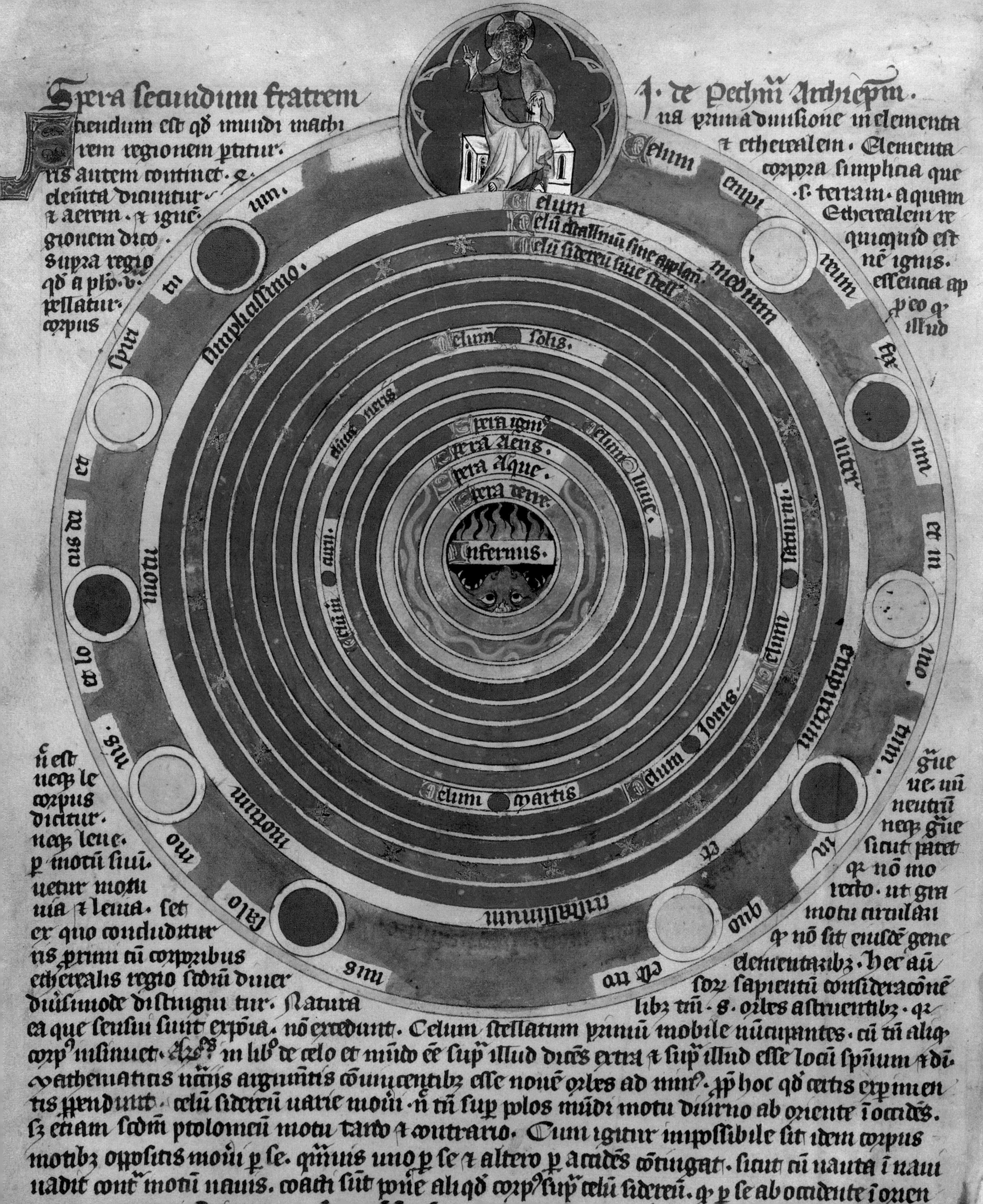

Spera secundum fratrem J. de Pechm archiepm.

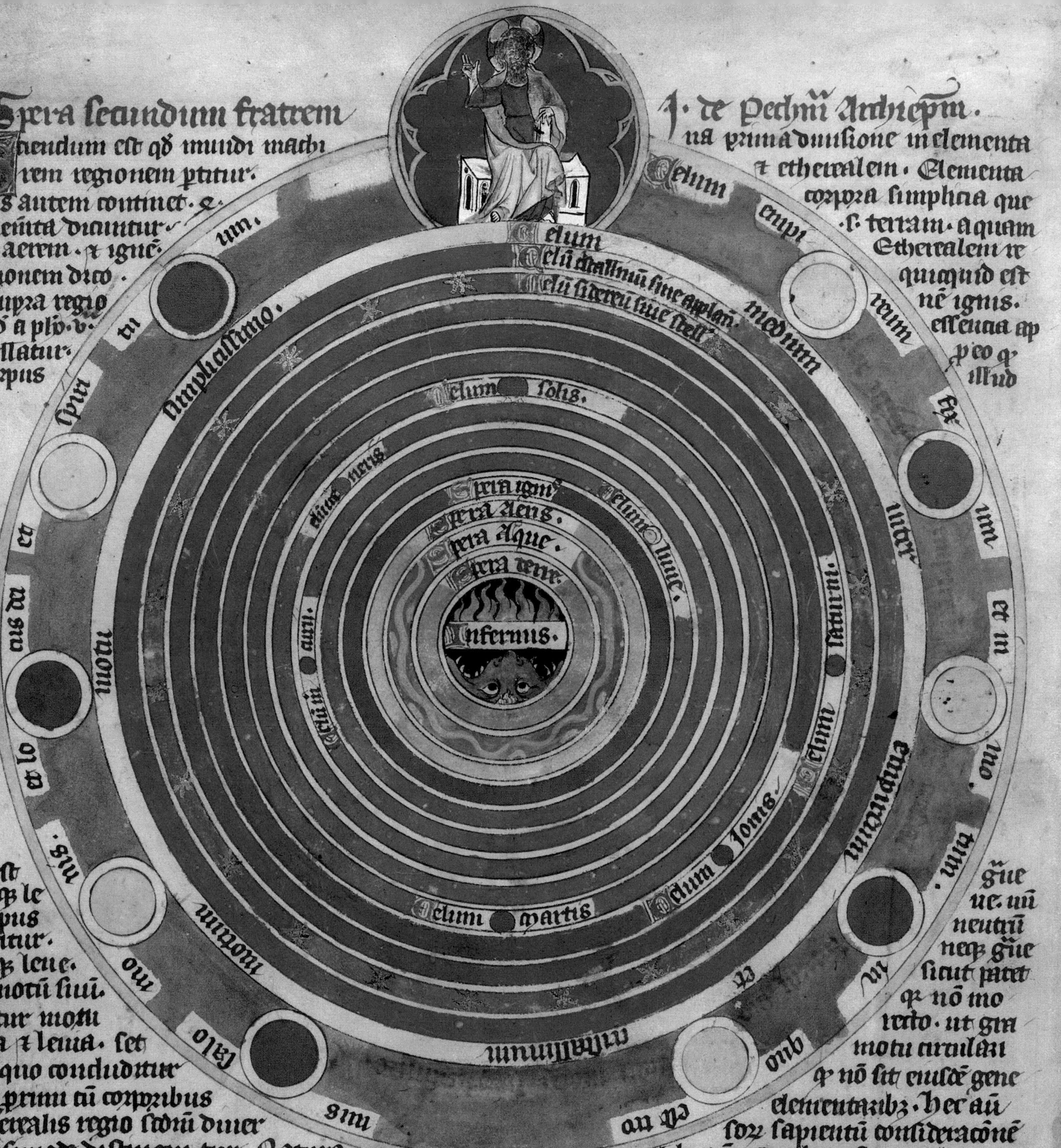

Celum empireum
Celum
Celum cristallinum sive aqueum
Celum sidereum sive stellatum
Celum solis
Celum veneris
Celum mercurii
Celum lune
Spera ignis
Spera aeris
Spera aque
Spera terre
Infernus
Celum saturni
Celum iovis
Celum martis

Sciendum est quod mundi machina prima divisione in elementarem regionem partitur et etherealem. Elementaris autem continet corpora simplicia que elementa dicuntur s. terram, aquam et aerem et ignem. Etherealem regionem dico quicquid est supra regionem ignis. quod a philosophis v. essencia appellatur pro eo quod corpus illud non est grave neque leve. unde corpus neutrum dicitur neque grave neque leve. sicut patet per motum suum quia non movetur motu recto. ut gravia et levia. sed motu circulari ex quo concluditur quod non sit eiusdem generis primum cum corporibus elementaribus. Hec autem etherealis regio secundum diversorum sapientum consideracionem diversimode distinguitur. Naturalibus tamen .8. orbes astruentibus. quia ea que sensui sunt exposita non excedunt. Celum stellatum primum mobile nuncupantes. cum tamen aliquod corpus insinuet Aristoteles in libro de celo et mundo esse super illud dicens extra et super illud esse locum spatium et di. Mathematicis variis argumentis convincentibus esse nonem orbes ad minus. propter hoc quod certis experimentis perpenderunt. celum sidereum variare motum non tamen super polos mundi motu diurno ab oriente in occidens. sed etiam secundum ptolomeum motu tardo et contrario. Cum igitur impossibile sit idem corpus motibus oppositis moveri per se. quamvis uno per se et altero per accidens contingat. sicut cum nauta in navi vadit contra motum navis. coacti sunt ponere aliquod corpus super celum sidereum. quod per se ab occidente in orien

1278–86

IN 1278 THE ARCHBISHOPRIC of Canterbury fell vacant and Edward wished to appoint his chancellor, Robert Burnell. The pope, however, overruled him, giving the position to John Pecham (or Peckham), who was installed the following year, an appointment that inaugurated 13 years of conflict between church and state. Pecham combined two characteristics that made him a formidable adversary: he was a zealous Franciscan of austere personal habits (even as archbishop he wore a ragged habit and went barefoot) and personal piety, and he was a brilliant theological controversialist, well able to argue his case with incisiveness and persistence. He arrived in his archdiocese determined to carry out far-reaching reforms and prepared to use the weapon of excommunication against anyone who stood in his way. The two most important topics over which he clashed with the king were the rivalry between common law and canon law and the issues of pluralism and non-residence – that is, clergy holding more than one living or being paid for serving a parish but not actually living and working there. This affected his relationship with the government because the granting of benefices was a standard (and cheap) way for the king to reward faithful service and remunerate men in royal employ.

In July 1279 Pecham called a convocation at Reading in which he set out his programme of root and branch reform. He threatened with excommunication any royal officials who infringed the church's rights, and, in order to make it quite clear what those rights were, he ordered copies of Magna Carta to be pinned to the doors of cathedrals and churches. Edward did not respond immediately, but, at the parliament held at Westminster in October 1279, Pecham was forced to back down in the face of opposition from several quarters.

In April 1282 Dafydd, the brother of Llewelyn-ap-Gruffydd, attacked Hawarden Castle. This was the overture to a determined attempt by the brothers to throw off English control and was followed by military action over a wide area. Edward summoned a large army to suppress this rebellion, advancing from Chester in the autumn, while a naval force occupied Anglesey. Archbishop Pecham made a vain attempt to broker a peace, but neither side wanted it. Edward believed that the

OPPOSITE **Astronomy and astrology**. *All branches of medieval 'science' (knowledge) were linked: theology (the queen of the sciences), cosmology, natural philosophy, medicine and alchemy. There was no doubt in the minds of scholars that man was the centre of God's creation and that the earth was the centre of the universe. Beyond Earth the heavenly bodies were arranged in concentric circles, and these bodies exercised influence over the earth and its inhabitants. The Greek philosopher, Aristotle, had taught that changes in human bodies were brought about by the movements of celestial bodies, which were part of a chain of influences emanating from God and descending through all the other levels of creation. This meant that important events ranging from the treatment of disease to royal marriages and the making of treaties should, ideally, take place when the alignment of heavenly bodies was 'favourable'. Astrologers were, therefore, employed to cast horoscopes for those rich enough to afford their services. This cosmological diagram from the psalter of Robert de Lisle (d.1343) was made by John Pecham (c.1220–95).*

Welsh were trapped in the northern part of the country, but Llewellyn broke out and faced the English in battle at Orewin Bridge in the Brecknockshire hills. Here he was killed and his force routed. Dafydd continued his resistance until April 1283, when he was handed over to Edward by some of his own followers and executed at Shrewsbury.

Edward was now determined to ensure the permanent submission of Wales. The backbone of his rule there was an impressive chain of great castles – Flint, Builth, Rhuddlan, Aberystwyth, Conwy, Caernarfon and Harlech – and he stripped the leading rebel families of their lands and imposed on the people the English administrative system. Four new counties were created – Flint, Caernarfon, Merioneth and Anglesey – and he also founded several new towns, which were to be peopled by English settlers. His 'pacification' of Wales completed the work begun by the Norman Conquest, two centuries earlier.

> Be circumspect in your dealings with the Bishop of Norwich and his clergy. Do not punish them if they hold pleas on purely spiritual matters.
>
> WRIT *CIRCUMSPECTE AGATIS*, 1286, *ENGLISH HISTORICAL DOCUMENTS 1189–1327*, ED. H.ROTHWELL, 1975, III, P.462

In April 1284, at Caernarfon, a fourth son was born to the king and queen and christened Edward. They had lost two earlier boys in infancy, and their only remaining son, the 12-year-old Alfonso, died in August of this same year. The infant Edward thus became heir to the throne.

In 1285, once the Welsh war was over, the problem with the church came to the fore again. During a parliament held at Westminster in the spring the clash of jurisdictions was brought up. Long debate led to the issuing of a royal edict that church courts should confine themselves to issues involving wills and marriages. The bishops protested and complained about the alleged malpractices of the king's justices, and in the Norwich diocese the bishop and his officers ignored the edict and continued to summon defendants in a variety of cases to appear before the church courts. The king responded by appointing a royal commission to examine complaints against the bishop's officials for overstepping their authority. Investigations continued throughout much of 1286, but these created more heat than light. Then the king, who was at the time in Paris, issued a conciliatory writ, *Circumspecte agatis*, in which he listed those issues that should be left to the church courts to decide.

OPPOSITE **Edward I and the Jews.** *Anti-semitism continued to be a feature of life in England long after the massacre of York at 1190. One cause of hostility was the Jews' economic power. As principal moneylenders they held hundreds of people, from the king downwards, in their debt. Because this community was so vulnerable kings were able to impose heavy taxes on them. In 1255 Henry III actually sold the Jews to his brother, Richard of Cornwall, which meant that Richard could gather all dues the Jews owed to the crown. However, Henry III gradually relied more on Italian bankers for cash. By the time Edward came to the throne he had no real need for the Jewish community and he gradually stepped up pressure on them. In 1275 he enacted a law forbidding them to practise usury and urging them to take up other trades. However, many trades were controlled by guilds that excluded Jews from membership. Hardship forced many into voluntary exile or a life of crime. In 1290 Edward expelled all Jews from his dominions. This image, with a marginal drawing of a Jew, is from the* Chronica Roffense *of Matthew Paris (early 14th century).*

1286–91

IN THE SPRING OF 1286 Edward crossed the Channel and was absent from England for three years. He was, by this time, highly regarded by his brother monarchs, and his advice and mediation were sought in various disputes. His main objective, however, was to establish his rule in Gascony as firmly as he had done in England. Edward still held the hereditary title Duke of Aquitaine, an area covering most of southwest France, but in reality the activities of local rulers and the intermittent encroachment of the French kings tended to limit his effective rule to Gascony. This territory was important to him bccausc of its flourishing (and therefore taxable) wine trade, its provision of money and troops to aid him in his wars, and its strategic position between the sea and the Pyrenees. Edward held this territory as a vassal of the king of France and, just as he sought to consolidate his control of Wales and (later) Scotland, so his French counterparts were endeavouring to extend their rule over the lands of their vassals. Edward spent the summer of 1286 in Paris and reached an agreement with Philip IV confirming his holding of most of Aquitaine, while he ceded the rest to the French king in return for payment.

Edward devoted considerable energy to revising the laws that operated in the various lands of Aquitaine and to establishing trustworthy men in office. This was a complicated exercise, since different customs and laws pertained in the regions, but the king's attention to detail indicated his commitment to the rule of law and to ensuring the rights of his subjects.

This concern did not extend to the Jews, however. This unpopular community was regarded by the church as the enemy of Christianity, and Jews were disliked by the people at large for their wealth and exclusivity. In 1287 Edward took a crusading vow, and in order to finance his proposed expedition to the Holy Land he took the popular step of confiscating all Jewish property and expelling the Jews from Gascony.

Edward I's castles

The castles Edward I built in Wales constitute his most enduring legacy. They were constructed at immense cost and occupied thousands of craftsmen and labourers for many years. Between 1276 and 1295 no fewer than 17 castles were built or rebuilt by the king and major English landholders as a means of preventing any fresh outbreaks of Welsh independence.

They were situated in strong defensive locations with access to the sea or a river giving good supply lines in the event of siege. Each stronghold was within a day's march of its neighbour to give an unbreakable chain capable of containing attack at any point. Many of them incorporated the latest developments in the construction of fortifications, including innovations that the king had noted in crusader castles. He was, in fact, probably the leading expert of his day in the art and science of castle building.

His new works appeared in two phases. Flint, Builth, Rhuddlan and Aberystwyth were built after the first Welsh war of 1277 to contain Llewellyn within his northern homeland. After the second war in 1282 Edward added Conwy, Caernarfon and Beaumaris castles to the ring, and he brought over from Savoy the master mason James St George and his team of specialists to supervise their construction.

New designs

Edward's castles shared several features, but they were by no means uniform because each had to be designed to take account of its site. The old motte-and-bailey arrangement was a thing of the past. Where possible, walls and towers were built in concentric circles, so that any invaders, having scaled the outer defensive ring, would find themselves confronted by another. The outer wall might be protected by a moat. A common feature was an abundance of round towers. One weakness of earlier fortresses had been their vulnerability at the angles where the walls met, and round towers provided the defenders with a much improved field of fire. Edward also made the utmost use of topographical features. Harlech Castle, for example, was perched on a steep scarp overlooking the sea, which protected one side, while a moat guarded the remaining faces. Edward employed 1,800 ditchers to construct a canal to bring supplies into Rhuddlan Castle.

A passion for castles

Caernarfon Castle was the most elaborate of the fortresses James St George built for Edward. Positioned beside the Menai Strait, its monumental polygonal towers were inspired by the defensive walls of Constantinople and guarded a building that served as a palace and administrative centre as well as a military stronghold. Edward's last castle, Beaumaris, on Anglesey, was the archetypal concentric-plan fortification, with a wide moat forming the outer defensive ring. Any attacker getting across the water would have had to scale the outer wall and then turn to right or left to find the entrance gateway to the inner ward, meanwhile coming under fire from strategically placed arrow slits. Passageways were provided with murder holes in the roof through which boiling oil could be poured on assailants. With 14 potential hazards to be overcome, Beaumaris was a veritable death-trap.

It was not only Wales that benefited (if that is the right word) from Edward's passion for castle building. Although he spent little time in his own

capital, this itinerant king invested £21,000 between 1275 and 1285 on extending and strengthening the Tower of London. He filled in his father's moat in order to enclose the fortress in a new curtain wall. The landward entrance was now guarded by two massive gatehouses and a barbican, which controlled access over a system of bridges. A new Watergate, protected by yet another tower, enabled the garrison to be supplied in the case of a siege, and Edward had two watermills set up so that the occupants of the fortress could be as self-sufficient as possible. The king was well aware of the strategic and economic importance of London and had not forgotten that the city had briefly fallen into rebel hands during the civil war. In 1285 he sacked the mayor and took the government of London into his own hands, placing Ralph of Sandwich, the Constable of the Tower, in charge as warden. For 13 years, England's capital city was kept under tight royal control.

ABOVE **Stonemasons and builders**. *In this image from a French translation of St Augustine's* City of God *by Raoul de Presles (early 15th century) there are displayed various building activities. A mason marks out stone preparatory to cutting, while other workers mix mortar, use a plumb line, chisel stone and carry building materials up a ladder. With so much castle building going on in England, masons were much sought after and highly paid.*

claimed the overlordship of the northern kingdom on the basis that Alexander had sworn fealty to him (although Alexander had always claimed that this applied to lands he held in England and not to his Scottish crown). Secondly, in 1288 Edward had negotiated with King Eric the marriage of little Margaret to his own infant son, Edward. There were several potential claimants to the Scottish crown, but all the leaders of the nation had agreed to this arrangement, which would unite the two countries.

The Maid of Norway's death threatened anarchy, and Edward intervened to prevent this and to assert what he considered to be his rights. He summoned the Scottish lords to meet him at Norham Castle, close to the border, and they reluctantly accepted his authority and swore fealty to him. Edward set up a united council of regency and a commission to consider the claims of the two main rivals for the crown, John Balliol and Robert Bruce – this is known in Scottish history as the Great Cause – and then went on a tour of several Scottish towns to receive the homage of the people.

Governing Aquitaine

The judges *in ordinary, each in his own judicatura ... shall investigate carefully the behaviour in their offices of all our bailiffs and hear everyone who has a complaint against the same and do swift justice ... A bailiff guilty of a minor offence shall be condemned to make good to the injured party and to pay to us one hundred shillings ... The judges (or one of them) shall assess the punishment for a greater offence according to its measure.*

FROM *JUDEX ORDINARIUS CITRA GARONAM*, EDWARD'S ORDINANCESS FOR THE GOVERNMENT OF PART OF HIS POSSESSIONS IN AQUITAINE, BRITISH LIBRARY, COTTONIAN MS, JULIUS E. I

1292–8

IN NOVEMBER 1292, after lengthy deliberations, Edward decided the Great Cause in favour of John Balliol, who was crowned before the end of the year and subsequently came to Norham to swear fealty to Edward.

The following year a dispute arose with Philip IV, which led to war when the French king used a clash between English and Norman ships as an excuse to assert his authority. Just as Edward summoned Balliol to Norham, Philip now

OPPOSITE **Statue of Queen Eleanor of Castile** *at All Saints Church, Harby, Nottinghamshire. On 11 September 1290 Edward and his queen arrived in the manor of Harby and probably stayed in a house there belonging to the Bishop of Lincoln. The queen remained at Harby while Edward travelled in the area on royal business. Between 27 October and 13 November the king presided over parliament in his manor of Clipstone. It was while he was riding back from there that he learned that his wife had contracted a fever and that her condition was deteriorating. He hurried back to Harby and supervised the efforts of physicians to cure her. He was inconsolable when she died on 28 November. This later statue adorns the church wall and a plaque within commemorates the sad event.*

demanded that Edward appear before him. Early in 1294 the king sent his brother Edmund instead, and an agreement was patched up. It involved the marriage of Edward to Philip's sister Margaret and the temporary ceding of Gascony to the French king. Philip subsequently reneged on the agreement and claimed that Edward had forfeited Gascony by his failure to answer the summons in person. Edward sent a military contingent to Gascony and prepared for war with France by forging a series of alliances with rulers in Germany and the Low Countries.

Welsh malcontents now took advantage of Edward's involvement with France to stage a rebellion. The leader, Madog-ap-Llewelyn, enjoyed widespread support from people who resented English-style administration and Edward's demand for troops to fight in France. The effectiveness of Edward's castle-based defence strategy was now put to the test and proved itself. With the exception of half-finished Caernarfon, all the royal fortresses survived Welsh attack, but Edward had to put on hold his plans for a major expedition across the Channel and marched into Wales at the head of an army with more than 30,000 infantry and hundreds of mounted knights. The campaign would probably have been over quickly had an attack by Madog on the king's baggage train not forced Edward to take refuge in Conwy for the winter. Again, the castle chain proved impregnable because the English were able to keep it provisioned by sea and river. In March 1295, at Maes Moydog, near Montgomery, an English force led by the Earl of Warwick fell upon Madog's army and slaughtered it. The rebellion rapidly collapsed, and Edward toured the country, receiving homage from the defeated rebels and ordered the building of his last Welsh castle at Beaumaris, Anglesey.

Meanwhile, fresh difficulties arose in Scotland. In 1294 Edward demanded that John Balliol provide soldiers for his French war. When the Scottish king agreed, a group of nobles and ecclesiastics set his authority aside, formed a regency council and opened negotiations with the French king. (This is usually regarded as the beginning of the combination of France and Scotland against England known as the Auld Alliance, which lasted for three centuries.) In March 1296 a Scottish force crossed the border, and the following month Balliol renounced his fealty to Edward, who responded immediately by invading Scotland. Any resistance collapsed rapidly after the capture of Dunbar (27 April), and Edward swiftly overran the Lowlands. In July Balliol surrendered. The

OPPOSITE **Knightly tournaments** *developed throughout these centuries and were strictly regulated in accordance with internationally acknowledged rules. This illustration is from the 14th-century* Ordinances of Armoury. *It shows a king, his courtiers and members of the public watching a combat of arms, while a herald marshals the event and acts as referee. Tournaments consisted of various contests and were not confined to jousts of mounted knights. In warfare knights often fought on foot and needed practice in wielding halberds, axes and swords. Plate armour had, by this stage, superseded chain mail. The combatants were encased, from head to toe, in metal. Death and injury sometimes resulted from such contests and it was to minimize the risks that strict rules and specialist armour were introduced. Eventually tournaments became little more than theatrical spectacles.*

ABOVE **Edward I and John Balliol, 1292**. *In this image from the* St. Albans Chronicle *Edward I is shown receiving homage from John Balliol (1249–1315) whom he subsequently installed on the Scottish throne by virtue of his own authority as feudal overlord. After a lengthy examination of the merits of various claims to the Scottish crown, in which the Scottish nobles participated, decision was given in favour of Balliol. Edward's feudal right acknowledged but exactly what it implied remained in dispute. When Edward had suits referred from Edinburgh to his own court in London it seemed to many north of the border that their independence was threatened by an English king who had installed a puppet to do his bidding.*

humiliated king is known in Scottish folklore as 'Toom Tabard' (Empty Coat) because of the insignia removed from his robes as a symbol of his submission. Edward made a victory tour of the kingdom and brought back to Westminster the Stone of Scone upon which Scottish kings had traditionally been crowned. Balliol was taken to England as a prisoner, and he remained there for three years before retiring to France.

The Welsh rebellion had cost Edward valuable time and money, and he now resorted to blatantly unjust measures to finance his French expedition, including seizing the wool that his merchants were exporting in order to pocket the profit. Parliament granted fresh taxes, but when the king asked for money from the church Pope Boniface VIII refused to sanction it. (At this point the pope was trying

ABOVE **Pope Boniface VIII** *(1293–1303), in an image from the 14th-century Italian MS* Bonifatii VIII Decretarium liber Sextus, *presiding over the college of cardinals. Boniface, born Benedetto Gaetani, made the most exaggerated demands of temporal power for the papacy. In his bull* Unam Sanctam *he asserted 'The spiritual and temporal swords are in the power of the Church. The spiritual is wielded* by *the Church: the temporal* for *the Church. The one by the hand of the priest; the other by the hand of kings and knights at the will and under the sufferance of the priest ... temporal authority is subordinate to spiritual authority'. Boniface provoked conflict with Edward I and Philip IV because both kings were raising funds from the clergy to fight their wars. In 1303 Boniface excommunicated Philip, who responded by sending an army to capture and imprison the pope. Though released after a few days, Boniface died of his treatment. One historian has written of this pope, 'He was admired by many, feared by all, loved by none.'*

to put an end to the Anglo-French war.) Edward's angry response, early in 1297, was to call a meeting of all the leading clergy and demand half their revenues, threatening to outlaw any who opposed him. 'Whoever of ye will say me nay,' he said, 'let him rise and stand up that his person may be known.' According to a contemporary source, the dean of St Paul's fell dead with fright on the spot. Thus browbeaten, the clergy gave in and gave the king what he wanted. Yet Edward still lacked the funds necessary for a major campaign, and he was forced to use the money he had collected for his planned crusade and to borrow still more heavily from Italian bankers. He was eventually able to sail in August 1297.

The French campaign was a disaster. While inconclusive fighting occurred in the southwest, Edward took a small army to Flanders to link up with his allies, but they deserted him. In October 1297 he made a truce with Philip. While peace terms were being worked out Edward returned to England in March 1298. His marriage to Margaret was confirmed and took place the following year.

Meanwhile, the position in Scotland had been reversed. As soon as Edward had departed for France a widespread revolt had erupted led by Robert Bruce (grandson of the earlier competitor for the throne), William Wallace, a charismatic knight, and Sir Andrew

OPPOSITE **The Stone of Scone**. *This block of sandstone was kept at Scone Abbey in Perthshire and was traditionally the seat on which Scottish kings sat for their crowning. In 1297 Edward I seized it, took it to Westminster and had a special chair constructed to house it. Most of Edward's successors used this chair at their coronation to symbolize the submission of the Scots.*

ABOVE **The French army** *campaigning in Flanders. This illustration, from the 14th-century* Chroniques de France ou de St Denis, *shows Philip IV attacking Lille in 1297. The Count of Flanders was an ally of Edward I. When peace was made between the two kings Philip was able to concentrate on Flanders and the count was forced to make his submission.*

Moray of Bothwell, and in September 1297 they defeated an English army at the Battle of Stirling Bridge. As soon as he returned from France Edward summoned his barons to join him in another Scottish invasion. Some declined to be involved until the king agreed additions to Magna Carta that would clarify still further the rights of king and subjects and confer new freedoms on the people, and it was with an army composed largely of Welsh, Irish and Gascon elements that Edward crossed the border in July. On the 22nd of the month, despite having been injured when his own horse threw him, the king led his men in the Battle of Falkirk. This was a resounding English victory, only Wallace's infantry having put up a heroic resistance. The Scots lost some 20,000 men.

By this time Edward's determination to pursue by military means what he considered to be his rights had alienated the French, the Welsh, the Scots, the church, the English magnates and the merchants. He was hugely in debt and had squeezed his subjects for money almost to the point at which they could pay no more. He continued to summon parliament frequently and could claim with some accuracy that he consulted his people on important matters of state. In the writs for the parliament of 1295 (often known as the Model Parliament) this principle was first clearly enunciated. 'What touches all should be approved by all,' the writ stated. Theory and practice did not always coincide, however.

1299–1307

THE SITUATION IN SCOTLAND continued to be disturbed, and Edward was determined to make his rule there a reality. However, he was forced to abandon a campaign in 1299 because his magnates refused to march with him, and Stirling Castle fell to Scottish attackers. He was back again the next year, reasserting his authority. Under instruction from the pope, the new Archbishop of Canterbury, Robert of Winchelsea, pursued the king into Scotland and there delivered the papal demand that Edward should abandon his overlordship of Scotland. 'By God's blood,' Edward retorted, 'I will defend with all my might what all the world knows to be my right.' In the parliament held at Lincoln in 1301 the king

OPPOSITE **Italian bankers**. *The Italian cities of northern Italy were ideally placed to take advantage of trade between the Mediterranean world and the kingdoms of western Europe. Cities such as Florence, Venice, Genoa and Pisa flourished and its merchants became extremely wealthy. They were able, from their surplus funds, to become moneylenders. They founded the first European banking houses. Families like Bardi and Peruzzi became very wealthy and powerful dynasties but the most famous house of all was the one founded by Giovanni Medici in Florence in 1397. He moved his premises out of the market place, into his own palace and established branches in European towns as far afield as London. Italian bankers lent money to kings and this put them in a position to influence political events. The Medici became financial agents for the papacy. By the end of the 15th century they were rulers of Florence, married into royal houses and provided the church with some of its popes.*

EDWARD II

Upon looking on him [Gaveston] the son of the king immediately felt such love for him that he entered into a covenant of constancy, and bound himself with him before all other mortals with a bond of indissoluble love, firmly drawn up and fastened with a knot.

'A CHRONICLE OF THE CIVIL WARS OF EDWARD II', *SPECULUM*, ED. G.L. HASKINS, 14 (1939), P. 75

was regarded with suspicion by many of his magnates. His advisers expected his successor to wrap up military affairs successfully, ease the tax burden on his subjects, respond to wise counsel and submit to equable laws. Unfortunately, the prince had scarcely been well prepared to assume such a role. He saw little of his father, lost his mother when he was six, had no brothers to influence him and scarcely knew his sisters, most of whom were married off before he was born or during his infancy. It is, therefore, scarcely surprising that young Edward should choose and become closely attached to his own companions. It was that, above all things, that would prove his downfall.

1307–11

EDWARD II SUCCEEDED his father on 7 July 1307 at the age of 23. For some years his closest companion had been Piers Gaveston, the son of a Gascon knight who had been brought up in the prince's household, and it may be that Edward doted on Gaveston as the accomplished elder brother he had never had, for the courtier was athletic, intelligent and cultured. It may also be that the relationship of the two young men was homosexual. What is clear is that Gaveston came to exercise complete dominance over the prince. Edward could refuse him nothing, and Gaveston took advantage of that to gain lands and favours. He also behaved with insufferable arrogance towards those whose noble birth gave them the right, as they thought, to be numbered among the prince's intimates and guides. 'I firmly believe,' wrote one chronicler, 'that had he borne himself discreetly and with

OPPOSITE **Queen Isabella (1292–1358).** *The daughter of Philip the Fair was married to Edward II at the age of 11. She was as strong-willed as she was beautiful and would prove to be the king's nemesis. From the outset Edward virtually ignored her and lavished affection on his successive favourites. The couple did, however, have four children. After the disaster of Bannockburn Edward abandoned his wife, and two of her ladies were killed in her ensuing flight. Frequently humiliated by her husband, Isabella's story reads like the plot of a Gothic novel. Edward's cruelty virtually drove her into the arms of Roger Mortimer. She eventually escaped to France in 1325 and returned the next year to put herself at the head of Edward's disgruntled barons. Edward II's death in prison, if not ordered by the queen, was certainly encompassed to remove any opposition to her rule. In 1330 Isabella experienced the final tragedy of forfeiting the affection of her elder son Edward III, who ordered Mortimer's execution. This representation of the queen is from a carved boss in Beverley Minster.*

deference towards the great lords of this land, he would not have found one of them opposed to him.'[2]

In February 1307 Edward I had ordered Gaveston's banishment because his son had tried to make over a large portion of his continental lands to his friend. When the king died in July one of Edward's first acts was to recall Gaveston and make him Earl of Cornwall. In November Gaveston married the king's niece, Margaret de Clare, sister of the Earl of Gloucester, and also received from the king large sums of money filched from the royal treasury. Edward had already sacked the treasurer and replaced him with another favourite, Walter Reynolds.

Gaveston's pre-eminence became plain to all in January 1308. Edward left for France and his marriage to Isabella, and he appointed Gaveston as regent during his absence. A group of nobles, led by the Bishop of Durham, meanwhile drew up a list of grievances that needed redress. They were concerned to see an end to the financial dislocation caused by the late king's wars, and, as ever, pressed Edward II to guarantee their legal rights. If anyone was in any doubt about the influence of the royal favourite the coronation on 25 February made the state of affairs

Apres le tres pre
du bon roy edou
ard regna sire
edouard son filz
lequel nasqui
en carnarenan.
Cestui roy edouard alla en france
et espousa dame ysabel fille du roy
de france le xxve iour de ianvier
lan de grace mille trois cens et viii.
Et le xxviiie iour de febvrier lan
apres ensievant il fut moult
solempnellement couronne a west
monstier par larcheuesque robert
de wincestre et de cantorbie ou la
presse fut si grande que sire Jehan
de bakewelle fut murtry en ceste
place. Et puis si tost que le roy e
douard de carnarvan fut couronnez
en enfraingnant le commande
ment expres du bon roy son pere il
narresta iamais nuit ne iour tant
quil eut envoye querir pierres de
gauaston qui estoit alors en gascon
gne lequel il ama tant quil lap

crystal clear. Gaveston enjoyed prominence in the high ceremonial of the religious service – to him were assigned the privileges of the carrying of the crown, the 'redeeming' of *curtana*, the sword of mercy (placed on the altar until redeemed by the king with an offering of gold), and the fixing of a spur to the king's left foot. These symbolic acts were of extreme importance to the nation's leading families, and their exclusion from them in the interests of the 'upstart' could not fail to arouse resentment. Worse followed at the coronation banquet. The banners on the wall behind the high table displayed the arms, not of England and France, but of Edward and Gaveston. The favourite appeared clothed in purple, the royal colour, and Edward paid more attention to him than to his queen or her French nobles. In his determination to demonstrate that he could and would rule as he wanted and with the advice of whoever he wanted, Edward succeeded in uniting many of the nobles against him right at the beginning of the reign.

A robber of the people

The people ought to judge him [Gaveston] as one not to be suffered because he disinherits the crown and, as far as he is able, impoverishes it. By his counsel he withdraws the king from the counsel of his realm and puts discord between the king and his people ... Since the lord king has undertaken to maintain him against all men on every point, entirely without regard to right reason ... he cannot be judged or attainted by any action brought according to law, and therefore, seeing that he is a robber of the people and a traitor to his liege lord and to his realm, the people rate him as a man attainted and judged, and pray that the king ... will accept and execute the award of his people.

ANNALES PAULINI, IN *CHRONICLES OF THE REIGNS OF EDWARD I AND EDWARD II*, ED. W. STUBBS, 1882, I, P. 263

In the parliament that assembled a few days later the nobles made their concerns quite clear by demanding that Gaveston's exile should be renewed. The assertion of their right to protect the crown *against* the king amounted virtually to a claim for the sovereignty of the people.

Edward's response was to reject the ultimatum, withdraw to Windsor Castle and prepare to oppose his critics by force. But when to the protests of his barons were joined those of the king of France and his own stepmother, Margaret of France, he gave way. But only temporarily. In June Gaveston was despatched to Ireland as the king's deputy – not quite the casting into oblivion his enemies had hoped for. Meanwhile, Edward appealed to the pope to annul the exile order, which he did in April 1309. Into the gap created by Gaveston's departure stepped

OPPOSITE **The marriage of Edward II, 1308.** *Illumination from Jean de Wavrin's,* Chroniques d'Angleterre, *Bruges (c.1470–80). In 1298 Edward's marriage had been arranged when he was 14 and his intended bride, Isabella of France, was eight. It was part of an Anglo-French peace package involving Edward I's marriage to Philip IV's sister, Margaret, as well as his son's union with Philip's daughter, Isabella. The new king crossed to France at the beginning of 1308 to do homage for Gascony and to marry his bride. The wedding was celebrated on 25 January with great pomp at Boulogne in the presence of a great concourse of French and English nobles. A month later Isabella was crowned at Westminster. Her husband's first snub of his wife occurred immediately after the ceremony. He gave to his favourite, Piers Gaveston, all the jewels that Philip the Fair had given to his daughter. It was an indication of worse to come.*

Whereas, through bad and deceitful counsel, our lord the king and all his men have everywhere been dishonoured and his crown has in many ways been debased and ruined ... we Robert, by the grace of God archbishop of Canterbury and primate of all England, and the bishops, earls and barons ... do ordain for the honour of God and Holy Church and of the king and his realm in the manner following.

PREAMBLE TO THE ORDINANCES OF 1311, *ENGLISH HISTORICAL DOCUMENTS 1189–1327*, ED. H. ROTHWELL, 1975, III, P. 529.

Gaveston

[Warwick] entered the gate *of the courtyard and surrounded the chamber. Then the earl called out in a loud voice, 'Arise, traitor, thou art taken'. And Piers, hearing the earl, also seeing the earl's superior force and that the guard which had been allotted was not resisting, putting on his clothes, came down from the chamber. In this fashion Piers is taken and is led forth, not as an earl but as a thief, and he who used to ride palfreys is now forced to go on foot ... Blaring trumpets, yelling people and savage shouting followed Piers. Now Piers had laid aside his belt of knighthood. He travels to Warwick like a thief and a traitor and, coming there, he is thrown into prison.*

VITA EDWARDI SECUNDI, ED. W.R.CHILDS, 2005, PP. 44–5

Hugh Despenser, the only leading magnate to support Gaveston. He now became Edward's principal adviser and urged the king to turn the tables on his opponents. By bribery and blandishment Edward achieved what he had had failed to achieve by stubbornness and bluster. In parliaments held in April and August 1309 Edward struck a bargain with the majority of the barons: political reform, including the removal of Despenser from court, in return for Gaveston's reinstatement.

The king failed to keep his side of the bargain, and at the parliament held at Westminster in February 1310 most of the leading magnates threatened to renounce their allegiance unless the king agreed to widespread reforms. Because he needed support in trying to restore his authority in Scotland Edward had to agree, and 21 'lords ordainer' were appointed to draw up a catalogue of demands.

The lords ordainer drew up a list of 41 items in need of reform, which fell broadly into five categories. First, the lords in parliament were to be the king's advisers and his principal organ of government, with power to vet all royal appointments. This was the first real challenge by parliament to the royal household as the seat of government. Secondly, Gaveston and other royal favourites were to be banished. Thirdly, the king might only wage war with baronial consent. Fourthly, parliament was to have more say in financial matters. Specifically, all revenue was to be paid into the Exchequer, not the household, for greater accountability, and the king should not service his debts by farming out the customs to foreign bankers. Finally, local government should be strictly regulated. Sheriffs should only be appointed by the chancellor and other senior officials.

While the lords ordainer were doing their work, Edward and Gaveston went to campaign in Scotland, but they fought no battles and did little more than plunder the Lowlands. The king stayed away from his capital as long as possible, unwilling to face his critics, as one anonymous letter writer observed: 'The king is in no mood yet for a parliament, but when the Earl of Gloucester and the council meet in London, he will have to do what they order.'[3]

Parliament eventually met in mid-August. Edward tried to resist the inevitable, rejecting the lords' demands over and again, but at last he offered to do everything they asked with one exception: 'You shall stop persecuting my brother Piers and allow him to have the earldom of Cornwall.'[4] But on this point, too, he eventually had to give way. The ordinances were published and distributed at various ceremonies in September and October, but Edward immediately once more sent to the pope for an annulment of this trespass on his royal power. Gaveston again went into exile but secretly returned before Christmas.

1312–16

ON 18 JANUARY 1312, when he was at York, Edward defiantly announced the return of his friend. Archbishop Winchelsey of Canterbury summoned a meeting of bishops and nobles for 13 March at which arrangements were made for Gaveston's arrest. For several weeks the king and favourite were on the run but, on 19 May, Gaveston surrendered at Scarborough. A deal was struck with the king, and by its terms the Earl of Pembroke assumed surety for his person and set out with him for Gaveston's castle at Wallingford, Oxfordshire. But faith in Edward was now wearing thin, and some of the opposing barons were convinced, probably correctly, that the king was trusting that the pope would come to the aid of his favourite. At Deddington, north of Oxford, on 10 June the Earl of Warwick led a dawn raid on the place where the prisoner was being lodged.

Roxburgh Razed

Now at the beginning *of Lent [1314] the Scots cunningly entered the castle of Roxburgh at night by ladders and captured all the castle except one tower, wherein the warden of the castle, Sir Gillemin de Fiennes, a knight of Gascony, had taken refuge with difficulty, and his people with him; but the Scots got possession of that tower soon afterwards. And they razed to the ground the whole of that beautiful castle, just as they did other castles, which they succeeded in taking, lest the English should ever hereafter be able to lord it over the land through holding the castles.*

CHRONICON DE LANERCOST, ED. J. STEVENSON, 1839, P. 225

At Warwick Castle the earl was joined by the earls of Arundel, Hereford and Lancaster (who was now the leading figure among the nobles opposing the king). They agreed that Gaveston should be executed, and, possibly after a makeshift trial, the prisoner was taken to nearby Blacklow Hill on 19 June, where two Welsh soldiers despatched him – one stabbed him, and the other cut off his head. This summary and brutal act probably put an end to one problem that would otherwise have run for years, but it created another in that it divided the barons and determined the king on vengeance.

On 13 November 1312 Queen Isabella gave birth to a son, christened Edward (the French king's wish to name him either Louis, or Philip was vetoed by Lancaster and his allies), and in December a peace of sorts was patched up between Edward and Gaveston's murderers. The issue of the favourite had gone, and Edward had engineered the appointment of his ally, Walter Reynolds, as Archbishop of Canterbury. It seemed that the king was well placed to resume the authority and respect he considered to be his due. During a visit to France in the summer of 1313, thanks to the mediation of Philip IV and Pope Clement V, a full reconciliation was made between Edward and the lords ordainer, and agreement was reached for an expedition into Scotland to bring Robert Bruce to heel.

RIGHT **Philippe IV, the Faire (1268–1314).** *This is a detail from an early fresco in the Palais de Justice (old Palais Royal) in Etampes showing the king handing over the barony of Etampes to Louis d'Evreux. In this section Marguerite de Valois, Philippe's niece, is depicted with an escort of knights.*

Coment le cõmoune gent checon leua a cõtre autre e uoudra autre occire p̃ le auer sen; par mes-
prise. E ceo est dunt nous esperoms been q̃ le iour de dreit iugemẽt forment aproche.

North of the border pockets of English rule existed around a few well-fortified castles and towns. Between 1311 and 1314, while Edward and his nobles were at loggerheads, Bruce had steadily picked off these centres of English authority until only Stirling and Berwick were left in Edward's hands. Stirling was besieged in June, and Robert Bruce's brother, Edward, raided at will south of the border. By this time the English king was already on his way with a formidable army of over 2,000 armed knights, 2,000 Welsh archers and 13,000 infantry. Edward crossed into Scotland and moved towards Stirling to raise the siege. Bruce prepared to meet the enemy at a battle site of his choosing at a ford near Bannockburn village, where the English would have to form into a narrow file to cross the river. This gave him a tactical advantage that outweighed the superior numbers of the enemy. The Battle of Bannockburn was fought on 23–24 June in three phases.

During the first phase Sir Philip Mowbray together with 500 knights heading for the castle found their way blocked by Scottish infantry armed with spears some 15 feet long. They charged this position, but, to their surprise, the pikemen

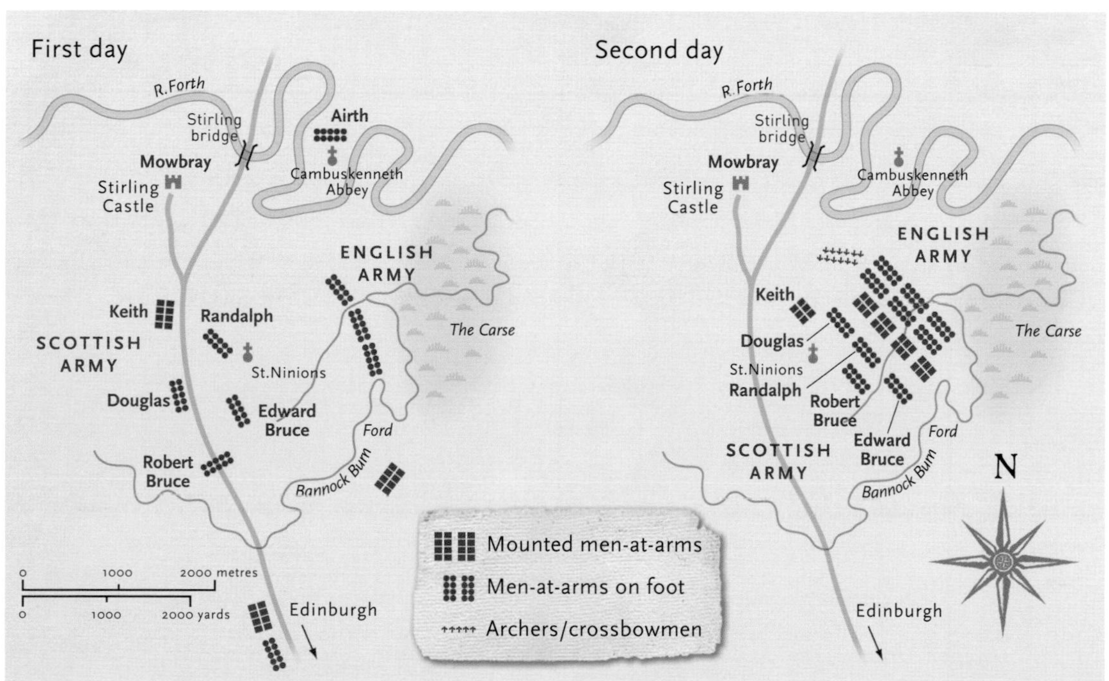

OPPOSITE **A 14th-century battle scene.** *This illustration from the* Holkham Bible Picture Book *(1327) gives a vivid impression of hand-to-hand fighting in the 14th century. It is believed by some to represent the Battle of Bannockburn but the precise location of the action scarcely matters. The artists who drew such pictures were rarely, if ever, witnesses to the events they portrayed. What is impressive about these scenes is the general atmosphere of violent confusion combined with individual representation of dead and dying men, panicking horses, the wielding of spears, axes, swords and longbows. Hundreds of book illustrations devoted to warfare have survived from these centuries – an indication of the prevalence of armed conflict in wars between nations, between kings and barons and between feuding barons.*

ABOVE **The Battle of Bannockburn 23–4 June, 1314.** *Contemporary accounts of the battle give varying descriptions of the engagements that took place over two days. On 23 June ill-disciplined forays by Edward's subordinate commanders were repulsed. On 24 June Edward's army were balked in their attempt to reach Stirling and were forced to offer battle in restricted and difficult ground where they could make no progress against the Scottish spearmen.*

It was ordained that the king should undertake no important matter without the consent of the council and that Lancaster should hold the position of chief in the council. CHRONICLES OF THE REIGNS OF EDWARD I AND EDWARD II, II, P. 224

held firm. Wave after wave of cavalry were cut down by the Scots. In the second phase, while the English were crossing the river, a young knight, Sir Henry de Bohun, spotted Bruce riding in front of the Scottish lines and, on a death-or-glory impulse, charged at him full tilt. As the two men clashed, Bruce felled the knight with his battle axe. This single combat greatly heartened the Scots. In the third phase the main battle took place the following morning. The English were camped with the river behind them, facing the Scottish position on a hillside opposite with a small gorge between the two armies. Bruce aimed to attack while the enemy were still crossing the gorge. However, the English vanguard reached the field beyond the gorge in good order and prepared to charge. Now their effort was ruined by divided counsels, Edward's commanders not agreeing on who should lead the attack. It was in some disarray, therefore, that the English knights smashed into Bruce's wall of pikes. Again, it was the infantry who prevailed. Soon there was confusion in the English ranks, those trying to retreat being hampered by those trying to press forwards. Then Bruce's infantry advanced, pushing the confused English back towards the gorge. They fell into it, their dead and wounded lying so densely packed that, as one observer said, 'a man could cross the gully dry-shod'.

Edward fled to Dunbar Castle and thence by sea to Berwick. There is no accepted estimate of the numbers of those who perished in the field and the gully and in trying to cross the River Forth, but, even if the Scottish claim of 30,000 slain is rejected as an exaggeration, the impact on national pride and Edward's reputation was dire. 'Oh, day of vengeance and misfortune, day of ruin and dishonour, evil and accursed day, not to be reckoned in our calendar, that stained the reputation of the English ... So many fine noblemen and strong young men, so many noble horses, so much military equipment, costly garments and gold plate – all lost in one harsh day, one fleeting hour!'[5]

At parliaments held at York in September, and in London in February 1315 and January 1316, Edward was progressively stripped of many of his powers. His inner circle was purged of 'bad influences', including Despenser and Walter Langton, and the Earl of Lancaster was appointed to lead the army in any further contests with the Scots.

1316–20

DURING THE NEXT few years the government of England was contested by various baronial factions, each pursuing its own interests. Hugh Despenser, now joined by his son, Hugh Despenser the Younger, feathered his own nest by supporting the king and obtaining from him grants of land and honours, while Lancaster built up an anti-court alliance in order to bolster his own power against the crown. Late in 1316 Edward turned for help to the new pope, John XXII, who responded by lending him money, ordering a truce to be agreed between England and Scotland and sending ambassadors to negotiate a comprehensive peace between the two countries. The papal agents were also under instructions to heal the kingdom's political divisions. Intermittent negotiations led, in October 1318, to a reconciliation between Edward and the Earl of Lancaster, which was confirmed in a parliament at York.

While these negotiations were in train, a man called John Powderham appeared at Oxford and declared himself to be the true king of England. His story of a cradle-switch that had enabled the current 'impostor' to claim the throne should have been laughable, and Edward was initially disposed to dismiss Powderham as a deranged fool of no consequence. However, there were plenty of people prepared to give the impostor a hearing on the basis of the fact that Edward seemed to lack all the characteristics of his father. The fact that Powderham was condemned to be hanged may suggest that his tale was a real embarrassment to Edward.

Important developments were also taking place in Scotland. Robert Bruce rejected the mediation of the pope. He had begun a siege of Berwick, the last English stronghold, at the beginning of the year and was too close

RIGHT **A crossbowman.** *Image from the Luttrell Psalter (c.1325–35). The crossbow is a very ancient weapon, dating from as far back as fifth-century BC China. It was capable of firing a metal-tipped bolt that was very effective against mail-clad knights. It could be fired with considerable accuracy and the skill needed to use it could be acquired quite quickly. Hand tensing required real effort, as is well indicated in this picture. Interestingly, the archer shown here is a monk.*

A la requeste con
templation z plai
sance de treshault
et noble prince
mon treschier seigneur z maistre
Guy de chastillon conte de blois
seigneur dauesnes de chymay
et de beaumont de scoonhove
et de la gode. Je iehan frois
sart prebstre et chappelain a mon

treschier seigneur dessus nome
Et pour le tamps de lors tresorier
et chanonne de chymay et de lille
en flandres ie me suis de nouvel
resueillie et entre dedens ma forge
pour ouurer et forgier en la
haulte et noble matiere de la
quelle du tamps passe ie me
suis ensonnie. Laquelle traitte
et propose les fais et aduenues

The collapse of the rebels was swift and complete for two reasons: Lancaster, always better at words than deeds, failed to come to the aid of the Marcher lords, and the king received support from Welsh leaders who rose against the Mortimers. On 22 January 1322 the Mortimers surrendered and were sent to the Tower of London, and Edward now marched against the northern lords. He seized Lancaster's castle at Kenilworth and eventually confronted the enemy at Burton upon Trent. After some desultory fighting, the rebels fled in confusion. Lancaster was tracked down and captured at Boroughbridge in Yorkshire on 16 March, and a few days later (on 21 March) he was brought before the king at Pontefract, speedily tried the next day, hustled outside the walls and despatched by a bungling executioner who took two or three blows to sever the earl's neck.

OPPOSITE **Queen Isabella enters Paris, 1325**. *The queen was desperate to get away from what had become a sham marriage and a court dominated by the Despensers. She was warmly welcomed by her brother, the new king, Charles IV. In this picture from* Froissart's Chronicles *(c.1400) she is shown entering Paris in great pomp with her two sons, though whether the actual event was quite as grand may be doubted.*

ABOVE **The execution of Thomas of Lancaster, 1322**. *The earl's futile rebellion and long-standing opposition to Edward's friends received their punishment on 21 March 1322. He was not allowed to speak in his own defence when tried before the king at Pontefract. He was sentenced to be hanged, drawn and quartered but, because of his royal cousinage, this was commuted to beheading. The next day he was executed outside the town wall. This depiction is from the Luttrell Psalter.*

The harshness of the king has today increased so much that no one, however great and wise, dares to cross his will. Thus parliaments, colloquies and councils decide nothing these days. For the nobles of the realm, terrified by threats and the penalties inflicted on others, let the king's will have free play. Thus today will conquers reason. For whatever pleases the king, though lacking in reason, has the force of law.

Vita Edwardi Secundi, p. 136

On 2 May the triumphant king called a parliament at York where, at last, he was able to get the Ordinances of 1311 revoked. Edward was now determined to follow up his victory by dealing with the Scottish problem. He led his army across the border, but Bruce declined to meet him in battle. The Scots retreated, wasting the land as they went, so that the English were deprived of food. Edward reached Edinburgh at the end of August but was then obliged to withdraw because his men were dying of starvation and sickness. Now Bruce pursued him and on 2 October inflicted a defeat on the English at Blackhow Moor in Yorkshire. Edward was not to be seen on the field of battle leading his forces. He was at nearby Byland when he heard that the Scots were on their way to capture him. He narrowly escaped with the younger Despenser and, after two weeks spent running and hiding, reached York. Queen Isabella's position was hardly less perilous. She was at Tynemouth Priory, well within the territory now controlled by the Scots, and had to make her escape by sea. A year of royal triumph had ended in yet another humiliation for Edward II.

1323–7

EDWARD COULD NOW FEEL that he was master in his own house. In May 1323 he agreed a 13-year truce with Robert Bruce. With peace came increased prosperity, and over the next few years he was able to clear the crown's debts and build up a healthy financial reserve. The Despensers continued to benefit from royal favour – Hugh the Elder was created Earl of Winchester and numerous gifts were showered on him and his son – and although the barons were far from content with this situation they were leaderless and the power of the royal favourites seemed unassailable.

Several prominent barons and churchmen suffered from the reprisals Edward inflicted after the civil war. Many more had to endure the personal animosities and arrogance of the younger Despenser, whose role was far more political than Gaveston's had ever been – he controlled royal business, assumed semi-regal state and frequently spoke in the king's name. The disaffection of the people showed itself in many ways. The Earl of Lancaster, for example, for all his weakness and ineffectiveness, was now regarded by some as a saint, and it was claimed that miracles were performed at his tomb. More seriously for Edward, his own queen was among those who developed a deep loathing for Despenser. Isabella resented the favourite's attitude towards her and the fact that her husband preferred his favourite's company.

Many of the malcontents who plotted against the regime or who even dreamed about overthrowing it looked to Roger Mortimer of Wigmore as their potential leader, but he was safely locked up in the Tower of London in quarters described as 'less elegant than were seemly'. Until August 1323, that is. Although officially sentenced to life imprisonment, Mortimer guessed that the king and Despenser would not fail to dispose of him if ever they felt he was a real threat, and he therefore contrived to do what, according to extant records, only one other prisoner had ever done before – to escape from England's most secure gaol.

The feast-day of St Peter ad Vincula, the patron saint of the Tower church, which was always celebrated by the garrison with heavy drinking, fell on 1 August. Mortimer's friends won the sub-lieutenant of the Tower, Gerald de Alspaye, to their cause, and he was able to make sure that the guards' drinks were spiked. To avoid incriminating himself, Gerald also consumed drugged wine after admitting the prisoner's friends. They attacked the wall of his cell with picks and crowbars until they had made a hole large enough to crawl through and to allow Mortimer into the king's kitchen. After that, with the aid of a rope ladder, he negotiated the roofs and walls and so reached the river, making his way, via Hainault, to Paris, where he presented himself to the new king, Charles IV, who had succeeded his brother, Philip.

King Charles was glad to receive him because a dispute had erupted between him and Edward over a skirmish on the border of Gascony, and this led in August 1324 to a French invasion of the English province. Long negotiations to resolve the crisis ended with an agreement for Queen Isabella to go to France as her husband's representative to discuss terms, and she left England in March 1325. The terms subsequently agreed were that Edward would

Mortimer flees

On Monday the Feast *of Saint Peter, on the Gule of August [Lammas Day, a time of harvest festival] at night, Sir Roger Mortimer, Lord of Wigemor, by means of a potion subtly made and given the same evening to the Constable and watch of the Tower, and to the other persons therein, escaped from the Tower of London, by a ladder skilfully made of cord, and fled to Porchester, where he took ship and crossed the sea, and so reached the dominions of the Court of Henaude [Hainault].*

'The French Chronicle of London, Edward II', in *Chronicles of the Mayors and Sheriffs of London*, ed. H.T. Riley, 1863, No. 16

Invasion defences

The king, by the advice of his councillors, had the Tower of London and other castles stored with provisions. Also, Sir Hugh Despenser, the son, had all the carpenters, masons and smiths taken, who were then in London and everywhere around it and caused all the turrets and crenelles in the Tower to be repaired and bars and bretasches [watchtowers] to be made at all the gates there of the very stoutest timber that in all England could be found and had mangonels [catapults], springals [snares] and other manner of engines made at great cost, and yet this availed him nothing, for his purpose was thwarted in another way. And all this was done through fear of strangers coming over in company with the queen.

'The French Chronicle of London, Edward II', No. 19

personally travel to Paris to do homage for his lands. He agreed, but at the last moment changed his mind. He was in a dilemma. He did not know who, if anyone, he could trust. Charles might renege on his agreement, and Mortimer was at large in France, as were other of the king's enemies, who might try to waylay him, possibly with the French king's connivance. Despenser was *persona non grata* in Charles's domain but, if he were left behind without Edward's protection, what might happen to him? Finally, Edward could not even be sure of his wife's intentions, for relations between the royal couple had broken down almost entirely. According to one chronicler, Isabella issued an ultimatum from her brother's court: 'Marriage is a joining together of man and woman, maintaining the undivided habit of life ... someone has come between my husband and myself, trying to break this bond. I protest that I will not return until this intruder is removed.'[6]

Edward finally accepted a compromise. He would confer on his 13-year-old son, Edward, his French lands, and the prince would do homage for them to his Uncle Charles, and in September the boy joined his mother at the French court. By the end of the year Isabella and Mortimer had become lovers, and the couple, together with their small band of compatriots, pledged themselves to the overthrow of the Despensers and, probably, the king. Charles declined to aid and abet them, and they travelled north to the duchy of Hainault, whose count, William, was a cousin by marriage of Isabella. He was prepared to back Mortimer's plans with men and *matériel* in return for a marriage treaty between his own daughter, Philippa, and the heir to the English throne. This news panicked Edward and the Despensers, who made urgent but belated plans to see off the threatened invasion.

When Queen Isabella and her small army landed at Orwell, Suffolk, on 24 September 1326, the true extent of the king's unpopularity soon became clear. As Isabella approached the capital Edward's followers simply disappeared. Within days he and Despenser were fleeing westwards, hoping to reach Despenser lands and gambling on the support of the Welsh. They may have pinned their hopes on reaching Ireland. No lords came to their support, however. Everyone looked to the queen and her champion, and soon London was in Mortimer's hands:

ABOVE **Queen Isabella with her army.** *Isabella is shown in this 14th-century illustration leading her troops at Hereford. Following her husband in his westward flight, the queen arrived at Hereford at the end of 1326 and spent a month there gathering her forces. This once important border town had declined in military significance after Edward I's subduing of the Welsh and the building of new castles in Wales. Hereford Castle was not fit for royal habitation and Isabella stayed at the palace of the bishop, Adam Orleton, one of her chief supporters. It was while at Hereford that Isabella received the news that Edward II had been captured and the Despensers executed.*

OVERLEAF **Queen Isabella and Prince Edward reach Oxford, October 1326** *as depicted in this illustration from the* Chronicles of the Court of Flanders *by the Master of Mary of Burgundy (fl. 1469–83). Isabella's westward march was virtually a triumphant procession. Barons and church leaders, weary with years of misrule by Edward and his favourites, flocked to her standard. Adam Orleton, Bishop of Hereford, preached a public sermon in which he denounced the Despensers and declared that Isabella and her son had come as holy pilgrims, rather than avenging furies, to rid the government of evil influences. Within days the queen learned that London had risen in her support. With the capital secure, she had no need to watch her back and could press on in pursuit of the king and his diminishing band of supporters.*

A letter was sent to London by the queen and her son and was fixed at daybreak upon the cross in Chepe, and a copy of the letter on the windows elsewhere ... to the effect that the commons should be aiding with all their power in destroying the enemies of the land, and Hugh le Despenser in especial, for the common profit of all the realm ... Wherefore the Commonalty proceeded to wait upon the Mayor and other great men of the City ... so much so that the Mayor crying mercy with clasped hands went to the Guildhall and granted the commons their demand and cry was accordingly made in Chepe that the enemies to the king, the queen and their son should all quit the City upon such peril as might ensue.[7]

The loss of London was crucial to the king's fortunes. With no capital and no army Edward could only try to evade his enemies. The fugitives – which was what the king and his friend had become – were pursued from castle to castle, refuge to refuge, until they reached Llantrisant, where they were captured on 16 November. Meanwhile, on 26 October, Prince Edward was proclaimed guardian of the realm at Bristol. The next day the elder Despenser was beheaded in the same city. His son survived until 24 November, when he met the same fate at Hereford.

On 7 January 1327 parliament met at Westminster to decide what to do with the ex-king. It was a question without precedent, and the solemnity of what they were about cannot have failed to impress itself on the minds of all present. Articles were drawn up listing Edward's faults: Edward was condemned as incompetent and

ABOVE **The execution of Hugh Despenser the Younger, 1326.** *After his capture, Despenser was brought to Hereford for trial and execution before Isabella and Mortimer. The queen must have enjoyed the grisly spectacle of the man who had systematically humiliated her over the years. Even by the standards of the day the execution was spectacular in its horror. The prisoner was led to a gallows 50 feet high wearing a tunic with his arms reversed and with a coronet of nettles around his head. Once hoisted onto the gallows, he was castrated, his entrails torn out and burned, after which his body was quartered and his head despatched to London and displayed on a pole on London Bridge. The illustration from* Froissart's Chronicle *(15th century) is not accurate in all respects.*

OPPOSITE **The tomb effigy of Edward II.** *Although Edward II was hated by most of his people and his death had been encompassed by the queen and Mortimer, he was accorded the honours of a royal funeral. His body was not taken to Westminster, for fear of the Londoners creating unseemly demonstrations. Instead it was conveyed to the nearby abbey church at Gloucester (now the cathedral). There is a certain irony about the fact that this most unpopular of kings now resides beneath one of the most impressive royal tombs in England. The fine alabaster effigy is surmounted by an intricate stone canopy. Exactly who created it and when remain unresolved mysteries.*

of being ruled by favourites; he had ignored the sound advice of mature barons and churchmen; he had behaved with brutality towards his own people; and his foreign affairs had been a disaster – he had failed to exert control over Scotland, had antagonized the French and had placed his continental lands in jeopardy. The fact that Edward had a male heir who was not far from reaching his majority made it easier for his subjects to contemplate setting aside their consecrated king.

Edward was being held at Kenilworth, in the castle of the late Earl of Lancaster that he had taken so triumphantly in 1322. It was there, on 20 January, that he was presented with a demand for him to resign the crown to his son. As a broken man, weeping tears of grief, Edward finally submitted to the inevitable. Prince Edward formally acceded on 25 January and was crowned on 2 February. It was agreed that the ex-king should be kept in comfortable, honourable confinement for the rest of his natural life, but this was never a realistic option, for he immediately became the focus of opposition to the new regime, and various plots were hatched to effect his release. For this reason Edward was moved, usually secretly and by night, from location to location until he reached Berkeley Castle, near Gloucester, on 6 April. Even here attempts were made in July and September to set him free. Such plots, in effect, sealed his fate, and on 21 September it was officially stated that Edward had died of natural causes. The truth is that the ex-king was murdered, probably on the direct orders of Mortimer and without the knowledge of Isabella and her son.

EDWARD III

About the time that young Edward had the crown thrust upon him by the machinations of his mother Isabella and her lover, Roger Mortimer, William Langland, the first poet of the English language, was born. He was writing his only extant poem, *The Vision of Piers Plowman*, during the closing years of the reign, so his reflections on the state of society must be seen as one sensitive observer's assessment of the state of England under the seventh Plantagenet king. The picture he paints is bleak indeed, and it is supported by the evidence of contemporary chroniclers and the verdict of most later historians.

Edward III's reign falls into two parts, divided by the appalling cataclysm of the Black Death (1348–50), but it was not only that natural disaster that was responsible for the decay of the existing social order. Feudalism was collapsing under the weight of its own complex (and often contradictory) structures. The power of the monarch was being challenged by parliament, which established an existence of its own, separate from the will of the king. The power of the church was being challenged by protesters at all levels of society. In foreign affairs the old disputes between the French and English kings over the vaguely defined area of Aquitaine expanded into a contest for the crown of France, setting in motion what would later be known as the Hundred Years War. The early stages of that war were marked by impressive English victories, and Edward enjoyed a reputation as a great warrior-king, but the fundamental issues between France and England remained unresolved at his death. The same can be said of Anglo-Scottish relations. Edward's campaigns north of the border succeeded only in strengthening the bonds between Scotland and France and reinforcing the Scottish kings' determination to achieve undisputed independence.

1327–30

THE YOUNG KING was provided with a council of peers and bishops, under the nominal headship of Henry, Earl of Lancaster (brother of the executed Thomas of Lancaster), a quorum of whom were to be constantly in attendance wherever Edward was. In reality, Mortimer and Isabella, the queen mother, controlled the government. This inevitably created conflict, especially when Mortimer used his position, quite brazenly, to accumulate lands and offices. At the parliament held in Salisbury in October 1328 he took to himself the title Earl of March – that is, the Welsh Marches – and it was quickly apparent that he was no better than the Despensers.

Grumbling against the regime soon turned to plots. Lancaster and other nobles refused to attend the 1328 parliament, and in January 1329 they mounted an armed rebellion, although this was swiftly suppressed by Mortimer. Lancaster and others were pardoned, but Mortimer took the opportunity to purge the upper reaches of society of the men he feared most, and the king's uncle, Edmund of Kent, was foremost among those executed (1330). Mortimer seems to have learned nothing from the fate of Edward II's favourites. He lived in a style of pomp and luxury that put the royal court in the shade, and one of his earliest displays of personal magnificence was a round table, normally the preserve of princes, where jousts and other feats of arms were staged amid gorgeous splendour.

Mortimer's reputation was further damaged by his poor handling of the Scottish problem. In the spring of 1337 an English army was assembled at York to march north and assert Edward's rights as overlord. The expedition was marred at the outset by a serious clash between Welsh archers and mercenaries hired to Mortimer and Isabella by their old friend, the Count of Hainault. The English army spent most of the summer trying to bring the Scots to battle but only succeeded in wasting time, money and energy in fruitless pursuit. Jean Froissart recorded the misery of the army, wandering the rain-drenched border country in search of their enemies. He tells us that the soldiers were offered food by the English peasants and had to pay 'sixpence for a badly baked loaf that was worth only a penny, and two and sixpence for a gallon of wine worth only sixpence'.[1]

OPPOSITE **Gold coin of Edward III**. *In 1344 Edward, like his father, experimented with a gold coinage. The most impressive item was the florin or double leopard, valued at 6 shillings. It was modelled on a contemporary French coin. Like Edward II's attempt to upgrade the English coinage, this was not a success. The florin and other new gold coins were soon removed from circulation. However, other gold coins first minted in 1351 did establish themselves. Foremost among them was the noble, valued at 6s.8d. (1/3 of a pound), which now made its first appearance.*

PREVIOUS PAGES **The seal of Edward III**. *In this seventh in the sequence of Edward's seals the king is shown wearing a coat of mail, a heraldic surcoat and a crested helmet. He holds a broadsword and a shield. His galloping horse has heraldic trappings and a plume (1364).*

Portrait of Edward III *by an unknown, probably 16th-century artist. This is a copy by the German artist, Hermann Goldschmidt (1802–66) of an original at Hampton Court.*

Following the death of Robert Bruce in 1329, Scotland descended once more into political anarchy. The new king, David II, was a child of just five years, and Edward Balliol, currently living in France, asserted his claim as the son of John Balliol, who had died in 1296. He asked for Edward's military help but the king (officially) declined to break his treaty oath. However, once Balliol had landed in Scotland and won a victory over David's supporters at the Battle of Duppin Moor (August 1332), Edward reconsidered his decision. Only after Balliol had suffered a reverse and fled across the border did Edward decide to act on his behalf. In May 1333 he brought his own army up to Berwick to join Balliol in laying siege

ABOVE **Edward III pays homage to Philip VI, 1329** *in an image from* Chroniques de France ou de St Denis. *What became the Hundred Years War began in the relationship between these two men. The 17-year-old Edward obeyed the summons to do fealty for his continental dominions but he did so reluctantly and demonstrated this by attending the ceremony wearing his crown, sword and crimson robe embroidered with the gilded 'leopards' of England. Tradition demanded that vassals should come bareheaded and unarmed before their liege lords. The clash of two proud spirits led to open war in 1337 when Edward gave refuge to a Frenchman fleeing from Philip's justice. Philip declared Gascony forfeit and Edward responded by asserting that his claim to the French crown was better than Philip's.*

The Battle of Halidon Hill

The site of the battle in 1333 was a broken ring of low hills surrounding a bowl of boggy ground. Edward took up his position on Halidon Hill and waited for Douglas to attack. Because of the soft terrain, both commanders dismounted their knights. Edward placed contingents of archers on both wings and relied on the fact that his enemy would have to attack uphill and come within range of the bowmen before they reached the hilltop. Douglas put his faith in his superior numbers and hoped to force the Anglo-Scottish host back towards the River Tweed. One chronicler indicates the misgivings of the defenders as they looked across the open ground at the Scottish host: 'When the English saw them they were very cast down ... but King Edward of England rode about everywhere among his army and encouraged his men well and nobly, and generously promised them good reward provided that they conducted themselves well against the great multitude of their Scottish enemies.'[2]

Douglas attacks

Douglas waited until late in the afternoon and then concentrated his attack on the left and centre, commanded by Balliol and Edward, respectively. Before they could begin the ascent to higher ground they encountered a deadly hail of arrows and retreated in disorder. Only on the English right did hand-to-hand fighting take place. Screaming their battle cries, the Scots charged 'with the ferocity of a lion against the foremost English line. A bloody battle developed there because the Scots struggled to reach the town and wanted to fulfil their oath; on the other hand the English resisted manfully. So most of the day was spent, until the English, by Divine favour, finally prevailed, and obtained the victory. In this prolonged struggle there perished 500 of the strongest and choicest of all the people of Scotland, in the spot called by the local inhabitants "Hevyside".'[3]

Douglas's men regrouped again and again, but they could make no headway and were eventually routed. Several heavily armoured Scottish knights struggled their way back to where their horses had been left, only to discover that their grooms had mounted the steeds themselves and fled.

The young English king learned from such experiences that infantry and archers were vital features of any good army. Earlier encounters had shown that the heroic and awe-inspiring charge of a body of armoured horsemen could be checked by unflinching pikemen, and now the effectiveness of a phalanx of bowmen had been demonstrated.

BELOW **The seal of Edward Balliol, king of Scotland (*c.*1283–1364).** *This impressive seal shows the unfortunate king seated on an elaborate throne and bearing crown and sceptre. However, he was only able to hold onto his position intermittently – 1332, 1333–4 and 1335–6.*

to the town. Sir Archibald Douglas arrived to relieve the town with a numerically superior force, outnumbering the army of Edward and Balliol by at least two to one, and battle was joined at Halidon Hill, to the north of Berwick, on 19 July. This engagement provided Edward with his first battlefield victory and was important in the development of military tactics.

Berwick was not Scotland, and, although their king was living in exile in France, the supporters of David II were not vanquished. Edward spent much of the next three years trying to bolster Balliol's claim, but every time he ventured deep into mountainous Scottish terrain his enemy simply left him to waste his efforts wandering around in hostile country looking for a fight. Meanwhile, the situation in France was deteriorating rapidly, and in November 1336 Edward had to make a truce with the Scots in order to concentrate on securing his territories across the Channel.

1337–47

EDWARD SPENT THE NEXT DECADE fighting a war on two fronts, which was horrendously expensive, achieved little and set the king at odds with his principal advisers.

The conflict with France was the result of a personal clash between two belligerent, violent, choleric and ambitious monarchs. Philip was under pressure from a domineering wife to assert his rights. As the first cousin of three kings of France, all of whom had died young and without male heirs, he had come unexpectedly to the throne, and there were others who contested his right. Some other claims, including Edward's, relied on succession through the female line, and to avoid the types of problem that, according to contemporary thinking, were inclined to attend rule by, or in the name of, women, Philip's predecessor had had the Salic Law enacted, but it was not universally accepted and Philip felt some vulnerability on that score. Therefore, he forcefully asserted his authority in all parts of his realm.

Aquitaine was a running sore, and there appeared to be no end to the border disputes between the French kings and the Anglo-Gascons, whose first allegiance was to the kings of England. In May 1337 Philip severed the Gordian knot by annexing Aquitaine. Edward had no intention of being deprived of his inheritance or of the considerable income he derived from his continental lands. However, he could not declare war on his feudal overlord without risking papal excommunication. He therefore asserted his claim to the crown of France as a *casus belli*, and from 1340 he quartered the arms of France with those of England on his coat of arms.

A state of war existed between the two realms, but this did not lead immediately to major military conflict. Both kings set about borrowing money and seeking allies for the coming contest, and Philip ordered naval raids on England's southern coast. In June 1340 Edward managed to put a stop to this. He was crossing to the Low Countries with a small army when he encountered a fleet of some 200 sailing vessels and galleys in the harbour of Sluys in the Scheldt estuary. Philip had spent months assembling this force and bringing ships round from the Mediterranean for a massive attack and possibly even an invasion, but in the bloody naval battle that followed on 24 June, the English routed their enemies and captured 190 French vessels.

After his success in the Battle of Sluys Edward went on to join his father-in-law, the Duke of Hainault, in the siege of Tournai in July, but the city proved impregnable. Meanwhile, encouraged and resourced by Philip VI, the supporters of David II had captured Edinburgh and Stirling. Edward, heavily in debt to his allies, was forced to break off the siege and seek a truce in September. He returned to England in a furious mood, insisting that his failure was entirely due to lack of funds and turning his wrath on his principal advisers. Ever since he had assumed full power those closest to him had been the brothers John and Robert Stratford, Archbishop of Canterbury and Bishop of Chichester, respectively. Both brothers had been entrusted at various times with the chancellorship – John 1330–34 and 1335–7; Robert 1337–8 and 1340. Neither had been enthusiastic about the French war, and their enemies now managed to arouse the king's suspicions against them. Edward dismissed Robert from his office of chancellor and had several senior judges and prominent

ABOVE **Medieval royal shield**. *This painted stone boss was discovered in London's Guildhall during 19th-century rebuilding works and is one of the earliest examples of the royal emblems of England and France being combined after Edward III laid claim to the French crown. The shield's quarters show France's gold fleurs de lys on a blue ground and England's gold 'leopards' on a red ground. The English beasts are correctly termed in heraldry 'lions passant guardant' (i.e. walking with faces turned to the viewer). These were often called, particularly by French heralds, 'leopards', presumably because they appeared less fierce than the erect 'lions rampant' depicted in other heraldic devices.*

ant le roy dan
pou et tou

The Battle of Sluys

King Edward ... *drew up his ships in line so that there was one shipload of men-at-arms between every two of archers, with a number of additional vessels full of archers kept in reserve as replacements ... When King Edward had properly deployed his fleet, he manoeuvred it so that the wind was on their starboard quarter, in order to have the advantage of the sun, which had previously shone full in their faces. The Normans ... drew up their own ships, with the Christopher, which they had captured earlier that year, in the van, now manned with Genoese crossbowmen. The fleet advanced to the sound of trumpets and other warlike instruments.*

A fierce battle broke out, each side opening fire with crossbows and longbows, and hand-to-hand fighting began. The soldiers used grappling irons on chains in order to come to grips with the enemy boats. Many noble feats of arms were achieved, both captures and rescues. The great Christopher was recaptured by the English, and all her crew killed ... The battle that followed was cruel and horrible. Sea-battles are always more terrible than those on land, for those engaged can neither retreat nor run away ... But [the English] fought so valiantly, with the help of those from the neighbourhood of Bruges, that they won the day. Their enemies were all killed or drowned, and not one escaped.

Froissart's Chronicles, pp. 103–4

LEFT **The Battle of Sluys, 24 June 1340**. *This vivid illustration from* Froissart's Chronicles *reveals a great deal about the nature of early naval warfare. The object was to grapple the enemy so that armed soldiers could board and engage in hand-to-hand combat. Archers provided covering fire to aid this process and, from the mastheads, other troops aimed spears at the enemy. Most harrowing was the fate of those who fell overboard. In their heavy armour they stood no chance of survival.*

merchants thrown into prison. He accused John Stratford, who had been president of the regency council in his absence, of deliberately starving him of funds.

For several months king and archbishop were involved in a heated correspondence, which was highly abusive on Edward's part. John stood his ground and demanded to be tried by his peers. This was the worst confrontation between king and archbishop since Henry II had fallen out with Becket, but John won the support of several barons, who persuaded Edward to issue a statute confirming the right of the leading men of the realm to be tried by their peers and not by the king's justices. Edward was shaken by this display of solidarity, and in October 1341 he was reconciled to the Stratfords. Nevertheless, as soon as he had the opportunity he revoked the parliamentary statute concerning the judicial rights of the ruling class.

Meanwhile, the new Duke of Brittany, John de Montfort, who was eager to establish his independence from Philip VI, offered to do fealty to Edward. This gave the English king another valuable foothold on the continent and, over the next two years, he campaigned in northern France, although he was hampered by lack of funds from mounting a major expedition. His failure to service his debts had contributed to the bankruptcy of his Italian bankers, and his shoddy treatment of parliament made it impossible to raise more taxes. When parliament was summoned in 1343, both Lords and Commons united to demand that statutes should not be unilaterally annulled by the king.

Determined to proceed with his military ambitions, in 1344 Edward organized a grand round table at Windsor. This magnificent festival emphasized the splendour of the monarchy and its spiritual identity with the Arthurian legends and the ideals of chivalry. All the leading nobles and knights of the realm were invited to take part in jousts and to display their combat prowess, and Edward vowed to found a military brotherhood or secular order of 300 knights, based on King Arthur's fellowship of the Round Table.

The castle at Windsor

At this time King Edward *decided to restore and rebuild the great castle at Windsor, first built by King Arthur, who instituted the noble Round Table there, from which so many good and valiant knights went out into the world to engage in brave and gallant feats of arms.*

FROISSART'S CHRONICLES, P. 128

OPPOSITE **Edward III taking advice**. *Robert, self-styled Count of Artois (shown on the left in blue), arrived in England in 1334 having fled from France after a quarrel with his brother-in-law King Philip VI. His dispute with the French king lay over his claim to the County of Artois, currently held by his cousin, Jeanne II, Countess of Burgundy. King Philip sided with Jeanne, confiscated Robert's property and imprisoned his family. In England Robert, by now an expert in the laws governing succession, encouraged Edward III to lay claim to the crown of France. In the subsequent Anglo-French campaigns he fought on the English side for Edward. He succumbed to dysentery and now lies buried in St Paul's Cathedral.*

r dist li contes que apre
ce que mess t. se fut pa

Whatever romantic ideals the king may have espoused, his immediate political objective was to unite England's military class behind him for the next projected stage of his war with Philip. He also made clever use of sermons and royal proclamations to draw attention to the perfidy of the French king in supporting David II and the threat to England's legitimate interests in Gascony and Brittany. On a less elevated level the propaganda pointed out the rewards that soldiers could expect from looting the towns and villages of the lands they conquered and ransoming French knights. It worked: Edward received the sanction and support of parliament for a massive invasion of France in 1346.

A force had been despatched to Gascony the previous year, and in July 1346 Edward gathered an army of 4,000 men-at-arms, 10,000 archers and an unspecified number of Welsh and Irish infantry at Portsmouth for a cross-Channel thrust. Despite his loud and frequently uttered claims to the French crown, Edward's real aims were more immediate: he needed, by plunder, to replenish his coffers and he intended to frighten Philip into renouncing his claims in Aquitaine.

He landed on the Normandy coast and made for Caen. Froissart describes the impact made on the citizenry who had never seen such an invasion force before: 'When the inhabitants saw the English battalions approaching in serried ranks, with all their banners and pennons flying in the breeze, and heard the archers roaring – for they had never heard or seen archers before – they were so terrified that nothing in this world could have prevented them from fleeing. They ran from the town in disorder ... falling over each other in their haste.'[4] They did well to flee, for those who stayed and tried to make a fight of it were slaughtered to a man. The English helped themselves to all the food they needed and sent wagon-loads of booty back home. They continued their marauding way through northern France, and it was not until they had crossed the Somme that news reached them that King Philip was approaching with a superior force. Edward had time to choose the ground for the coming battle and placed his men in defensive formation on rising ground overlooking the River Maie, close to the village of Crécy.

The course of the battle (on 26 August 1346) was largely determined by the contrasting tactical abilities of the generals. Edward had learned how to use longbowmen and dismounted knights. Philip not only relied on the traditional

OPPOSITE **Knights being taught to joust**. *This French illumination on vellum is from a 15th-century version of the earlier* Roman du Graal *(*The Romance of the Grail*), c.1200–1210 by Robert de Boron. The Arthurian legends were as popular in France as in England and the poems that made up the* Roman *told the stories of Arthur, Merlin and the knights of the Round Table. These stories were vital in providing an honourable, chivalric mythology to justify knightly combat and giving it a religious gloss. The Holy Grail story related the adventures of the cup used by Jesus at the Last Supper, its transfer to Avalon and its quest by Perceval (Parsifal). The picture shows knights being schooled using poles instead of lances.*

RIGHT **The capture of Caen, 1346**. *Caen was a city divided into two parts by the River Odon. Bridges linked the old city with its castle to a newer, prosperous suburb. The defenders concentrated on defending the latter because it was the obvious target of soldiers eager for loot. Edward III directed his assault at the sparsely defended old town. He rapidly lost control of his troops, who swarmed across the bridges and crumbling walls and became engaged in running battles through the streets. He was never able to direct a disciplined assault on the castle because his men could not be distracted from a five-day plundering rampage. Most of Caen was raised to the ground and those citizens who failed to escape to the country were slaughtered. French losses numbered about 5,000. As Edward moved on to Crécy and other battles it seemed that he might well make good his claim to the French crown.*

se leuerent
Si approuchierẽt la grosse

deployment of his resources, but he weakened them by poor battlefield direction. His army arrived at the site after a long march, when his men were tired and the sun was low in the west and shining into their eyes. He first ordered his vanguard to charge, then decided that it would be better to wait until the next day. Receiving conflicting orders, some of his men turned back while others pressed on. Out of range of their targets and pierced by English arrows, the Genoese crossbowmen fell back, throwing down their bows. The king, who on sighting the English changed colour 'because he hated them', lost control of the situation. Seeing the Genoese flee, either he or his brother, the Duke of Alençon, shouted, 'Slay these rascals who get in our way!' while his knights, 'in haste and evil order', slashed at the archers in their effort to cut a way through. Out of this terrible tangle in their own ranks, the French launched attack after attack on the enemy, but the disciplined line of England's longbowmen, stiffened by the long practice their weapon required, held firm and sowed confusion and death by their missiles. Then English knights advanced on foot, preceded by archers and supported by pikemen and murderous Welsh with long knives, who went among the fallen and slew them on the ground.[5] The fighting went on almost until midnight, and mopping up operations continued the next day. While Edward lost probably fewer than a hundred men, French casualties were on a horrendous scale. It is estimated that some 13,000 to 14,000 of Philip's troops and allies fell at Crécy, including the cream of French nobility.

News from home provided a further boost to English morale. In a battle at Neville's Cross near Durham in October the Scots were heavily defeated, and several of

OPPOSITE **The Battle of Crécy, 26 August 1346.** *This legendary battle is regarded by some historians as marking the end of the rule of chivalry in medieval warfare. Whether or not this is so, what emerged clearly from the battle was the superiority of the longbow over the crossbow. This is the point of the 14th-century miniature shown here, which is now in the Bibliothèque de l'Arsenal, Paris. Every returning longbowman was rewarded with an acre of land and tax exemptions. It was not just the skill of the archers that carried the day. Efficient organization played an important part. Each bowman was given two quivers of arrows. Other supplies were carried in the baggage train and brought to the archers by servants, who were also sent into no man's land to retrieve shot arrows. In medieval warfare good administration was as important as valour.*

The longbow

The success at Crécy *and other significant battles of the 14th century was in large measure due to the longbow. This simple weapon had been in use for generations for hunting, but the Welsh perfected it as a weapon of war. Edward I recognized its value and ordered peasants to become proficient in its use, but it did not come into its own as a standard piece of military equipment until the reign of Edward III. Before that, the crossbow was the favoured long-range hand weapon. In the hands of a practised bowman the longbow was a formidable weapon. Strong and portable, the longbow was made from a single piece of yew. It was about 6 feet in length and fired a shaft more than 4 feet long. It had an average range of 300 yards and could be fired with sufficient force to penetrate chain mail and even plate armour. But its main advantage was its rapid rate of fire. Unlike the crossbow, which had to be cranked up for each delivery, the longbow was capable of loosing off eight shafts a minute. It was the machine gun of its day. Even the most hardened knight might be daunted by a relentless rain of metal-tipped arrows, and at Crécy the English army had somewhere between 6,000 and 10,000 archers, which means that the advancing French horsemen were confronted by a deadly barrage of at least 50,000 arrows a minute.*

Crécy legends

The celebrated English victory *has given rise to many legends surrounding the king's son, Edward, Prince of Wales. The 16-year-old prince was given command of the vanguard so that he could 'win his spurs'. He was, supposedly, sent into battle wearing black armour so that his men would recognize him easily and was thereafter known as the Black Prince, but this story has its origins in the 16th century and there is no indication that it was used in the prince's lifetime. He is supposed to have assumed his heraldic badge of the 'Prince of Wales Feathers' and the motto* Ich Dien *('I serve') after the battle, and it is claimed that they were derived from the arms of John, the blind King of Bohemia, who fell at Crécy, fighting for the French. Young Edward, impressed by the king's bravery, is supposed to have adapted John's arms of black vulture wings. This, too, cannot be proved, and there may well be a more pragmatic origin for the badge that has been used ever since by princes of Wales.*

BELOW **Effigy of the Black Prince**. *This gilt-copper effigy of Edward, Prince of Wales, the 'Black Prince', made soon after his death in 1376, surmounts his tomb in Canterbury Cathedral, where he specifically asked to be buried.*

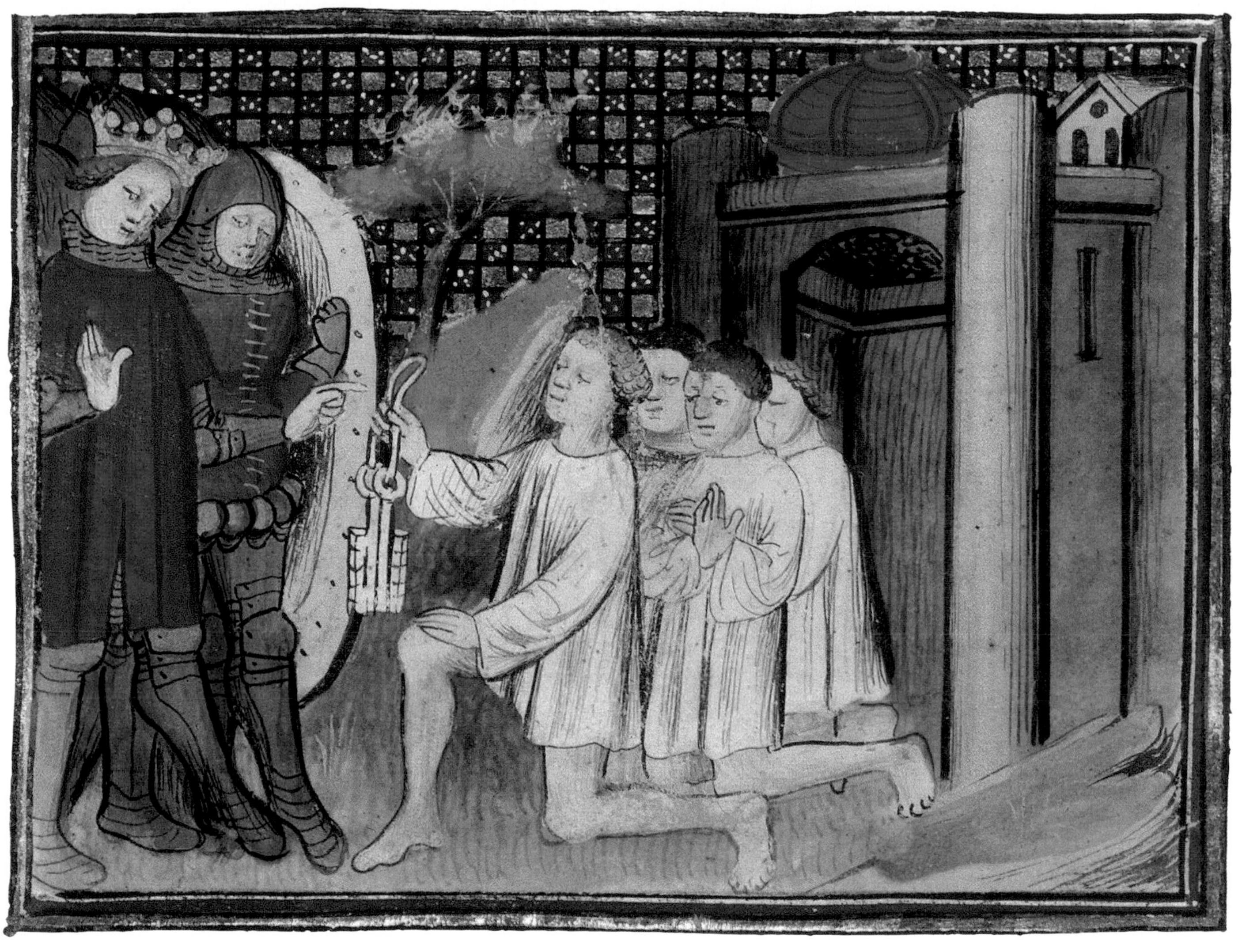

their leading men were taken prisoner. Among them was King David II, who was paraded through the streets of London on a large black charger on his way to the Tower. On the continent King Edward continued northwards and laid siege to the port of Calais, which would provide him with a useful base for further forays into France. The town resisted for almost a year, but Philip's forces were so depleted and demoralized that they were unable to come to its defence, and Calais capitulated in August 1347. During this campaign Edward employed small cannon, and this is the first instance of the use of artillery in field operations, further evidence of Edward's strategic and tactical creativity.

ABOVE **The surrender of Calais, 3 August 1347**. *Edward set about the siege of Calais methodically and patiently. He entrenched it round to prevent counterattack by the defenders. He had reinforcements brought from England. He built what was, in effect, a town providing his men with as many of the 'home comforts' as could reasonably be supplied. Then he settled to an 11-month siege. When they had given up all hope of relief the besieged garrison asked for terms. Edward insisted not only on total surrender, but also on a demonstration of his power. Six burghers were to be sent out clad only in shirts and with halters round their necks to present the city keys. This done, they were to be executed before the walls. Only with great reluctance was Edward persuaded to spare the lives of the hapless citizens. This scene is illustrated in* Froissart's Chronicles.

1348–56

KING AND NATION were in exultant mood. The victories, proclaimed from market crosses and lauded from pulpits, fired the public imagination. Soldiers returned as heroes with tales to tell and money to spend. It was said that those who returned from this campaign brought with them so much booty that no woman in the realm lacked for some graceful gown or valuable trinket. Edward basked in the glory of having achieved the most spectacular military success of any English monarch, and he toured the country during the early months of 1348, staging a series of tournaments, and revived his grand design of founding an order of chivalry.

The celebrations and self-congratulation did not last long, however, and in the summer of 1348, at about the time that Edward was creating his martial brotherhood, one of the worst disasters (perhaps *the* worst disaster) ever to hit England struck – the Black Death.

The plague had taken less than two years to arrive from Asia, and within weeks it travelled from the south coast to London. Then it made its inexorable way along the nation's highways and byways. Within a year there was no corner of the realm that was not affected: villages fell empty and silent, and town populations were decimated. By the end of 1349 between a third and a half of Edward's subjects had been struck down. One chronicler recorded its coming 'like black smoke' or a 'rootless phantom', which was indiscriminate in destroying young and old, male and female. There were not enough living to bury the dead. Corpses lay in the streets – animal as well as human, because there were few left to care for flocks and herds. In London and other cities, where streets had become open sewers choked with bodies, rubbish and human and animal filth, other diseases thrived. The pestilence was carried by the bacterium *Yersinia pestis*, which lived in fleas feeding on black rats, and the crowded, unsanitary dwellings in which most people lived enabled it to spread with alarming rapidity.

The dreadful pestilence

The dreadful pestilence *penetrated the sea coast by Southampton and came to Bristol, and there almost the whole population of the town perished as if it had been seized by sudden death; for few kept their beds more than two or three days, or even half a day. Then this cruel death spread everywhere around, following the course of the sun. And there died at Leicester in the small parish of St Leonard more than 380 persons; in the parish of Holy Cross 400; in the parish of St Margaret's, Leicester, 700; and so in every parish, a great multitude.*

KNIGHTON'S CHRONICLE 1337–1396, ED. G.H. MARTIN, OXFORD, 1995, P. 12

OPPOSITE **Death's grim harvest**. *The horrors of the Black Death left a deep and long-lasting impression on all the people of Europe. This French illuminated manuscript, which dates from around 1503, shows death driving his wagon and collecting the bodies of men and women from all classes of society.*

la mort
laure

Windsor and the Order of the Garter

Starting in 1344, Edward spent 20 years turning the already impressive castle at Windsor into the finest royal residence in Europe. For his great tournament of 1344 he built a great 'House of the Round Table', some 66 yards across, intending it to be the headquarters of the order he projected for 300 knights. His objective was to associate the Arthurian legends, then centred on Glastonbury, with Windsor and the crown.

He needed to tie the nobility more closely to himself if he was going to succeed in his wars in France and Scotland. He had to proceed against opposition from many church leaders, who condemned tournaments and the chivalric ideals that lay behind them. Military 'games', they insisted, were dangerous – as one critic said, they were just a complicated way of committing suicide – and vainglorious, encouraging the sin of pride. Lechery was a very real threat because women were encouraged to admire and reward their macho champions. Knights should be employing their talents on crusade, fighting for Christian truth, and not competing with each other in obedience to romantic legends. Such grumblers were fighting a losing battle, however. The thrill of martial combat and the elaborate spectacle of the joust appealed to combatants and spectators alike.

A more exclusive order

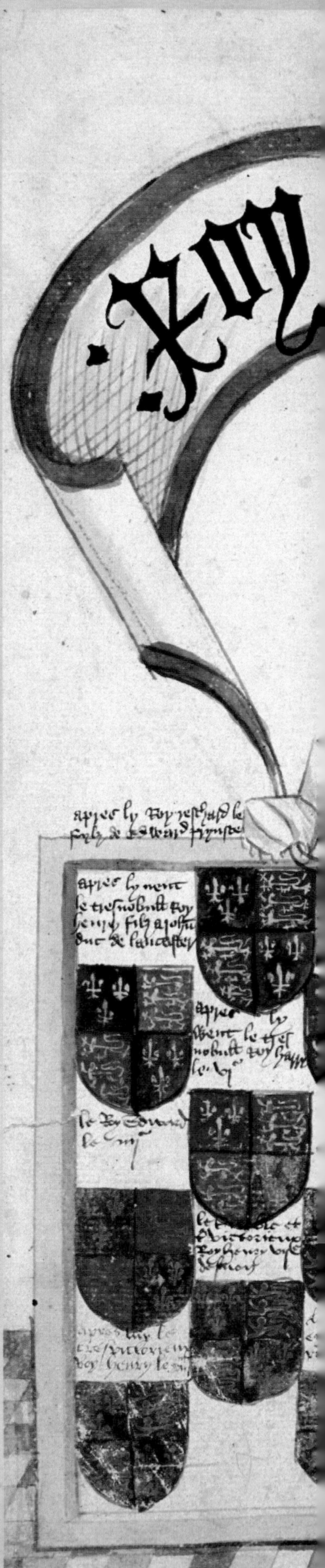

Edward did not persevere with his building plans in 1344, probably because he ran out of money, and the House of the Round Table was demolished in the 1360s, when his ideas turned in other directions. After his spectacular successes in northern France in 1346–7, the king decided to create a more exclusive order of chivalry to reward those who had given outstanding service in the recent campaign. Building at Windsor recommenced in order to provide the order with an impressive home, and an elaborate ceremonial was ordained to set the chosen members apart from other prominent men of the realm. Edward had a practical reason for this: he wanted to elevate men of real military talent above those who were merely prominent in his army by reason of noble birth. Several men of knightly rank were among the first members of the order, but they were not provided with lands or aristocratic titles. They formed a military elite under whom nobles would be prepared to serve because of their intimate connection with the king. Its emblem was a garter of gold embroidery on a blue ground to be affixed just below the knee (where it would be visible in battle) bearing the motto, *Honi soit qui mal y pense* ('Evil be to anyone who despises it'). The colours – blue and gold – were those of the French royal arms, and it seems likely that their choice was closely bound up with Edward's French claims. The motto defied anyone to hold those claims in scorn. The popular myth that a

trivial incident gave rise to this grand and important order of chivalry may well have been started by the French to do precisely that – to ridicule Edward's ambition. According to this story, the Countess of Salisbury (with whom Edward was reputed to be sexually involved) dropped her garter at a court function, and the king retrieved it to save her embarrassment. Why the emblem should have been a garter is not clear, and one suggestion is that the item of clothing in question was originally a belt. The Most Noble Order of the Garter was the first secular order of chivalry. The French king, John II, instituted the Order of the Star in 1351, but it had a very short life.

Windsor

The ordinances for establishing the order were dated 6 August 1348. They provided for a college of 24 canons to be established in St George's Chapel, Windsor, and 24 poor knights (the number was later increased to 26). Over the next two decades masons, carpenters and glaziers were constantly in attendance at Windsor as Edward refurbished the chapel, built extensive royal lodgings, towers, cloisters and an imposing gatehouse. The castle became a statement about monarchy, Arthurianism and national prestige. Above all, it was a focus for the loyalty of England's political classes.

LEFT **Edward III as founder of the Order of the Garter** *in an image from* William Bruges's Garter Book, 1440. *This order of chivalry had first been mooted in 1344 and was to include 300 knights. By 1348 the number had been whittled down to 26 of the king's own close companions. Those chosen were enjoined never, by fleeing a battle, 'betray the valour and renown which is ingrafted in constancy and magnanimity'.*

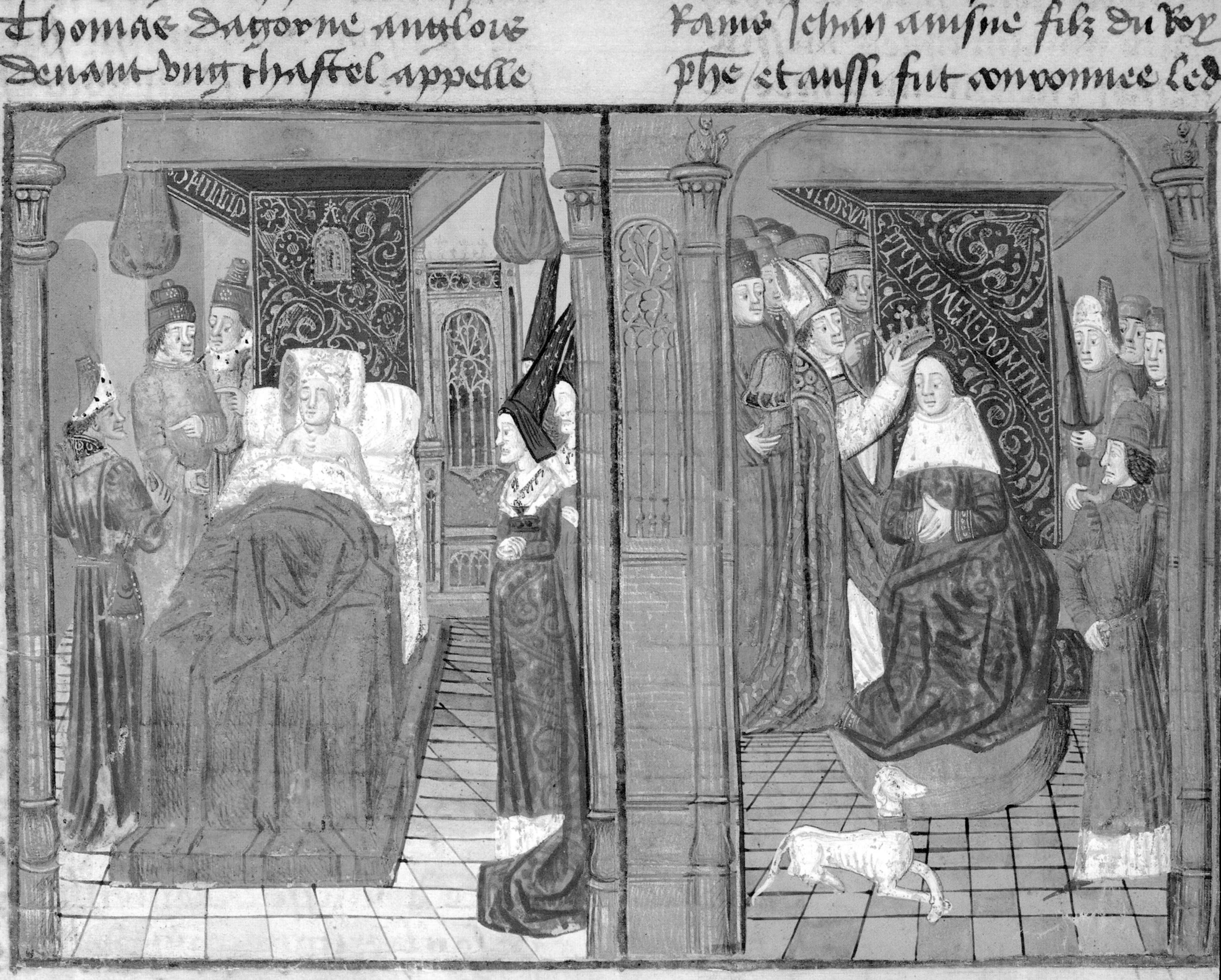

ABOVE **The death of Philip VI and coronation of John II, 1350** *are both depicted in this illustration from* Froissart's Chronicles. *In 1350 French fortunes were at a low ebb. The humiliating defeats inflicted by the English and the loss of Calais were bitter blows and these were followed by the Black Death. Taxation had alienated the Estates (France's parliament) and Philip had forfeited his son's affections by marrying Blanche of Navarre, who had been designated for his son. Philip enjoyed little respect and it was even said that the real power behind his throne rested with Queen Joan. John II (known as John the Good) did little to raise the prestige of the crown. Not only was he defeated at the Battle of Poitiers, he was taken as a prisoner to England. John II was allowed to return in 1360 in order to organize the raising of an enormous ransom. However, in 1363, he announced his intention of returning to England, preferring to live in comfortable captivity than shoulder the burdens of rule. He actually died in London the following year.*

The plague took two forms. Bubonic plague produced swellings or buboes in the groin or armpits, high fever and delirium, and it was extremely contagious. Those caring for victims were highly likely to contract the disease themselves as a result of direct contact. The worse manifestation occurred once the lungs were infected. This produced pneumonic plague, which was highly infectious and could be caught by airborne droplets coughed up or sneezed by the sufferers.

The social and economic upheavals were devastating. Crops were not harvested. Fishing boats were laid up in harbour. Mining came to a standstill, and, because there was not enough metal to mint new coins, commerce and government expenditure could not be sustained. Deserted homes lay open to looters, and because the law courts did not sit regularly there was every incentive to turn to crime. Foreign trade came to a halt when ports were closed for fear of admitting new plague-bearing vessels. At a time when people were more than ever in need of the consolations of religion priests were not to be found, either because they had died or had fled from their afflicted flocks. More fundamentally, the feudal hierarchy based on land tenure in return for service broke down. Landowners in desperate need of labourers to till their fields were obliged to pay whatever money wages surviving workers demanded. In the early days of the pestilence a ploughman could receive 2 shillings a week; by 1350 this had risen to 10 shillings. Landowners who could not compete in the labour market staved off bankruptcy by selling chunks of their estates at knock-down prices. And beneath all the tragedy and turmoil lay the psychological impact of the Black Death, which profoundly changed people's attitudes.

> God is deaf nowadays and deigneth to not hear us,
> And prayers have no power the plague to stay.
>
> Anonymous poet, 1349

The royal court kept away from London and all major centres of contagion. The parliament summoned for 1349 was cancelled, and Edward and his council ruled by decree. In June 1349 they issued the Ordinance of Labourers, designed to protect the landowning class by pegging wages at their pre-plague levels and forbidding workers from travelling from their own villages to sell their labour to the highest bidder. Though reinforced by parliament in 1351, this decree was a dead letter – certainly as long as the crisis lasted – and it did not help when Edward ordered the mayor and corporation of London to clean up the capital. They would gladly have done so if they could have found enough labourers in a city that had lost 30,000 inhabitants.

Edward's plans for the Order of the Garter went ahead regardless. It had its inaugural meeting, amid much festivity and splendour, on 23 April 1349, St George's Day, but there was no enthusiasm for renewing the French war – both countries were preoccupied with minimizing the internal disruption caused by the plague. In August 1350 Philip VI died, leaving a country weakened by war and plague to his son John II, known as John the Good. In the same month another

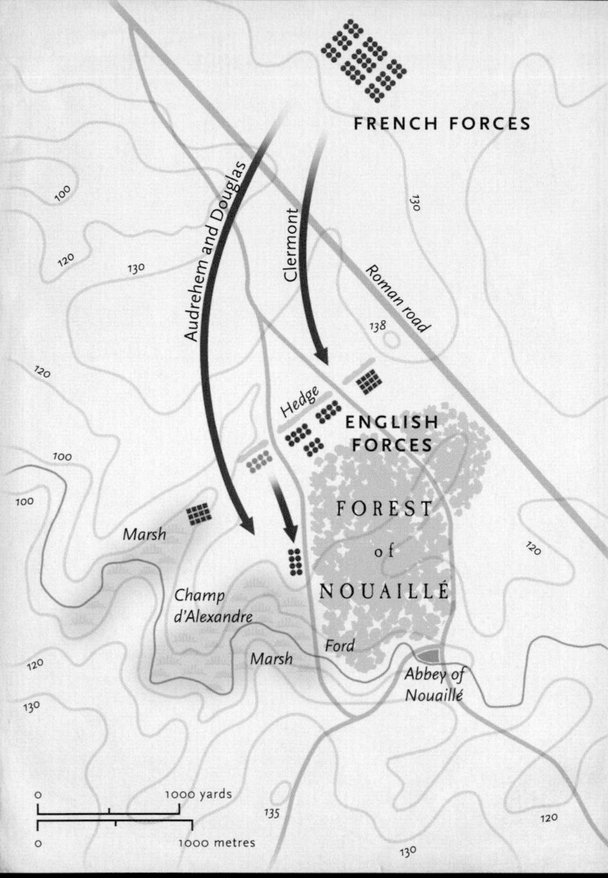

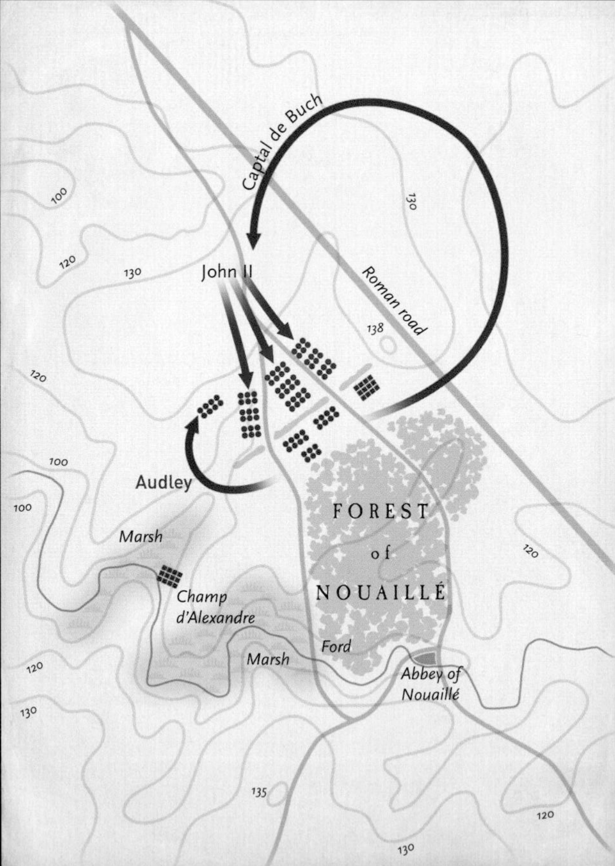

OPPOSITE **The Battle of Poitiers, 19 September 1356.** *The Black Prince took up a strong defensive position similar to that adopted by the English at Crécy, in a plain surrounded by natural obstacles such as marsh and forest. He dismounted his knights and placed them in divisions with archers defending their flanks. A mounted unit, led by Jean de Grailly, Captal de Buch, were concealed in the forest. The French advance was contained, at which point de Grailly's horsemen cut off the French retreat.*

ABOVE **The Cardinal of Périgaud tries to broker a peace** *in this illustration from the* Chronicles of the Court of Flanders. *While the two armies and Poitiers were preparing for battle the Cardinal of Périgaud rode out from the town in the hope of persuading Prince Edward and King John to agree truce terms. He shuttled back and forth between both camps but discovered the leaders to be intransigent. All he achieved was a one-day cessation of hostilities, during which both sides completed their preparations. According to Froissart the French became so fed up with the cardinal's interference that they told him to 'go back to Poitiers or anywhere else he liked, and not to bring them any more proposals, or it might be the worse for him'.*

would be forced to pay ransom. Just how important ransom was in 14th-century warfare is indicated by Froissart's account of the capture of King John. The prince sent out riders to a hilltop to see what they could discover about King John: 'They saw a great host of men-at-arms coming towards them very slowly on foot. The King of France was in the middle of them, and in some danger. For the English and the Gascons ... were arguing and shouting out: "*I* have captured him, *I* have." But the king, to escape from this danger, said: "Gentlemen, gentlemen, take me quietly to my cousin, the Prince, and my son with me: do nor quarrel about my capture, for I am such a great knight that I can make you all rich."'[6]

1357–68

WITH TWO RIVAL KINGS in captivity, Edward III was in an excellent bargaining position, but either he overplayed his hand or he had no intention of reaching a negotiated settlement. He demanded a ransom of 4 million écus and control of all of western France, from the Channel to the Pyrenees, in return for renouncing his title to the throne. His terms having been rejected, he invaded France again in 1359 and made straight for Rheims in order to be crowned in the traditional coronation place of French kings. Finding the city too well defended, he lifted the siege in January 1360 and went instead on a raid through Burgundy. He was hoping for another decisive battle, but a severe winter took so much toll on his army that he was obliged to open talks again. After much haggling, King John's ransom was reduced to 3 million écus and Edward renounced his claim to all French territory except Calais and Aquitaine and neighbouring territory, but the issue of sovereignty over disputed lands was left on hold. This vague settlement was ratified by parliament in January 1361.

OPPOSITE **Edward III and John II.** *After his capture at Poitiers, King John became Edward's guest/hostage in England. He was in the invidious position of being both Edward's feudal overlord and also his prisoner. It was an awkward situation and it was never resolved because John's ransom was never paid and he died in honourable captivity in the Savoy Palace, between London and Westminster, the most magnificent residence in the capital, scarcely less splendid than Edward's own palace.*

ABOVE **A fragment of a remembrance roll.** *Medieval kings had to transact an enormous amount of financial business. The Exchequer, therefore, had to keep a register of business. This was the remembrance roll and it was kept by an officer called the King's Remembrancer. In this particular roll, dating from 1361, someone has drawn pictures of a royal messenger and a pikeman.*

This year the plague returned, although not as seriously as 13 years previously, and from this point a noticeable change in Edward's behaviour was noticed. The vigour and decisiveness of earlier years was gone, and it seems that the king's mental faculties were failing. His decline coincided with the accession of a new and talented king in France. Charles V ascended to the throne in April 1364 on the death of his father, and he was bent on reversing the humiliation Edward had inflicted on his country and his family.

ABOVE **King Charles V vested with spurs.** *Charles V (ruled 1364–80) was the French king who initiated national recovery after the previous disastrous two decades. This contemporary image from* The Coronation Book of Charles V *(1365) shows a detail from the coronation ceremony. Philip the Bold, Duke of Burgundy, fixes golden spurs to the king's feet while the Archbishop of Rheims stands ready with the anointing oil, and the sword and crown lie on the altar.*

OPPOSITE **Edward III and David II reach an accord, 1357.** *This is an illustration from an English manuscript of 1386–99. After 11 years of honourable confinement in England, most of it spent at Odiham Castle in Hampshire, the Scottish king was repatriated on the promise of 100,000 marks (equivalent to £66,666, the mark only being an accounting unit and not a coin) ransom. This sum was never fully raised and, though David married Margaret Drummond in 1364, he died without heir in 1371 and was succeeded by his nephew, who reigned as Robert II, last monarch of the House of Bruce.*

Edward was now more inclined to pursue peaceful means to obtain control of Scotland. David II had been released in 1357 on agreeing to pay a large ransom in annual instalments. This was a great burden on the Scots, and Edward hoped to negotiate acceptance of his sovereignty in return for cancelling the debt. In November 1363 David, who was still childless, agreed to try to persuade his countrymen to convey the crown to Edward and his heirs after his own death. In return, Edward would cancel the ransom and restore those parts of Scotland he controlled. But the Scottish nobles would have none of this deal, and at the same time Charles V, instead of formally relinquishing his claim to Aquitaine, as required by the vague 1361 treaty, looked for a reason to occupy the territory. The ageing king could see no end to his two major problems.

1369–77

THE SUMMER OF 1369 was disastrous for Edward III. Charles devised an excuse to renew the war and sent troops into Aquitaine. In response, Edward hurriedly summoned parliament and secured a vote of taxes. That done, he revived his claim to the French crown and began assembling his troops. It was at this point, just as he was preparing to cross the Channel at the head of his army, that personal tragedy struck. 'The good queen of England that so many good deeds had done in her time, and so many knights succoured, and ladies and damosels comforted, and had so largely departed of her goods to her people, and naturally loved always the nation of Hainault where she was born; she fell sick in the Castle of Windsor, the which sickness continued in her so long that there was no remedy but death.'[7]

The king had already formed an attachment for a mistress, Alice Perrers, but there is no evidence of a serious estrangement between Edward and Queen Philippa. From this point, Alice exercised a growing and disastrous influence over the monarch. In 1370 the Prince of Wales, who was organizing the defence of Aquitaine, fell ill. From a litter he oversaw the long siege of Limoges, and when it fell he ordered the execution of 3,000 inhabitants – men, women and children – then fired the city. But such fearsome demonstrations could not stave off defeat. The year 1372 was one of military disasters. Charles V overran much of Aquitaine, and an English fleet was defeated in the Channel. Edward's fourth son, John of Gaunt, who had been created Duke of Lancaster in 1361, was sent to aid

ABOVE **John of Gaunt, Duke of Lancaster (1340–99).** *The fourth son of Edward III, who was to play an important role during the early years of Richard II's reign, was born at Ghent and the name of 'John of Ghent' was corrupted into 'John of Gaunt'. This portrait on vellum is from the* Benefactors' Book of St Albans Abbey *(c.1380).*

OPPOSITE **Illustration from Walter de Milemete's** De nobilitatibus, sapientiis, et prudentiis regum. *This splendidly illustrated treatise on kingship was presented to Edward III right at the beginning of his reign and, in this image, the young king is shown on horseback and at table. It was written by a clerk of the royal court who later took up residence as a fellow of King's Hall (later Trinity College), Cambridge. It was based on a work,* De Secretis secretorum, *supposedly written by the Greek philosopher, Aristotle, for the edification of Alexander the Great, his pupil. Such manuals advising kings how to conduct themselves were increasingly common in the 14th century.*

[illegible]
re secundum consuetudinem regu
bilium et age quod decet te agere.

Cesp
dera
dio
bun
pre
uo.

tas c
di fi
ta h
suc

tatis laborem medico. scilicet equitando
[illegible]

Parliament charged [William Wykeham] with several serious misdemeanours and exactions which the king certainly knew about because of specific notorious charges and loud complaints made by the people.

The Anonimalle Chronicle 1333–1381, ed. V.H. Galbraith, Manchester, 1927, p. 55

England's ally, the Duke of Brittany, but instead went on a looting expedition in eastern France. He and the Black Prince were at loggerheads and vying for influence with their father. In August King Edward took ship with his army for another campaign in France but weeks of foul weather prevented him making a landing and he was forced to return home. In 1375, Pope Gregory XII mediated a truce, agreed at Bruges, between Edward and Charles. It was a humiliating climb-down after years of spectacular success, and it was very unpopular with England's leading men.

By 1376 the Treasury was drained dry, and the government was forced to summon parliament in April. This assembly, which was held from 28 April to 10 July, became known as the 'Good Parliament' because, in the name of the people, the Commons attacked court corruption and maladministration. The king no longer enjoyed the respect that he had had

ABOVE **French and English forces clash outside Brest, 1353** *in this illustration from* Froissart's Chronicles. *As a popular adage of the time ran, 'He is not the Duke of Brittany who is not Lord of Brest'. The city was an important and strongly defended garrison town which had been ceded to the English in 1342. In the intermittent conflict between English and French forces of the latter years of Edward III's reign, this stronghold was important but Edward was never able to use it as a centre from which to extend effective control over Brittany. In 1373 Bertrand du Guesclin, Constable of France, who was known as 'the Eagle of Brittany', led an army up to the walls of Brest in an attempt to capture it for the king of France. However, the English defenders, fighting under the command of the Earl of Salisbury, held out against du Guesclin's army.*

in his heyday because, as was widely known, he was now completely controlled by Alice Perrers and John of Gaunt, both of whom were unpopular. The new parliament was determined to clean up the government, and they stripped the council of those advisers they did not like and had Edward's mistress sent away from court. By withholding funds they imposed new councillors on the king.

The only member of the royal inner circle who still commanded respect was the Black Prince, but in June he died. Lancaster and his friends at court lost no time in dismissing the Good Parliament. They removed the new councillors from office and imprisoned one of the parliamentary ring-leaders. Alice Perrers was allowed back to court.

By the end of September Edward's body, like his mind, was failing. He survived through the autumn and winter and was able to attend the Garter ceremony in April 1377, but he died on 21 June, probably of a stroke.

The development of parliament

The greatest political change *of the 13th and 14th centuries was the emergence of a bi-cameral parliament. The word 'parliament' meant originally a 'parleying', a meeting of the king with the leading nobles and churchmen to discuss major issues. Very occasionally representatives of rural and urban communities might be summoned to this* curia regis *(royal council), usually when the king needed extra support in dealing with the barons.*

Parliament increased in influence for two main reasons. As feudalism declined kings were obliged to hire mercenaries to fight their battles instead of relying on feudal levies. Frequently short of money, they had to persuade their subjects to pay taxes. Secondly, shire and town communities were becoming more self-conscious. By 1300 English society consisted not just of three 'estates' – crown, nobility and church; the communes (or commons) expected to have some say in matters of policy and taxation. The parliament of 1295 consisted of nobles, senior clergy, two knights from each shire, two burgesses from each major town and representation of the lower clergy (by the 1330s the lesser clergy were meeting separately in the lower house of convocation). The members met in separate chambers as the House of Lords and House of Commons.

Significant advances in the status of parliament occurred at the beginning and end of Edward III's reign. In 1327 parliament endorsed the dethronement of Edward II. The Good Parliament of 1376 was the first to impeach (take legal action against) ministers of the crown. It was also the parliament in which the House of Commons first elected its own chairman (the Speaker). Mercantile development and the spread of land tenure gave merchants and knights a secure power base from which to bargain with the government. They could make agreement to pay taxes dependent on legal reforms or other policy changes.

RICHARD II

RICHARDVS
R ANGLIA II

The social dislocation caused by repeated visitations of the plague provides the backdrop to this troubled reign. In 1400 the population was less than half what it had been before the Black Death, and the economic hardship and psychological malaise felt at all levels of society led to the Peasants' Revolt of 1381 and to the emergence of Lollardy, the 'English heresy', in the 1390s. To these disturbances were added unfinished business in Scotland and France, renewed conflict between king and parliament, and the challenge for the crown of John of Gaunt and, later, John's son, Henry Bolingbroke. Richard's fate – deposition and murder – echoed that of his great-grandfather.

1377–80

RICHARD BECAME KING at the age of ten because both his father, the Black Prince, and his elder brother, Edward, had died. On 16 July 1377 the boy king rode in a splendid procession through London to Westminster Abbey for his coronation, thus establishing a custom that was to be maintained for 300 years. The solemn and lengthy service may well have instilled into the boy a profound sense of the sacredness of monarchy, but he had inherited a country whose international reputation had declined over the previous decade and whose diminished population was weighed down with war taxes and rising prices. In February 1377 a cash-strapped government had imposed, for the first time, a universal poll tax, which brought more people than ever before within the scope of revenue collection.

Only weeks after the coronation a French raid on the south coast from Rye to Plymouth demonstrated England's vulnerability and military weakness. The attackers landed at several points, looting at will, and they burned Hastings and captured the prior of Lewes to hold him to ransom.

OPPOSITE **The coronation of Richard II (1367–1400).** *Richard, second son of the Black Prince, was only ten when he came to the throne. The lengthy ritual of the coronation, on 16 July 1377, was quite an ordeal for him. He almost fell asleep before it was over and had to be allowed to rest before being brought into Westminster Hall to preside over the coronation banquet. It was Richard's misfortune that he never did develop the qualities necessary for effective kingship. For many years national affairs were dominated by his powerful uncles. No one tutored him in the skills of government or guided him in the wise choice of policies and advisers. Image from* Chroniques de France ou de St Denis.

PREVIOUS PAGE **Richard II.** *This portrait in oil on panel is by an unknown artist and was probably painted in the late 16th century.*

The Lords and Commons are agreed that ... contribution should be made by every lay person in the realm ... males and females alike, of whatsoever estate or condition, who has passed the age of 15 years, of the sum of three groats, except for true beggars, who shall be charged nothing.

ROTULI PARLIAMENTORUM, ED. J. STRACHEY ET ALL., 1767–77, III, P. 90

No official regent was appointed, though two of his father's trusted companions, Sir Simon de Burley and Sir Aubrey de Vere, were appointed as knights of the household to guide the boy king. John of Gaunt, Richard's uncle, who had dominated the political scene since the death of the Black Prince, took no official position in government, largely because of the opposition of parliament, but the king looked to him for support and guidance, and Lancaster was thought of – rightly – as the leading political figure in the country. Richard, though young, was regarded as possessing full royal power, but parliament claimed the right to appoint a council to assist him. Another factor in the dynamic of government was the king's household. Richard was, in practice, dependent on his day-to-day companions, who came to be regarded with suspicion as 'favourites'. Among them was Robert de Vere, Earl of Oxford, who was probably introduced to the court by his uncle, Aubrey, and who later emerged as Richard's closest friend. The supervisory councils were unable to exercise effective control over the expenditure of the royal household, which, from an early date, was regarded as excessive.

The Isle of Wight captured

On the 21st day of August, *the French less by manly force than by good luck, captured the Isle of Wight, an island one might say impossible to take; it would never have been captured by anyone if it had been protected by an efficient guard. But the careless lack of concern of the islanders brought destruction upon them ... [The French] collected together the loot they had brought from the island, and forced the islanders to extort from the friends they had outside the island the sum of one thousand marks of silver in return for saving their homes from fire and the rest of their possessions.*

Chronica Monasterii S. Albani, Thomae Walsingham ... Historia Anglicana, ed. H.T. Riley, 1863, I, p. 340

In 1380 parliament decreed an end to the councils that had been its own creations, and it was this muddled constitutional situation that contributed to Richard's development of extreme opinions about the sacred nature of kingship and the absolute power wielded by the monarch.

1381

THE RISE OF LOLLARDY was only one manifestation of a serious social dislocation of English society. 'In the iiii year of King Richard's reign the commons arisen up in divers parts of the realm ... the which they called the hurling time.'[1] This 'hurling' or commotion erupted in several places. For example, at York in November 1380, 'various malefactors among the commons' drove the mayor, John Gysburn, out of the city, smashed their way into the guildhall with axes, seized one Simon Quixlay, forced him to become the new mayor and made all the members of the city council swear allegiance to him. Such incidents were but preludes to the rising in southeast England known as the Peasants' Revolt. The grievances of the common people were many and acutely felt but what brought matters to a head was the poll tax, voted in 1380.

OPPOSITE **Richard II – The Westminster Portrait (*c.*1390).** *Richard was a generous and enthusiastic patron of the arts and was also ardent in the assertion of the sacred nature of kingship. Both these qualities came together in his commissioning of this portrait, which is now in Westminster Abbey. This remarkable image in the International Gothic style by an unknown artist is as much about the splendour of royalty as it is about presenting a true likeness of the young king. Richard sits on a throne, staring straight out at the beholder. He grasps the orb and sceptre, the symbols of authority, and is situated in a gold-leaf 'heaven', often used by artists for representing saints or biblical characters. The portrait presented Richard as an icon and was intended to evoke awe and veneration of the king, bordering on worship.*

John Wyclif and the Lollards

In the aftermath of the Black Death the ecclesiastical hierarchy had lost much of the respect traditionally accorded to it and widespread indignation was directed at every level of the priesthood. The papacy itself was in turmoil.

From 1309 to 1378 the popes resided at Avignon as protégés of the French kings (with whom England was at war) , and the following years, 1378–1417, were known as the 'great schism' because rival popes, based at Rome and Avignon, competed for the loyalty of Christian Europe. Wealthy bishops and abbots were resented for their ostentation and their unwillingness to share the financial burdens placed upon laymen, and many parish priests had not been forgiven for deserting their flocks during the plague years.

Discontent

Fundamental to the general discontent was a widely held belief that the clergy were more interested in collecting their tithes and taxes than in fulfilling their responsibilities or setting a moral example. At the same time, there existed among many lay people a desire for a deeper, personal spirituality. John Wyclif (*c.*1330–84), an Oxford scholar and preacher, attacked the church hierarchy in his lectures and sermons and attracted the attention of John of Gaunt, who was campaigning against the interference of Rome on English affairs. The duke found Wyclif a valuable ally and encouraged his anticlericalism. This was the background to the emergence of what has been called the 'English heresy', Wycliffism or Lollardy.

In February 1377 the Bishop of London ordered John Wyclif to be examined in St Paul's Cathedral on the content of his recent sermons. The Duke of Lancaster turned up to support his preacher, got into a furious row with the bishop and threatened to drag him down from his throne by the hair. Thus protected, Wyclif developed his beliefs in greater detail. He began to consider the doctrinal basis of the church's institutions and to question their validity. Fundamentally, Wycliffism was all about authority. The scholar began by reflecting on the relationship between church and state and ended by rejecting the claims of the church's hierarchy not only to temporal authority but also to spiritual authority. The power wielded by the clergy over the laity was based on their sacerdotal function as mediators between man and God.

Priesthood set men apart from their neighbours by virtue of their ability to 'make God' in the mass, to hear confession and to pronounce absolution. Wyclif rejected these claims in a series of books. For the authority of the 'Bishop of Rome' (as Wyclif called the pope, to indicate that he had no authority in England) he substituted the Bible. 'All Christians, and lay lords in particular, ought to know holy writ and to defend it,' he wrote in his treatise On the Truth of Holy Scripture (1387). 'No man is so rude a scholar but that he may learn the words of the Gospel.' But the only Bible available in England was the Vulgate, written in Latin and accessible only to scholars and a minority of educated clergy.

The 'Wycliffites'

By this time, Wyclif had attracted many followers. Some were his students at Oxford, men who went on to be parish clergy or royal servants. From this pool of 'Wycliffites' there emerged English translations

OPPOSITE **A Lollard gospel.** *Like the monks copying and adorning the Latin Bible, the Vulgate, in their scriptoria, some of Wyclif's followers lovingly made copies of English Bibles and Bible fragments. The Lollards studied these forbidden books and read them to one another in secret gatherings. From time to time the bishops hunted down these 'heretics' and burned any Lollard books they could find. This page is the beginning of Matthew's Gospel, written early in the 15th century.*

of various parts of the Bible. How far Wyclif himself was involved in this process we do not know, but the English Bible, in whole and in parts, was spread in steadily widening circles, as fresh copies were made and circulated secretly in order to prevent their discovery by the church authorities.

Wyclif died in 1384, but his followers continued his work, circulating not only the Scriptures but also English versions of the master's writings. These disciples came to be known as 'Lollards', a term of ridicule from a contemporary Dutch word, *loller*, which was applied to itinerant unorthodox preachers. The Lollards gathered in secret groups to read the Bible and discuss their ideas. They tended to marry 'within the faith', and by the early 15th century Lollard cells were established in London and rural areas within about a 60-mile radius of the capital. However, these people had no central organization and no agreed body of doctrine. They represented a section of the populace critical of the existing establishment, who felt free to decide, on the basis of personal Bible study, what they would believe.

Matheus 241

here biginnyþ þe newe testa
ment þe firste plog on mathew
Mathew þat was
of iudee as he
is set first in
ordre of gos
pelers: so he
wroot first þe
gospel in iudee
and fro þe office of a tolga
derere: he was clepid to god
whan þis mathew hadde pre
chid first þe gospel in iudee
and wolde go to hethen men: he
wroot first þe gospel in ebrew:
and lefte it in mynde to cris
ten men of þe iewis: fro whi
che he departide bodili: ffor as
it was nedful þat þe gospel
were prechid to þe confermyng
of feiþ: so it was nedful
þat it were writun also azens
heretikis. Thouz many men

thew is undirstonden bi man:
for he dwelliþ principali aboute
þe manhede of crist. Mark is
undirstonden bi a lioun: for he
tretiþ of cristis rising azen. Luk
is undirstonden bi a calf: and
tretiþ of presthod. Jon is un
dirstonden bi an egle: and writiþ
hizliere þe sacramentis of heo
li priuitees of þe godhede. ffor
loþe crist whom þese gospele
ris discriuen: was a man born
of þe uirgyn. He was a calf: in
offring or dying on þe cros
He was a lioun: in rising azen
And he was an egle: in assen
cioun. Ever þe manhede of crist
is signified in man presthod is
signified in þe calf. Rewme
is signified in þe lioun. And
þe sacrament of godhede is
signified in þe egle. That is
bi þese foure beestis it is decla

Court at Brentwood in Essex

A certain Thomas Bampton *... held a court at Brentwood in Essex ... He had summoned before him a hundred of the neighbouring townships and wished to have from them a new subsidy ... Amongst these townships all the people of Fobbing gave answer that they would not pay a penny more because they already had a receipt from him ... On this Thomas menaced them strongly, and he had with him two sergeants-at-arms of our lord the king; and for fear of his wrath the people of Fobbing took counsel with the people of Corringham, and the folk of these two townships made levies and assemblies, and sent messages to the men of Stanford-le-Hope, to urge them to rise too, for their common profit. And then the men of the three townships came together to the number of a hundred or more and with one assent went to Thomas Bampton and roundly gave him answer that they would have nothing to do with him nor give him one penny. On this Thomas ordered the sergeants-at-law to arrest these folks and put them into prison; and the commons rose against him and would not be arrested, but tried to kill Thomas and the two sergeants.*

THE ANONIMALLE CHRONICLE 1333-1381, ED. V.H. GALBRAITH, MANCHESTER, 1927, P. 134

'The Lords and Commons are agreed that ... contribution should be made by every lay person in the realm ... males and females alike, of whatsoever estate or condition, who has passed the age of 15 years, of the sum of three groats, except for true beggars, who shall be charged nothing.'[2] However, the tax realized only two-thirds of the required sum and provoked widespread complaint. Instead of paying heed to the public mood, the government sent commissioners in May 1381 to make up the deficit.

An attempt by commissioners at Brentwood, Essex, to gather the tax sparked what appeared to be a spontaneous reaction, although it had probably been planned between malcontents in Essex and Kent. Groups gathered on both sides of the Thames, and their ugly mood indicated the profound hatred they felt for the existing regime. They armed themselves with longbows, axes and knives and were not slow to use them. Some had served in recent campaigns across the Channel, were used to violence and had no love for the 'officer class'. They seized Rochester Castle, broke into houses and abbeys, opened jails and released the prisoners, and took grain from barns and cattle from fields to feed their swelling number. At Canterbury Cathedral they told the monks to elect a new archbishop because the days of the present incumbent, Simon Sudbury (who, as chancellor, they blamed for the tax), were numbered. Everywhere they forced people to swear an oath to 'King Richard and the true Commons'. People who refused were murdered or had their houses burned down. One group, as a broad hint to those they met, carried three decapitated heads with them. While missionaries were despatched to carry the message to

OPPOSITE **Feudal labourers.** *In this detail from a page of the Luttrell Psalter (c.1325–35) two women are shown bending down to cut the corn with hand sickles, while a man, who has tucked his sickle into his belt, follows to bind the grain into sheaves. Under the feudal system manorial serfs had to spend several days a year working their lords' land. The Black Death had struck at the root of this system. Shortage of labour meant that many landlords had to pay labourers to tend their fields.*

neighbouring shires, the Kentish host camped on Blackheath and sent a message to the king, who had taken refuge in the Tower, asking him to meet them.

On 13 June Richard set out across the river with a flotilla of barges filled with men-at-arms. By this time the rebels had achieved some degree of overall organization and chosen as their leader Wat Tyler of Maidstone. The shouts that went up from the thousands of rebels, though expressions of loyalty, must have been heart-chilling to the young king and his attendants, who halted their boats well offshore. Worse followed when Tyler and his lieutenants began shouting their demands: 'Give us John of Gaunt!' 'Give us Sudbury!' 'Give us Hob the Robber!' (Robert Hales, the treasurer). The royal party beat a hasty retreat. Exactly what the leaders of the insurgents hoped to achieve is probably impossible to know now – their demands were more a passionate denunciation of the existing order than a coherent programme of reform – but they certainly wanted Richard's 'evil councillors' to be punished. The wild rhetoric of their preachers spoke of complete social levelling. Quotations from the Bible to the effect that God had created all men equal suggest possible Lollard influence.

All feudal service was to be abolished. The rebels called for free hunting and fishing rights for all, not just major landowners, the distribution of church lands among the people, the repeal of the Ordinance of Labourers and all other legislation restricting the rights of working men to sell their labour as and when they would. If acted upon, these ultimatums would have completely undermined the existing economic and social structure. The church taught that everyone should be content to remain in that station to which God had called them, and the civil authority enshrined social division in its laws. For example, a Sumptuary Law of 1363 had divided the population into seven classes and decreed what kind of clothes each was permitted to wear. Thus, for example, no one under the rank of gentleman might wear velvet or shoes having points of more than 2 inches in length, and no serving woman might have a veil costing more than 12 pence. Only by exercising rigid control could the crumbling feudal system be preserved. Without it there would be anarchy, and it was anarchy that Wat Tyler and his men were offering.

By this time many Londoners had declared support for the rebels. The city had its own problems. It housed a growing semi-criminal underclass of beggars, unemployed artisans, ex-soldiers, fanatical preachers and 'barrack room lawyers', who had nothing to lose by joining the insurrection, and they now opened the bridge to a detachment sent from Blackheath. Some stayed on the Surrey side to burn down the archbishop's palace at Lambeth. On the other side of the Thames, Lancaster's sumptuous residence was attacked by a frenzied mob, which smashed ornaments and furniture, burned tapestries, threw gold and silver plate into the river, hammered jewels into dust and then blew up the ransacked building with three barrels of gunpowder. Other orgiastic demonstrations of the protestors' fury took place as the Kentish men marched through the city. There was nothing to stop them. John of Gaunt had an army, but it was hundreds of miles away campaigning in Scotland. No courtier-lord could have counted on the support of his tenantry as the 'democratic' contagion spread.

By nightfall on 13 June the Kentish rebels were camped on Tower Hill, and the Essex host was beyond the wall at Mile End. Richard and his court were, in effect, under siege, and it was

LEFT **The arrest of royal officers, 14 June 1381.** *Rebels broke into the Tower of London looking for the hated Archbishop Simon Sudbury, the chancellor, and Robert Hales, the treasurer. The officials took refuge in St John's Chapel in the White Tower but claiming sanctuary did not save them. They were dragged out to Tower Hill with two of their companions. There they were beheaded over a fallen tree trunk, which was used as a makeshift block. This is the first recorded use of Tower Hill as a place for public executions. Thereafter successive governments employed it for the same purpose. This image from* Froissart's Chronicles *suggests, erroneously, that Sudbury and his companions were murdered within the Tower.*

The sermon of John Ball

The sermon of John Ball, Priest, at Blackheath

And so that his teaching might reach more people, at Blackheath where 200 thousand people had gathered he began his sermon in this way:

When Adam delved and Eve span
Who was then a gentleman?

And continuing the sermon he had begun thus he strove, through the words of the proverb he had taken as his text, to maintain and prove that all men were created equal by nature from the beginning and servitude was introduced through unjust oppression of wicked men contrary to the will of God.

Chronicon Angliae: Auctore Monacho Quodam Sancti Albani, ed. E.M. Thompson, 1874, p. 321

ABOVE **John Ball preaching to the rebels.** *The rebels wanted to believe that their actions not only were justified but also had divine approval. John Bull, who had a long history as a turbulent priest, obliged by assuring his hearers that God had created all men equal and that rebels and gentlemen claimed powers and privileges to which they had no right. When the revolt collapsed, John Ball fled to Coventry, where he was captured, tried before the king at St Albans and executed as a traitor. Image from* Froissart's Chronicles.

by no means certain that the Tower garrison would take up arms against their own countrymen. There was only one person who had the respect of the insurgents, one person to whom they would listen. The nation's fate rested on the 14-year-old king.

The next morning Richard rode out to Mile End with an armed escort. There Tyler presented the rebels' demands and the king promised that they would be granted, demurring only at handing over his hated ministers to immediate lynch law. Richard maintained remarkable poise and dignity, but while he was calmly 'reviewing' the peasant host a group rode off to the Tower. They entered with no show of resistance, dragged Sudbury from the chapel in the White Tower and took him out to Tower Hill for execution in front of the crowd. According to one chronicler, the job was bungled and the archbishop did not die until he had received eight strokes in the neck and head. Other royal confidants on whom the peasants laid hands were also summarily despatched.

This bloodletting and easy success went to the rebels' heads, and any order in their ranks broke down. They went back into the city as a rampaging rabble, intent on loot, and by so doing they forfeited the support they had hitherto enjoyed. On 15 June Richard called for another meeting at Smithfield, outside the western wall of the city. He went out to meet Tyler with a large retinue whose armour and weapons were concealed beneath their robes. The rebel leader demanded that everything they itemized was to be written in a chart and sealed by the king. Richard agreed. Then Tyler and the mayor of London, Sir William Walworth, fell into an argument. Swords were drawn, and Tyler received a mortal wound. The crowd, stunned by this departure from the script, wavered and Richard seized the initiative. 'I am your leader,' he shouted, 'follow me.' He spurred his horse and some of the rebels fell in behind him. Others did not.

ABOVE **The dagger of William Walworth (d.1385).** *This weapon, in the possession of the Fishmongers' Company, is reputed to be the one used by William Walworth to kill the rebel leader, Wat Tyler. Walworth was twice Lord Mayor of London (1374 and 1381). He was a prosperous member of the Fishmongers' Company, a supporter of John of Gaunt and a merchant who lent money to King Richard. For his services against the rebels he was knighted and granted a pension.*

In the confusion Walworth was able to ride back into London and raise a contingent of citizens and the Tower garrison to come to the king's rescue. A few ring-leaders were rounded up but most of the rebels, who may have amounted at one point to between 80,000 and 100,000 men, were allowed to disperse. Eventually, about 150 of them were tried and executed for treason.

ABOVE **The death of Wat Tyler**. *In this illustration from* Froissart's Chronicles *King Richard is shown twice, witnessing Tyler's death and addressing the rebels. One record states that Tyler attacked the lord mayor with his dagger and that Walworth then drew his 'cutlass' (not his dagger) and struck the rebel leader on his neck and head. In the ensuing scuffle one of the king's guards stabbed Tyler to death. When the rebels saw their leader fall they began firing their arrows. It was at this point that the young king rode up to them and called on them to follow him. Another account claims that Tyler was carried half-dead to a nearby hospital where Walworth subsequently discovered him, had him dragged out and summarily beheaded.*

1382–6

IN JANUARY 1382 RICHARD WAS MARRIED to Anne of Bohemia, the 15-year-old daughter of the late Emperor Charles IV. It was a diplomatic marriage, aimed at providing England with a powerful ally against France, but there is no evidence that any real advantage was gained from it. Anne's large foreign entourage provided another subject for the opponents of the court to grumble about, and they claimed that the queen's attendants added considerably to the expenses of an already spendthrift king. However, Richard, who, of course, had not seen his bride before her arrival, developed a deep affection for her, and she exercised a calming influence on him.

Now married and with the success of suppressing the revolt behind him, Richard took firm control of the government and began to assert his own style of kingship, even though he continued to feel overshadowed by his uncles, especially

the Duke of Lancaster. The king relied to a great extent on his close friends, particularly Robert de Vere and Michael de la Pole, and he showered gifts and offices on his favourites. In 1383 de la Pole became chancellor and two years later Earl of Suffolk. He was unpopular with many of the nobles for advocating peace with France, for although they did not like paying for war they liked even less the thought of agreeing an ignominious end to hostilities. Two factions had clearly emerged: while the royal uncles led a 'traditionalist' party committed to pursuing the old Plantagenet continental claims, Richard's young friends promoted peace and a sophisticated style of court life modelled on that of France. At the same time de Vere was rocketed to even higher office: he was given the title Marquess of Dublin with vice-regal authority in Ireland. What particularly galled many of the nobles was that the rank of marquess, which took precedence over the rank of earl, was a novelty in England. And then in 1384 and 1385 de Vere and de la Pole even tried to bounce the king into putting Lancaster on trial for treason. The move failed, but Richard signalled his defiance in 1386 by taking another step in the elevation of de Vere. He made his friend Duke of Ireland, thus putting him on a par with Richard's uncles, the dukes of Lancaster, York and Gloucester.

Following further cross-border incursions, Richard assumed command of an invasion of Scotland in July 1385. His army scoured the Lowlands as far as Edinburgh but, as so often in the past, was unable to bring the Scots to a pitched battle. Lancaster counselled pressing deeper into

The plot against Lancaster

During that same time *[1385] serious trouble broke out in England for the Duke of Lancaster when the young king and his youthful associates plotted his death. They had agreed among them to arrest him suddenly and make him stand trial before the justice Robert Tresilian, who had rashly undertaken to pass sentence upon him in whatever charges they brought against the duke. However, the duke was forewarned by one of the council and, taking measures for his own safety, he wisely withdrew, hastening as soon as he could to his castle of Pontefract, reinforcing this thoroughly with weapons and provisions. As the result, the nature of the dispute which occurred was now no longer a private one, but even became public knowledge, and the hatred each had for the other only grew stronger ... Lady Joan, the king's mother, refused to put up with the troubles of the kingdom, and though not strong and used to luxury, and hardly able to move about because she was so fat, nevertheless neglected her own tranquil way of life, and gladly took upon herself the troublesome journey first to the king, and then to the duke, sparing no expense whatsoever and pleading with them humbly until she achieved her desire to restore peace and concord between the two men.*

THE CHRONICA MAIORA OF THOMAS WALSINGHAM, EDS. J. TAYLOR, W. R. CHILDS AND L. WATKISS, OXFORD, 2003, P. 751

OPPOSITE **Richard II greets, Anne of Bohemia, 1381**. *This marriage seemed to be an important diplomatic coup. Earlier talk of an alliance with France had fallen through. The sister of King Wenceslaus of Bohemia was 'on the market' and Charles V of France was eager to secure her as a wife for his son. With the aid of Pope Urban VI (reigned 1376–89), who was violently anti-French, Anne was 'snapped up' for Richard. In May 1380, terms were agreed whereby, in return for his sister, Wenceslaus was to receive a loan of £15,000. The princess landed at Dover on 18 December 1381, and the wedding took place the following 14 January. Image from* Froissart's Chronicles.

Rumours of French invasion

The rumour spread *throughout England, that 600 ships were being directed hither, together with a numberless army which would fill the whole soil of the kingdom like locusts; and straightaway, as though there was no hope of salvation, not only the people but also the army, once well-trained now weak as women, once so courageous now full of fear, once so stout-hearted now weak and nerveless, began to panic, and they discussed not resistance nor fighting but flight or surrender.*

CHRONICA MONASTERII, II, P. 127

the country, but Richard overruled him and returned to London. It was by now clear that Richard was no warrior like his father and grandfather and that he bitterly resented attempts to force him into the same mould as his predecessors. Fortunately, he was able to rid himself of one of his uncles. Lancaster had ambitions to win the crown of Castile, to which he had a claim through his wife, the daughter of the late king, and in July 1386 he set off for Spain with a small army, partly paid for by a loan from Richard. However, this only brought to the fore the king's second uncle, Thomas of Gloucester, who, with his ally, the Earl of Arundel, maintained opposition to the favourites.

John of Gaunt's departure coincided with a new invasion threat from France. Charles VI assembled the largest fleet that had ever been seen in the Channel, and de la Pole went to parliament to demand a massive subsidy to pay for national defence. Worried as they were by the military threat, parliament refused the demand. In fact, they refused to contract any business at all until the chancellor had been removed from office. Richard rejected this attack on his prerogative to choose his own ministers, but Gloucester and Arundel told the king that he would have to negotiate with parliament. This he refused. But his uncle reminded him of the fate of Edward II, in effect threatening to depose Richard if he proved obdurate. De la Pole was impeached by the Commons, tried and condemned to imprisonment, but Richard overruled the sentence and de la Pole remained at court. Internal politics in France meant the feared invasion did not materialize, but that did not ease the constitutional situation. Parliament had set up a commission to enquire into all aspects of government and make recommendations, and it required the king to abide by them.

OPPOSITE **John of Gaunt in Portugal.** *In 1385 John decided to make good his claim to the kingdom of Castile. He had married Constance, Infanta of Castile, in 1371, whose father, Pedro IV, had died in 1369. The throne had then been grabbed by Pedro's illegitimate son Henry II (known as 'Henry the Bastard'). John claimed the crown in right of his wife and styled himself 'King of Castile' but lacked the power to make good his claim. Henry II died in 1379 and was succeeded by his son, John I. In 1383 John I laid claim to the crown of Portugal. This was contested, successfully, by John of Avis (known as 'John the Great' of Portugal). John of Portugal asked for the assistance of John of Gaunt, who saw this as his opportunity to overthrow John of Castile and seize the kingdom. The illustration shows John of Gaunt on the left, beneath his coat of arms, dining in state with the Portuguese king. The subsequent military campaign achieved nothing, but a marriage alliance was made between John of Castile's son, Henry, and John of Gaunt's daughter, Catherine. In return for a substantial payment John of Gaunt abandoned his claim.*

1387–8

RICHARD DISTANCED HIMSELF literally from the work of the parliamentary commission by going on a tour of the country to drum up support and also to obtain from some – well-chosen – judges the opinion that parliament had acted illegally in imposing its will on their anointed king. However, as soon as he returned to the capital in November 1387 he was confronted by a delegation of nobles led by Gloucester and Arundel. They demanded the arrest and trial of de Vere, de la Pole and three other close royal attendants on charges of treason. De Vere had recently offered the king's family a personal insult by divorcing his wife, a granddaughter of Edward III, in favour of one of the queen's ladies-in-waiting, and Richard's acquiescence in this action was the final straw that turned his uncles and their friends against him. Their demand was, in effect, a declaration of war.

The decline of chivalry

What lay behind much of the conflict between the 'old' and 'young' factions at court was a cultural shift. The technology of warfare was changing. The importance of the longbow and of foot soldiers armed with deadly pikes, the appearance of cannons and the use of gunpowder to destroy fortifications were steadily rendering obsolete the medieval knight and the elaborate code of chivalry that surrounded him with a romantic mystique. Even the honour of knighthood itself was commonly being awarded not only for outstanding bravery on the field of battle but also for administrative or political services to the crown. Jean Froissart, who might be thought of as the high priest of chivalry and who was writing his *Chronicles* in these years, treated war as the business of heroes. Here is a typical example from his account of the Anglo-Scottish wars:

'The young Earl of Douglas had performed wonders. When he was wounded, he lay where he fell, for the blow on his head was mortal ... Sir John Sinclair asked the Earl; "How goes it, cousin?" "Not very well", was the reply. "But thank God few of my ancestors have died in their beds. You must avenge me, for I am as good as dead ... raise my banner for it is certainly on the ground; it fell from the hand of David Campbell, my valiant squire who refused a knighthood from me today, though he was the equal of any knight in courage and loyalty" ... Sir James Lindsay and the Sinclair brothers followed these instructions, and succeeded in rallying a number of the Scottish troops, who drove back the English ... The battle was extremely hard fought from beginning to end, but the behaviour of the Scots throughout was chivalrous in the extreme; whenever they took a prisoner, they treated him like one of themselves.'[3]

But the contemporary French poet Eustace Deschamps was thoroughly embittered by the war with England that had been going on all his lifetime, and he satirized the behaviour of the splendidly clad knights who played at war in the tiltyard:

> *You who are arrayed like bridegrooms,*
> *You who talk so well when you are in France*
> *Of the great deeds you will do,*
> *You go to conquer what you have lost:*
> *What is it? Renown that for so long*
> *Honoured your country.*
> *If you seek to recover it in battle,*
> *Display your hearts, not your fancy clothes ...*
> *You are not now on the Grand Pont in Paris.*[4]

In 1385 a body of Austrian knights were slaughtered by Swiss pikemen. They had developed new techniques of infantry warfare and could move around a battlefield with swift and disciplined mobility. Of the 900 splendidly accoutred knights the Swiss encountered at Sempach, they left 700 dead on the field of battle. This was the warfare of the future.

OPPOSITE **Richard II holding court.** *Richard's tragedy lay in weaknesses in his own character and in the fact that he was untrained for kingship. He carried to excess the courtly pomp and ceremony introduced by his grandfather Edward III and tried by impressive luxury to convey an impression of unchallengeable authority. He spent enormous sums of money on costly garments and, according to one chronicler, kept 10,000 people at his courts who, at Christmas 1398, consumed daily 28 oxen and 300 sheep. But his personality did not support his pretensions. He had a stammer and was subject to violent mood swings. In this early 15th-century illuminated capital the king is shown handing a letter to a knight.*

De Vere raised an army in Cheshire and marched south to come to Richard's aid. At Radcot Bridge, Oxfordshire, on 20 December he was met by an army led by John of Gaunt's son, Henry Bolingbroke, Earl of Derby. De Vere's men began to desert before battle was even joined, and the duke took flight, plunging into the river, making his way across country and taking ship for the continent. He eventually reached Paris, where he found de la Pole and other court exiles. De la Pole died soon afterwards in 1389, but de Vere next moved to Louvain in the territory of the Duchess of Brabant. There he was accidentally killed during the course of a boar hunt in 1392.

The royal dukes, Bolingbroke and Arundel, and their allies, the 'lords appellant', called a new parliament in February 1388. It is known as the 'Merciless Parliament' because it carried out a thoroughgoing purge of all Richard's most trusted companions and councillors, most of whom were executed. Having achieved this, the lords appellant seemed satisfied and made no attempt to take over the government or impose permanent restrictions on the king. That was a tactical mistake.

ABOVE **Death of Robert de Vere, 1392.** *All the powerful men of England, from the king downwards, used exile as a means of distancing 'undesirables' from positions of influence. Important exiles were often received at foreign courts because they were perceived as possibly useful tools in international diplomacy. Robert de Vere's flight, with Richard II's connivance, in 1388 took him to the French court and, subsequently, to the territory of the Duchess of Brabant who gave him the use of one of her castles near Louvain. There de Vere socialized with the local gentry and, while his life was reasonably congenial, he still held out hope for a recall to England and for reinstatement by his friend King Richard. This hope would almost certainly have been realized had he not been gored by a boar while out hunting, as shown in this illustration from a French manuscript of c.1410–15. In 1395 Richard had de Vere's embalmed body returned to England for honourable burial.*

The death of Michael de la Pole

That summer *[1389] the instigator of treachery, the cesspool of avarice, the charioteer of treason, the receptacle for malice, the disseminator of hatred, the fabricator of lies, that evil tell-tale, notorious for his deception, an artful back-biter, and a traitor to his country – I mean Michael de la Pole – breathed his last in Paris. He had been earl of Suffolk, and royal chancellor, but he was an evil counsellor who deserved to spew forth his treacherous spirit in a foreign land. His personal wealth, which he had there, was given to his colleague Robert de Vere, formerly duke of Ireland, who had fled to France with him.*

THE CHRONICA MAIORA OF THOMAS WALSINGHAM, I, P. 879

1389–96

IN MAY 1389 Richard declared that, now he had reached the age of 21, he was assuming sole responsibility for government. He acknowledged that poor counsel had previously created problems and promised that, in future, he would appoint better advisers. He gave every indication of having turned over a new leaf. Lords and Commons believed that they had achieved their objective, and this seemed to be confirmed when John of Gaunt returned in November and was warmly welcomed by the king. Gaunt had been successful in his Castilian venture. He had forced his rivals to recognize his claim to the crown and then resigned it in favour of his daughter, Catherine, who was then betrothed to his rival's heir. Leaving Spain, he was appointed lieutenant of Guisnes, a fortified town adjacent to Calais, which had been in English hands since 1360. In 1390 he was appointed Duke of Aquitaine and put in charge of peace talks with France.

Richard had embarked on serious negotiations. After 50 years of hostilities most of his subjects had become accustomed to regarding France as an inevitable enemy, but the argument of 'no war taxes' was a powerful one. The sticking point, as ever, was the status of Aquitaine. Richard was prepared to do homage for the duchy to Charles VI, but parliament would not countenance this. Thus little was achieved after years of discussion beyond the extension of the truce between the two countries. Tensions between the king and the lords appellant remained, but they were kept under control. They might, conceivably, have remained so had it not been for a tragedy that struck Richard in 1394 when, in June, his 27-year-old queen died of the plague. Richard was completely overcome with grief. He had the Palace of Sheen, where Anne had died, razed to the ground, and he planned an extremely elaborate and costly funeral at Westminster. The Earl of Arundel

arrived late for the service and then asked permission to leave. The distraught king, furious at what he considered disrespect for the memory of his beloved queen, snatched a staff from one of the attendants and felled the earl with it, drawing blood. This meant that Anne's obsequies had to be halted while the clergy carried out a ritual purification of the church. Arundel was sent to the Tower but released after a week, when Richard had calmed down.

In 1394 Richard took an army of 5,000 men across to Ireland to deal with a revolt against the government there. His campaign was successful, and most of the Irish leaders submitted to him over the following months, but he had to hurry home in May 1395 to deal with complaints by the bishops against Lollards in high places. Several courtiers and members of parliament who were high in the king's trust and had served in diplomatic or military capacities were known to espouse heretical views and to be protecting Lollards from the ecclesiastical authorities. Recently, notices had been nailed to the doors of St Paul's Cathedral and Westminster Abbey denouncing the clergy and propounding unorthodox opinions.

Richard frightened his heretical courtiers into submission and ordered the University of Oxford to expel anyone suspected of Lollardy, but he now began to give signs of his defiance of his critics. In November he had the embalmed

ABOVE **The death of Anne of Bohemia, 7 June 1394,** *from* Froissart's Chronicles. *The queen's sudden death was a double tragedy. It removed the one person who had exercised a moderating influence over Richard and it aggravated his quarrel with the Earl of Arundel. Arundel had been banished from court but subsequently recalled. The earl, either angry or genuinely confused by the king's treatment, appeared late at the queen's funeral, thus trampling on Richard's grief. Richard's intemperate reaction was precisely the kind of behaviour Anne would have soothed had she been alive. The growing alienation of Arundel and his friends contributed considerably to the final crisis of the reign.*

OPPOSITE **Art MacMurrogh confers with the Earl of Gloucester, 1399 in a illustration** *by the Virgil Master in Jean Creton's* Histoire du Roy d'Angleterre Richard II, *1401–5. MacMurrogh (1357–1417) was the native king of Leinster who resisted Richard II's attempts to extend English rule in Ireland. In 1399 he agreed to meet Richard's representative in an open space beside a brook. His appearance impressed the chronicler: 'He was of large stature, wonderfully active, very fell [fierce]'. MacMurrogh declared that he would accept no terms that did not guarantee his complete freedom of action. Richard II was furious but was quite unable to bring MacMurrogh and his followers to heel.*

Sir John Clanvow on Lollards

Clanvow, a cultured man, *poet and friend of Geoffrey Chaucer, belonged to a group of Lollard knights at the court of Richard II who were, the chronicler, Henry Knighton, said, 'the strongest promoters and most powerful protectors of Lollard preachers'.*[5] *Clanvow himself wrote: 'Such folk the world scorneth and holdeth them lollers and losels [good-for-nothings] fools and shameful wretches. But surely God holdeth them most wise and most worshipful ... And therefore take we savour in those things ... and reck [care] we never though the world scorn us or hold us wretches. For the world scorned Christ and held him a fool ... And therefore follow we his traces and suffer we patiently the scorns of the world as he did.'*[6]

body of de Vere brought back from Louvain for interment in his family tomb. He petitioned the pope to canonize Edward II as a holy martyr. In March 1396 the truce with France was extended for another 28 years and to cement the friendship of the two kingdoms Richard agreed to marry Isabella, the seven-year-old daughter of Charles VI. In September he crossed to France and spent several days with his bride's father in a specially created camp near Calais, where he sought to impress everyone with a sumptuous and expensive display of royal splendour. News of the marriage was not well received by parliament, not least because it would be several years before Isabella could provide an heir to the throne.

1397–8

THE KING WAS NOW BUILDING UP his own body of supporters by handing out titles and grants of land. As royal vassals these new men could be relied on to provide Richard with armed men when required, so having pacified Ireland and made peace with France, the king now felt strong enough to dispose once and for all of all thosc who cncroached upon his prerogative. In January 1397 parliament presented a petition complaining about the extravagance of the court. This time Richard moved swiftly and decisively, ordering the arrest of Thomas Haxey, who had drafted the petition. Haxey was charged with treason and condemned but, as a clergyman, spared capital punishment. But the king's action had served its

OPPOSITE **Isabella of France betrothed to Richard II, 1396.** *Richard's marriage to the daughter of Charles VI of France secured peace between the two countries and extended the existing truce by 28 years. The ceremonies accompanying the betrothal, depicted in this image from* Froissart's Chronicles, *took place over four days between Guisnes and Ardres and were lavish in the extreme and, according to the chronicles, cost Richard £200,000. Despite the obvious advantages of peace, the alliance did not please those Englishmen who were committed to recovering English territory in France.*

ABOVE **Richard II presides over a tournament.** *In this 15th-century manuscript illumination the king is shown in his pavilion watching mounted knights jousting with lances. On the left trumpeters play and on the right members of the public watch from an enclosure. Richard was always an observer and never a participator in these warlike games. His more martial nobles never regarded Richard as 'one of us'.*

en
bien
par
sans
charles roy de frãc
roy de
Richart roy dangletre:

purpose of cowing parliament. Over the next few months rumours abounded of plots and counter-plots, supposedly hatched by the king against his noble opponents and vice versa. On 10 July Richard struck. He invited Gloucester, Arundel and their colleague, the Earl of Warwick, to a feast. Gloucester and Arundel were wary enough not to attend, but Warwick arrived and was immediately arrested. At the king's urgings Arundel's brother, the Archbishop of Canterbury, persuaded the earl to give himself up, and on the same day Richard rode to Gloucester's Essex manor and arrested him in person.

OPPOSITE **The crowns of England and France, *c.*1396.** *This stunning image shows Christ's crown of thorns between the crowns of Richard II and Charles VI and illuminating them with golden rays. The legend above the centre crown reads, in French, 'peace to you', (on the left) 'in good faith' and (on the right) 'in perpetuity'. The gilt letters 'IHS'* (in hoc signo – *'in this sign' – a reference to a vision given to the Emperor Constantine, which inspired his conversion to Christianity) appear over the arms of France and England. This work by Philippe de Maizières (c.1327–1405) puts a religious gloss on the amity between the two countries sealed by the marriage of Richard and Isabella.*

ABOVE **The arrest of the Duke of Gloucester, 11 July 1397,** *from* Froissart's Chronicles. *On the previous evening the king had ordered Richard Whittington, Lord Mayor of London, to call out the city militia to accompany him on the 35-mile ride to Gloucester's house at Pleshy, Essex. The duke came out to meet him and submitted to arrest. Observing, 'By St John the Baptist, dear uncle, all this will turn out for the best', Richard ordered the prisoner to be taken to Calais. In captivity there Gloucester conveniently 'died'. The picture shows Richard and his uncle parting company. A ship stands ready to transport Gloucester across the Channel.*

Richard had planned in detail what was to happen to his principal enemies. He feared the reaction of putting his uncle on trial, and so Gloucester was taken to Calais and confined in the castle there. According to Froissart his end came quickly: 'Just before dinner, when the tables were laid in the castle and the duke was on the point of washing his hands, four men came out of the next room and putting a towel round his neck they strangled him, two of them pulling at each end. They then undressed the body, put it between the sheets, with the head on a pillow, and covered the bed with four coverlets; they then went back to the great hall and let it be known that the duke had had an apoplectic fit.'[7]

On 17 September parliament was convened, overawed by a contingent of 2,000 royal archers. On the 20th of the month Arundel was tried, found guilty and bundled through the streets of London to Tower Hill and there beheaded. People crowded to witness Arundel's end but not to rejoice in the death of a traitor. A great deal of sympathy was felt for him, and he was immediately claimed as a martyr, Londoners flocking to his tomb. It may have been partly as a result of this reaction that Richard commuted Warwick's sentence (on 28 September) to imprisonment on the Isle of Man.

The king may have hesitated to shed blood, but he pursued an ever-widening circle of people who had in any way supported his enemies. He resorted to fines and new laws. Thus, for example, the counties of Essex and Hertfordshire, where Gloucester had exercised considerable influence, had to pay £2,000 for their pardon. London and other towns were obliged to accept fresh charters that considerably increased the power of the crown in their affairs. But by thus overplaying his hand, Richard provoked considerable hostility, as a monastic chronicler moralized: 'What bitter feelings the whole people felt towards him. But he was driven on by his own destiny ... Therefore he made very great preparations throughout the whole of Lent [1399], and especially extorting money, demanding horses and wagons, commandeering supplies of corn, meat and fish everywhere for his departure and paying nothing; not taking into account the fact that, "Property acquired by evil means brings no good fortune". And that the more he accumulated unjustly of the property of his subjects, the more he justifiably incurred their hatred.'[8]

But the outcome of events would be decided not by popular disaffection, but by rivalries among the king's kindred and their allies. Richard had no children by his first wife, and it was certain that he would have none by Isabella for at least five or

Ghostly visions

After this man's [Arundel's] death, the king was troubled by various visions in his sleep; indeed as soon as he began to sleep, the ghost of the earl seemed to float before his eyes, and to threaten him and terrify him by pointing with his finger as if he were saying with the Poet: 'Now also I come as a ghost to remind you of your deeds and my bony form haunts your face.'

CHRONICA MONASTERII, I, P. 225

ABOVE **Richard banishes the dukes of Hereford and Norfolk, 1398.** *This was the event, shown in this image from* Chroniques de France ou de St Denis, *that hastened the king's downfall. The two recently elevated dukes were both critics of the regime but they fell out. Hereford accused Norfolk of treachery. Richard, at the height of his powers, having recently cowed parliament, summoned them to settle their dispute by single combat on 16 September at Gosford Green, near Coventry, then intervened and had both men banished instead – Norfolk for life and Hereford for ten years. Within a year Oxford and also John of Gaunt were dead. Richard then made the mistake of extending Hereford's banishment to a life sentence and confiscating his lands. This last*

six years. This raised the probabilities of a disputed succession and, perhaps, eventually another royal minority. John of Gaunt believed that the crown should be passed down through his line, which, in effect, would mean that Henry, Earl of Derby, recently promoted to the dukedom of Hereford would ascend the throne. For Richard's triumph to be complete he had to neutralize the last of his close relatives, and the chance came, in 1398, when Hereford fell out with Thomas Mowbray, Duke of Norfolk. Norfolk had been captain of Calais at the time of Gloucester's death and, from Richard's point of view, knew too much.

We have no documentary evidence for the ensuing strange events, but it is obvious that Richard saw a way of killing two birds with one stone. He decreed that the rival dukes should settle their dispute in single combat at Coventry on 16 September. On the day all was ready for the trial of arms before a large crowd when the king stepped down from his gallery and stopped the contest. He then banished both dukes, Hereford for ten years and Norfolk for life. A year later, Norfolk died in Venice.

1399–1400

IN FEBRUARY 1399 John of Gaunt died, leaving only the Duke of Hereford as an aggravating thorn in Richard's flesh. Under the terms of his banishment, Hereford was entitled to return to take up his inheritance, but in order to prevent this the king simply changed the rules. He revoked Henry's licence to return and extended his term of banishment to life. The exiled duke was then at the French court, and Richard was confident that Charles VI would not jeopardize the Anglo-French concord by aiding his brother king's enemy. In June 1399 he paid another visit to Ireland to deal with matters there.

The French king, however, was suffering from bouts of insanity and was in the hands of court factions. At this time the Duke of Orleans was effectively in charge, and he gave Hereford permission to launch an invasion from French soil in order to score over his pro-English rivals. Henry landed on the Yorkshire coast in July. His 'army' amounted to no more than a few hundred retainers, but it grew rapidly in size. All the magnates who had grievances against the king now had a leader to follow. The Duke of York, who was regent during the king's absence, threw in his lot with Hereford, and Richard's most dependable troops were with him in Ireland.

By the time the king landed in Wales on 11 August everything was already lost. Richard had too many enemies, and within days his own troops were deserting in droves. By 2 September he was lodged in the Tower as Henry's prisoner.

Hereford set up a commission to give a show of legality to the action he had decided to take. Its carefully chosen members agreed that Richard had forfeited his right to rule by virtue of his 'perjuries, sacrileges, sodomitical acts, dispossession of his subjects, reduction of his people to servitude, lack of reason and incapacity', and on 29 September Richard, according to the official version of events, bowed to the inevitable and renounced the crown. The next day parliament confirmed his abdication and hailed Hereford as king. A deposed king always posed a threat to those who had deposed him – he would inevitably become a focus for plots and rebellions – and it is unlikely that Richard did not calculate what his end would be. He who regarded Edward II as a martyr to divine kingship may well have steeled himself to the same fate. He was taken from the Tower under disguise, moved to various places of concealment and eventually arrived at Pontefract Castle. There, probably on 14 February 1400, he died. Exactly how he met his end will never be known. His body was taken to St Paul's Cathedral for funeral and then interred in the royal manor of Kings Langley. It was not destined to remain there long.

ABOVE **Richard II imprisoned in the Tower of London, 1399.** *Richard came face to face with his enemy at Flint Castle on 19 August and, two days later, he set out for London as Henry Bolingbroke's prisoner. At Lichfield he made a feeble attempt to escape by climbing out of a window but was soon recaptured. On 2 September he was brought to the Tower of London and imprisoned there. There are conflicting reports of the manner of his arrival. One relates that Henry marched him through the city along streets lined with jeering people but Froissart's account asserts that he was taken into the fortress under cover of darkness. There he remained for the rest of the month while Bolingbroke and his associates made all the necessary legal arrangements for the King Richard's voluntary abdication and his nomination of Duke Henry as his successor. On 29 September Richard made his formal surrender of the crown to a group of lords and on the following day, in Westminster Hall, the duke was placed upon a vacant throne and began his reign as Henry IV. Despite the tension surrounding these dramatic events, the transfer of power was carried out in an atmosphere of remarkable calm.*

RIGHT **The funeral of Richard II** *from a manuscript of the second half of the 15th century. The deposed king was taken to various castles in the weeks following his abdication and ended up in Pontefract, Yorkshire. In January 1400 there was an abortive rising by some of his supporters. Henry had probably already decided on the ex-king's death but this attempted coup sealed his fate. Sometime in February he died, by what means is unknown. The official story was that in his despair he refused food and pined away. Arrangements were made on 17 February for his body to be carried to London. But the obsequies befitting a king were denied him. After his body had been publicly displayed in St Paul's Cathedral, Richard was interred unceremoniously in the friars' church at Kings Langley, Hertfordshire.*

Henry IV

Henry 4th
K. of Engd

The nature of Henry's acquisition of the crown led inevitably to several challenges on behalf of claimants with a better title, and internal disruption encouraged the Scots and Welsh to wage war against the regime. By the time Henry had established his authority he was dogged by ill health and by the challenge of his popular, charismatic son, Prince Henry. By the turn of the 15th century vernacular English had established itself as a written language favoured by poets as against Latin or court French. Geoffrey Chaucer and William Langland provide vivid pictures of the lives of all classes of contemporary men and women.

1400–4

IT WAS ONE THING to get rid of King Richard but quite another to persuade everyone to accept King Henry. There was no disguising the fact that the man who now wore the crown was a usurper. Much as Richard had been unpopular, many Englishmen resented the way he had been removed, and there were some who persisted in believing that he was still alive.

Disruption in England frequently encouraged freedom fighters in Scotland and Wales, and in the closing weeks of 1399 Henry led an army into Scotland in response to serious border raids. As usual, the Scots offered no fixed battle. On his way back from the border, Henry learned that a Welsh champion, Owain Glyn Dwr, had proclaimed himself Prince of Wales and raised much of northern and central Wales

ABOVE **A gold coin of Henry IV.** *Throughout his reign the king was short of money because parliament declined to grant him the taxes he required. This, and the scarcity of bullion, forced him in 1412 to issue a new coinage. The noble was reduced in weight by 12 grains. The design was also slightly changed: the king was still represented on a ship, to denote England's mastery of the Channel, but the fleurs de lys on his shield were reduced from four to three, bringing English usage into line with French.*

PREVIOUS PAGE **King Henry IV** *(1367–1413) in a portrait in oil on canvas dating from the 17th century.*

King Richard alive?

A friar minor came to the king ... and said that 500 men ... had agreed to meet together on the plain of Oxford on Midsummer Eve and go thence to seek King Richard ... and there is in the convent of Leicester a master of divinity, an old man, who ... says that King Richard shall fight against you ... The king called the archbishop and other lords and the friars were brought before him ... Then said he to the master ... 'Do you say that King Richard still lives?' The master answered, 'I say not that he lives but I say that if he lives, he is in truth the King of England.' The king said, 'He resigned.' The master answered, 'He resigned against his will in prison, which is not according to law ... He would not have resigned ... if he had had his freedom, and a resignation made in prison is not free.' The king said, 'I have not usurped the crown, but I was chosen thereto by election.' The master answered, 'The election is void, if the true and lawful possessor is alive, and if he is dead, he is dead because of you, and if he is dead by your deed, you have lost all the right and title that you might have had to the crown.' [The friars were charged with treason and elected to be tried by jury but] neither men of London nor of Holborn would condemn them; and then they had an inquest of Islington and they said, 'Guilty'. [The friars were hanged at Tyburn] and afterwards the men of the inquest who condemned them came to the [friars' convent] praying their forgiveness and said that unless they had said that the friars were guilty, they would have been slain.

English Historical Documents 1327–1485, ed. A. R. Myers, 1995, IV, p. 185

BELOW **Richard II giving the crown to Henry Bolingbroke** *in a illustration from* Froissart's Chronicles. *Throughout his reign Henry carried the stigma of being a usurper. He always had the need to impress on critics that Richard had resigned willingly.*

against English rule, and an inconclusive campaign in the autumn of 1400 failed to suppress the rebellion. The French also refused to acknowledge the change of regime in England. There were arguments about the return of Isabella, the late king's young widow, or, more specifically, her dowry. She eventually returned to France – minus the dowry – in 1401. Charles VI's recurrent bouts of insanity – he sometimes insisted that he was made of glass and should not be moved – placed real power in the hands of the dukes of Orleans and Burgundy, who vied for supremacy. At first, the anti-English Orleans had the upper hand, and it was he who arranged in January 1401 for Prince Louis, Charles's heir (dauphin) to be made Duke of Aquitaine. The following year he concluded a new treaty with Scotland and, in 1403, sent troops to invade Aquitaine. Throughout these years there was running naval warfare in the Channel.

War on three fronts raised acute financial problems for Henry, but, as usual, when he approached parliament they raised issues of court expenditure. The last thing the king needed was civil war with his own nobles, but that is what now broke out. Having embraced the principle 'might is right', Henry laid his occupation of the throne open to challenge. The Percys were the dominant family in the north – Richard had made Henry Percy Earl of Northumberland – and Henry had relied heavily on the earl and his kinsmen during his bid for power. He rewarded them handsomely, not only lavishing them with lands and offices but also relying on the earl as his main adviser. His brother, Thomas Percy, Earl of Worcester, was brought onto the king's council and placed in charge of naval affairs. Northumberland's son, Henry, known as Hotspur because of his vigorous belligerence in dealing with Scottish marauders, became the major administrator of royal authority in Cheshire and north

Du couronnement du roy henry /
duc de lancastre / Quy se fist du con-
sentement de tout le comun dangleterre / Et de la maniere de la feste
quy si tint. Le chapitre
En lan de nostre seigneur
mil cccc / vng moins /
aduint en angleterre ou
mois de septembre / et le
darrain iour dicellui mois par vng
estoient / Et la fut tout ledit peu-
ple assamble a Westmoustier ce mar-
di deuant dit / present le duc de lancastre et ses gens / Et la calenga le
duc de lancastre le royaulme dangleterre / et requist a estre roy par trois
manieres de cas / Premierement par
conquest / Secondement pour tant
que il se disoit estre droit hoir de la couronne / Et tiercement par ce que le

OPPOSITE **Naval warfare** *as depicted in* Froissart's Chronicles. *Poor relations between England and France, which refused to acknowledge the Henrician regime, along with piracy, provoked continuous fighting in the Channel. Throughout the Hundred Years War control of the Channel remained of vital importance. France had the larger navy, which was stationed in harbours from Dieppe to St Malo, but Calais provided a haven on the continental coast for English shipping.*

ABOVE **The coronation of Henry IV, 13 October 1399.** *As one way of establishing his authority Henry ensured that his coronation would be as spectacular as possible. In the Tower, on 11 October, he conferred the Order of the Bath on 40 new knights (this order, founded by Richard II, later fell into disuse until revived by George I in 1725). On 12 October he made a grand procession through the city to Westminster attended by 6,000 knights, soldiers and dignitaries. He was greeted by cheering crowds, helped in their revelry by fountains flowing with red and white wine. The illustration shows Henry arriving at the abbey on 13 October, the feast of St Edward, under a canopy of blue silk carried on silver poles. The left panel represents Henry being crowned by two archbishops and ten bishops.*

ABOVE **Henry Percy, Earl of Northumberland** *(1342–1408) swearing an oath on the consecrated host in an illustration by the Virgil Master in the* Histoire du Roy d'Angleterre Richard II. *In the Middle Ages solemn oaths were enormously important in establishing the allegiance of men to their feudal overlords. Only by promising 'before God' to fulfil their obligations could they give convincing expression of their loyalty. Henry IV desperately needed the support of his great barons, especially the Percys, who were supremely powerful throughout the north of England. Driven by jealousy and mistrust, the king managed to alienate the Percys into rebellion in 1403. After his defeat the earl protested his continuing loyalty and Henry spared his life. However, the anger Northumberland nursed against the king erupted in rebellion again in 1405.*

Wales. In all, the king relied heavily on this clan in dealing with difficulties on the Scottish and Welsh borders.

In the autumn of 1402 the Earl of Douglas launched a major raid deep into England. Northumberland and his son intercepted the Scots at Humbleton Hill, in the Cheviots, near Wooler, and during the battle English archers again proved their worth, and the Scottish force was all but annihilated. This convincing victory showed up Henry IV's earlier less-than-glorious military leadership and, more importantly, led to a serious dispute between the king and his generals.

The main cause of the Percys disaffection was the lack of financial support they received for their military action. They could, reasonably, claim that they were providing loyal and valuable service that was not being recognized or recompensed. Henry, far from being alert to the importance of keeping the Percys close to the throne, seems to have gone out of his way to antagonize them. Hotspur had taken Douglas prisoner at Humbleton Hill and claimed the right personally to receive ransom for him, but Henry insisted that the Scottish lord be handed over to him.

Then, when young Percy asked for permission to ransom his own brother-in-law, Sir Edmund Mortimer, currently being held captive by Glyn Dwr, this, too, was refused. The king had good reason not to see Mortimer set at liberty: Edmund belonged to a family with a better claim to the crown, and Henry suspected that he might, in fact, be intriguing with Glyn

RIGHT **A statue of Sir Henry, 'Hotspur', Percy,** *at Beverley Minster, Yorkshire. Hotspur (1364–1403), eldest son of the Earl of Northumberland, was regarded by chroniclers (and later, Shakespeare) as the very embodiment of chivalry – bold, brave and honourable. Sir Henry certainly served courageously and effectively against the Scots and the Welsh but his ungovernable temper and headstrong nature limited his military achievements and, as one biographer has said, we should regard him as 'a doughty fighter rather than a skilful soldier'.*

The Battle of Shrewsbury

After that there had fallen on either side in most bloody slaughter to the number of 16,000 men, in the field of Berwick ... two miles from Shrewsbury ... victory declared for the king who had thus made the onslaught. In this battle, the said Lord Percy, the flower and glory of chivalry of Christendom, fell, alas! And with him his uncle. Whereby is the prophecy fulfilled: 'the cast-off beast shall carry away the two horns of the moon.'

Chronicon Adae de Usk, ed. E.M. Thompson, 1904, p. 29

Dwr. To prevent Mortimer making trouble he sent men to seize all his plate and jewels. At the parliament in October Hotspur and the king had a fierce argument. Henry denounced the young Percy as a traitor and drew his dagger against him. At this Hotspur stalked out, shouting, 'Not here, but in the field!' Relations were patched up for the time being, but in November Mortimer, either stung by Henry's action or simply revealing himself in his true colours, married Glyn Dwr's daughter. A month later he issued a call to all his friends to join him in an attempt either to restore Richard, should he still be alive, or to place his own young nephew, Edmund, Earl of March, on the throne.

In July 1403 Hotspur responded to this appeal and led a small army to the Welsh border in order to make common cause with the self-styled Prince of Wales against Henry. He was joined by his uncle, the Earl of Worcester. The king responded quickly, marching across country to face the Percys before they could link up with their Welsh allies. He reached Shrewsbury before them, and on 21 July a decisive battle was fought in the hamlet of Berwick, to the northwest of the town.

It was the speed and cunning of King Henry's response that was the undoing of the rebels. Had he delayed another day he would have faced the combined forces, not only of Hotspur and Glyn Dwr, but also of the Earl of Northumberland, who was racing across country to come to his son's aid. Hotspur's men actually gained an early initiative, but their leader was severely wounded when he raised his visor and an arrow struck him in the face. Either this killed him or disabled him so severely that he fell soon afterwards. That was really the end of the battle. According to one chronicler, the king had taken care to avoid a similar fate by sending two knights into battle wearing armour identical to his own. The Earl of Douglas, fighting alongside Hotspur, reputedly exclaimed, 'Have I not slain two king Henries with my own hand? 'Tis an evil hour for us that a third yet lives to be our victor.'[1] Thomas of Worcester was captured and executed immediately after the battle. Northumberland surrendered, was arrested, tried for treason but found guilty only of the lesser charge of trespass. The king pardoned him but stripped him of several of his offices. Henry was in a dilemma: he knew that Percy was nursing thoughts of revenge but he needed him to keep the Scots at bay and he knew also that throughout much of the north people felt a greater loyalty to Northumberland than to the king.

OPPOSITE **The Battle of Shrewsbury, 21 July 1403.** *This image is from the* Beauchamp Pageants, *which was published in the Netherlands (late 15th century). This engagement was significant in that it confirmed Henry IV in possession of the crown. The Percys renounced their allegiance for personal reasons but also because Henry had claimed the throne instead of simply fighting for the restoration of his confiscated lands; because he had murdered Richard II; and because he had levied taxes without parliamentary consent. Hotspur and his uncle, Thomas, Earl of Worcester, rejected the king's peace terms. The initial stages of the Battle of Shrewsbury went against the king but Hotspur, characteristically making a death or glory charge against the royal standard, was killed by an arrow and his army dispersed. Henry made terrible examples of the surviving leaders of the revolt and, thereafter, his position was secure.*

William Langland and Geoffrey Chaucer

By 1400 a brisk trade in vernacular books was developing. The processes of copying and binding books were no longer the preserves of the monks, and such secular writings as poems, chivalric romances and ribald satires were as much in demand as devotional works and Lollard tracts. Among the most popular authors were William Langland and Geoffrey Chaucer. Although very different, both writers reflected on contemporary life and they provide us with real insights into the way ordinary people lived at the turn of the 15th century.

Little is known about Langland. He lived through most of the second half of the 14th century, was a minor cleric, spent some years in London but probably spent most of his time in Worcestershire, around Malvern. His only work was a long allegorical poem, *The Vision of Piers Plowman*. It describes a series of dreams that come to the narrator, Long Will. In his quest for virtue Will encounters allegorical characters such as 'Favel' (Falsehood) and 'Meed' (Acquisitiveness) and 'Do Well'. The poem is a moralistic reflection on the state of English society. It tries to discern the application of the Bible and traditional church teaching to life as it really is, and the gloomy picture it presents of corrupt clergy and a legal system weighted against the poor comes close to reflecting criticisms voiced by Lollards and the rebelling peasants of 1381. Monks, for example, came in for a lambasting:

RIGHT **A portrait of Geoffrey Chaucer** *(1342–1400) from a manuscript of the* Canterbury Tales *in the British Library. Chaucer was a versatile poet and storyteller with an intimate knowledge of all sorts and conditions of men and women. His own experience embraced military service, the life of the royal court, government administration and mercantile activity.*

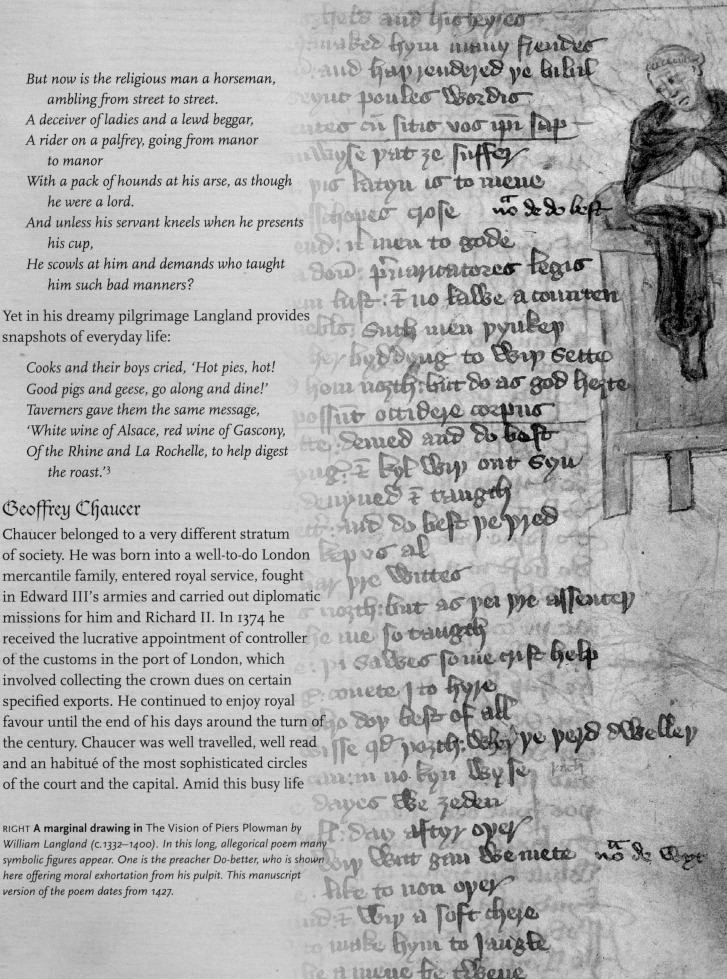

But now is the religious man a horseman,
ambling from street to street.
A deceiver of ladies and a lewd beggar,
A rider on a palfrey, going from manor
to manor
With a pack of hounds at his arse, as though
he were a lord.
And unless his servant kneels when he presents
his cup,
He scowls at him and demands who taught
him such bad manners?

Yet in his dreamy pilgrimage Langland provides snapshots of everyday life:

Cooks and their boys cried, 'Hot pies, hot!
Good pigs and geese, go along and dine!'
Taverners gave them the same message,
'White wine of Alsace, red wine of Gascony,
Of the Rhine and La Rochelle, to help digest
the roast.'[3]

Geoffrey Chaucer

Chaucer belonged to a very different stratum of society. He was born into a well-to-do London mercantile family, entered royal service, fought in Edward III's armies and carried out diplomatic missions for him and Richard II. In 1374 he received the lucrative appointment of controller of the customs in the port of London, which involved collecting the crown dues on certain specified exports. He continued to enjoy royal favour until the end of his days around the turn of the century. Chaucer was well travelled, well read and an habitué of the most sophisticated circles of the court and the capital. Amid this busy life

RIGHT **A marginal drawing in** The Vision of Piers Plowman *by William Langland (c.1332–1400). In this long, allegorical poem many symbolic figures appear. One is the preacher Do-better, who is shown here offering moral exhortation from his pulpit. This manuscript version of the poem dates from 1427.*

he managed to write several poems, most of which were extremely popular with the cultured elite.

The most famous of all Chaucer's works, *The Canterbury Tales,* was written towards the end of his life and was unfinished at the time of his death. It is a group of verse stories ostensibly told by a party of pilgrims to wile away their journey from London to the shrine of Thomas Becket at Canterbury. The poet presented pen portraits of the travellers, a cross-section of society ranging from an impecunious university student to a knight, several grades of clergy and a much-married Wife of Bath.

These brilliant, well-observed cameos of Chaucer's contemporaries and the stories they told are witty satirical comments on the times, sometimes moralistic, sometimes bawdy, sometimes refined, sometimes vulgar but always witty. Here a pardoner (a cleric licensed to sell papal pardons and indulgences) boasts of his oratorical skill:

I stand like a clerk in my pulpit,
And when the common people
have taken their places
I preach as you heard me before,
And tell a hundred more tall stories.
Then I go to great lengths to stick out my neck
And nod upon the people to both
east and west,
As a dove does sitting on a roof.
My hands and tongue are both so
eagerly active
That I am a delight to behold when
I am at work.[4]

There were a rising number of writers in the vernacular by the early 15th century. No longer was it necessary to produce books in French, Latin or Italian to be considered cultivated. The English language, or, rather, the language spoken in the southeastern part of England, was contributing to the distinct identity and sense of nationhood that were beginning to emerge.

LEFT **The Pardoner, a character from Chaucer's *Canterbury Tales*,** *in an image from the Ellesmere Manuscript (1400–10). This ecclesiastic with a bag of pardons 'come from Rome all hot' was exposed by the poet as a con man. He is shown carrying a richly jewelled cross to impress people. When they resorted to him he sold them false relics, such as pigs' bones, purporting to be the bones of long-dead saints. By hawking his frauds, 'In one day he collected more money than [a poor husbandman] could earn in two months'.*

1405–6

ALTHOUGH THE EARL OF NORTHUMBERLAND had been restored to favour, the personal losses he had sustained and the decline in his influence at court estranged him from the king. Early in 1405 he re-established contact with Glyn Dwr and Mortimer, and they planned further rebellion. It involved the kidnapping of the young Earl of March, whom Henry kept in honourable confinement at Windsor, proclaiming him the rightful king and dividing the nation between Northumberland, Mortimer and Glyn Dwr. The first part of the plan went well: the Earl of March was successfully snatched. Once again, however, the king acted swiftly and recaptured the boy en route for Wales after a few days. Then, in May, as Henry was preparing another Welsh campaign, he heard that Northumberland, Richard Scrope, Archbishop of York, and Thomas Mowbray, the Earl Marshal, were gathering their forces in the north. Scrope had papers pinned to the doors of all the York churches denouncing Henry as a usurper, a wastrel and a breaker of promises. The king sent the Earl of Westmorland, a bitter enemy of the Percys, to intercept the rebels. He persuaded Scrope and Mowbray to disband their army, giving assurances that their grievances would be addressed, then he promptly arrested them. When Henry arrived in York he had the two men tried and condemned, and he personally led them outside the city to the place of execution (8 June).

When the archbishop should die he said, 'Lo, I shall die for the laws and good rule of England.'

An English Chronicle 1377–1461, ed. J.S. Davies, 1859, p. 21

Henry Percy fled into Scotland. Henry, meanwhile, had fallen ill, and poor health was to dog him intermittently for the rest of his life. At the end of the summer, however, he was fit enough to campaign in Wales, but the Glyn Dwr problem remained unresolved and was intensified by the arrival of French troops, sent to aid the rebels. In August 1405 2,500 French soldiers landed at Milford Haven, and they remained in Wales until March 1406. With their support, Glyn Dwr was able to gain control of southern Wales and cross the border towards Worcester. The Earl of Northumberland joined his former allies there. However, when the French left, disappointed by the lack of dissident Englishmen ready to join their cause, the tide of war turned. Northumberland hurried back to France to seek more aid from Orleans, but the duke was too involved in his own problems to render fresh assistance. (He was assassinated by agents of the Duke of Burgundy the following year.)

The parliament that assembled on 1 March 1406 was known as the Long Parliament because it remained in almost continuous session until 22 December. The main reason for this was another breakdown in the king's health. Henry seems to have suffered from various illnesses, some

The French came to … the harbour of Milford with 140 ships, having lost almost all their horses, owing to the lack of fresh water. Lord Berkeley and Henry Pay burnt 15 of their ships in the same harbour. The Frenchmen laid siege to the town of Carmarthen and took it, having first allowed the defenders the right to keep all their goods and chattels and transfer themselves whithersoever they pleased.

Chronicia Monasterii S.Albani, Thomae Walsingham … Historia Anglicana, ed. H.T. Riley, 1863–72, II, p. 272

psychosomatic, and one monastic chronicler asserted that Henry had been struck down with leprosy for having Archbishop Scrope executed. While there is no basis for this, it is very likely that the insecurity of his position and the constant criticisms of those who regarded him as a usurper did not help his mental condition. In May Henry asked for a permanent council to help him carry the heavy burden of government, and a total of 17 prominent lay and ecclesiastical lords were appointed.

The burning issue was, as always, finance. Between 1399 and 1404 six treasurers had come and gone, each unable to balance the books. Parliament produced a comprehensive programme for the reform of the royal finances and set up a smaller council, headed by Prince Henry (now 19 years old) specifically to oversee this aspect of government. Young Henry was now gathering a considerable personal following. He had been appointed Prince of Wales in 1399 and had been involved in several campaigns against Glyn Dwr, and

Finances

Revered and gracious lord, *because the revenues of your kingdom are burdened so outrageously that there can be no relief … will your gracious highness abstain now from charging me beyond my power to pay or else hold me excused for not accomplishing your said letters and commandment? For truly, reverend lord, there is not in your Treasury at the moment enough to pay the messengers who are to bear the letters which you have ordained to be sent to the lords, knights and esquires to be of your [parliament].*

Letter from Lawrence Allerthorpe, treasurer, to the king, December 1401, *Anglo-Norman Letters and Petitions*, ed. M.D. Legge, 1933, No. 331

many people now looked to the heir rather than the ailing and not spectacularly successful king. The prince was impatient for more authority and had his own ideas about the running of the country. He was a vigorous young man, an already experienced field commander and a prince untainted with the stigma of having usurped the crown.

All was not gloom and despondency for the semi-invalid king, however. In 1406 his younger daughter was married to Eric VII of Norway, Sweden and Denmark. In the same year, Prince James, heir to the Scottish throne, was captured while en route to France. He was destined to remain a prisoner in England for 18 years.

1407–13

HENRY MIGHT WELL have thought it ironic that several of his more tenacious problems resolved themselves at a time when his own powers were failing. The death of Orleans and the dominance of the Duke of Burgundy over the mentally ill French king were good news. Early in 1408 the rebellion of the Percys

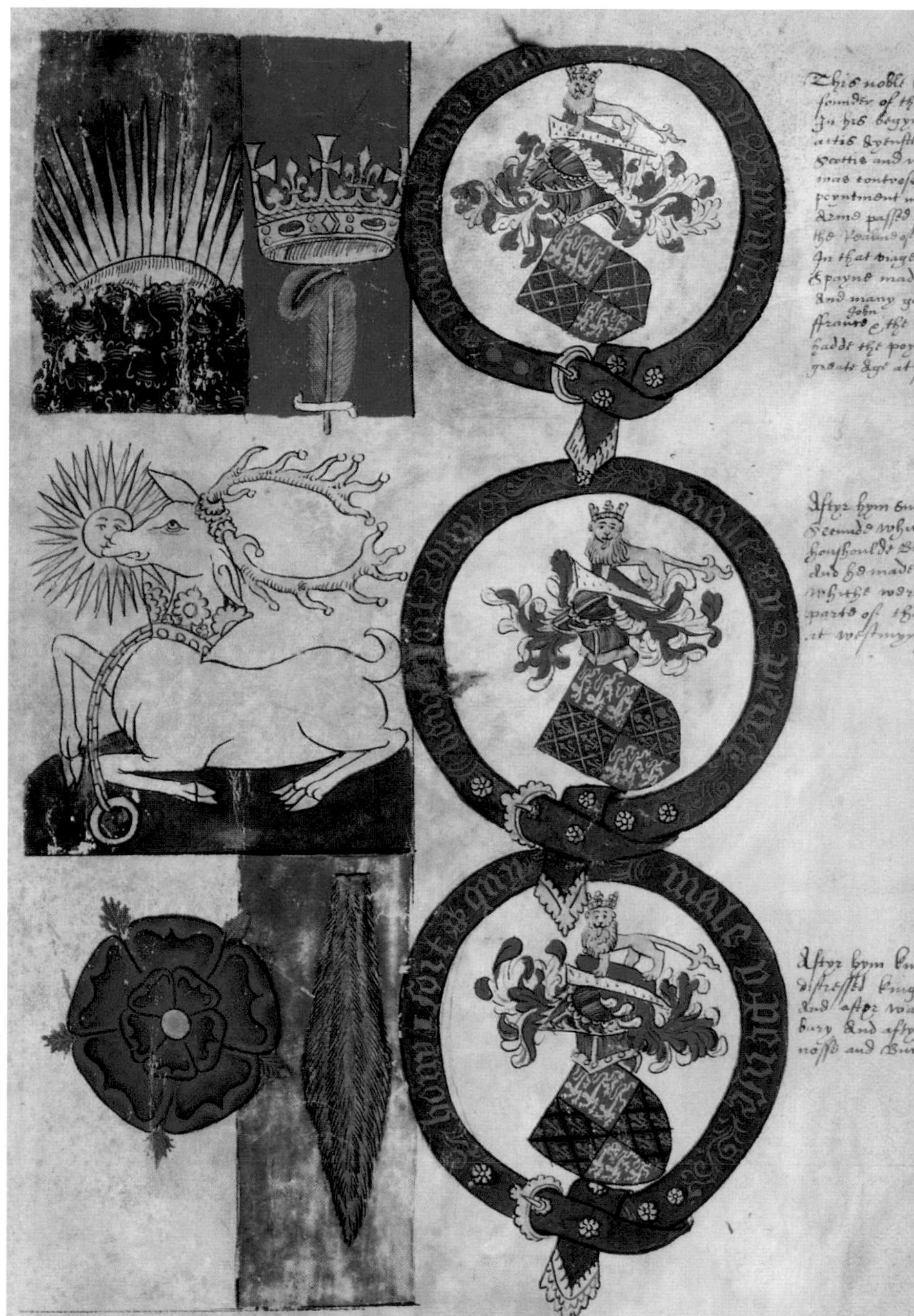

ABOVE **Royal badges**. *In the 14th century the custom developed among the leaders of society of adopting simple emblems for personal display and distribution to their followers as symbols of loyalty. They were distinct from heraldic devices and were almost equivalent to written signatures; they easily identified their owners. Examples are the Prince of Wales's feathers and the white hart of Richard II. This detail from* Writhe's Garter Book *dates from c.1640 but is based on the records kept by royal heralds. It shows the sunburst of Edward III, the white hart of Richard II and the red rose of Henry IV.*

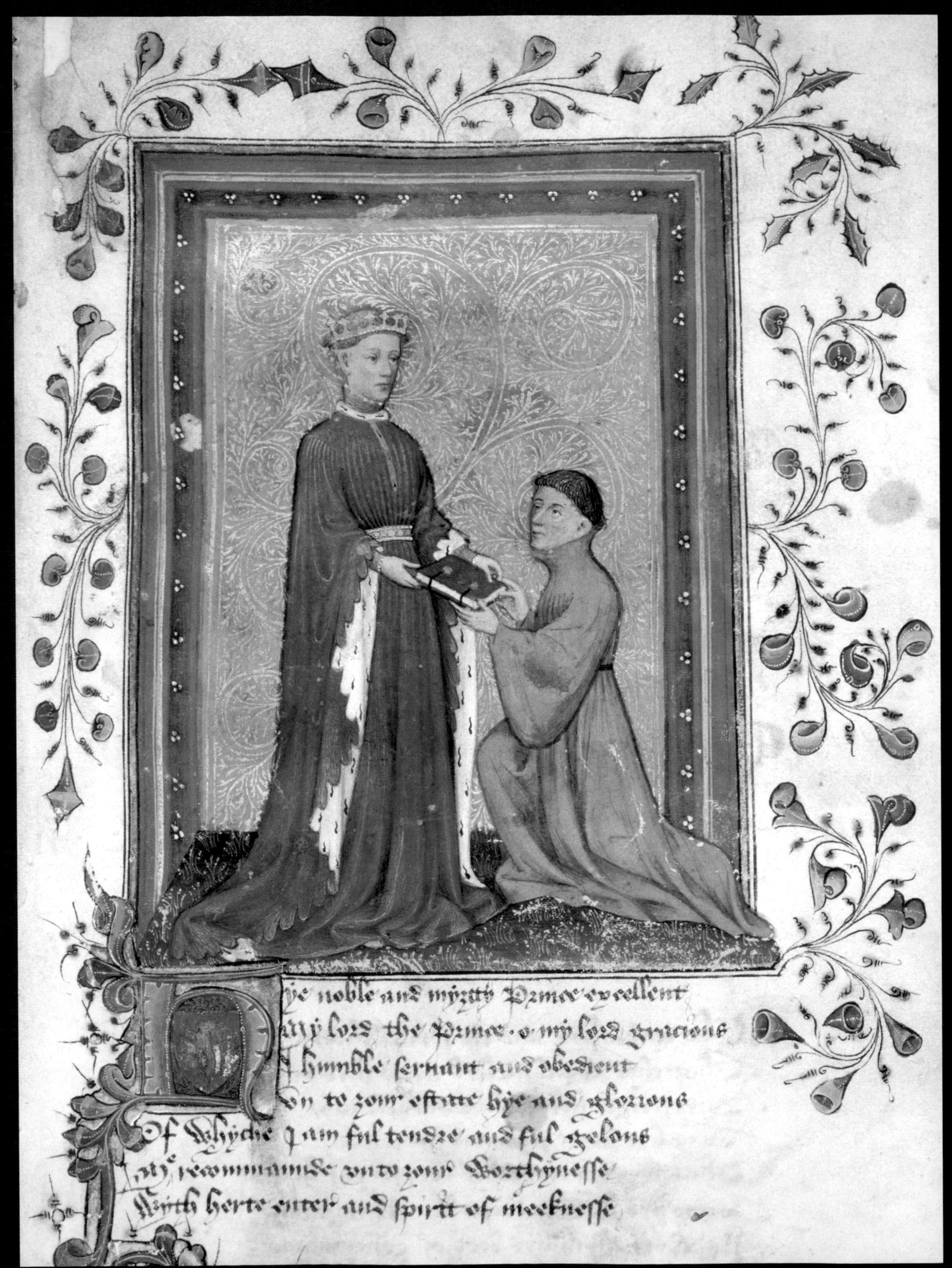
Hye noble and myzty Prince excellent
My lord the Prince · o my lord gracious
I humble seruant and obedient
Un to zour estate hye and glorious
Of whyche I am ful tendre and ful zelous
Me recommaunde vnto zour worthynesse
With herte enter and spirit of meekenesse

finally came to an end. The Earl of Northumberland had returned to Scotland. In February he crossed the border with a small army, hoping its ranks would be swelled by English malcontents, but this did not happen, nor was Glyn Dwr, whose fortunes were on the wane, able to come to his aid. On a snow-swept Bramham Moor, south of Wetherby, he met a force of Yorkshire levies assembled by the sheriff, Thomas Rokeby. During the scrappy battle that followed Northumberland was killed. The next year, Mortimer, last of the major English rebels, died during the siege of Harlech Castle. Owain Glyn Dwr withdrew into the mountains of north Wales and ceased to be a serious threat.

OPPOSITE **Thomas Hoccleve and Prince Henry, 1411**. *Hoccleve was a clerk in the office of the Lord Privy Seal. He was also a scholar and poet. In 1411 he completed his* Regement of Princes, *a verse manual on the virtues to be cultivated and the vices to be avoided by Christian monarchs. Hoccleve was also careful to justify the Lancastrian claim to the throne. In this illustration from the Arundel Manuscript the author is shown presenting a copy of the* Regement *to Henry of Lancaster, heir to the throne.*

ABOVE **Wax seal of Henry IV, 1411**. *The king, mounted on a galloping horse, brandishes a chained sword. His armour, like his shield and the trappings of the horse, bears the arms of England and France. Henry's helmet is surmounted by a lion crest and the same crest is carried by the horse. This particular example of the royal seal is from a document that ratified a trade agreement between England and Flanders, dated 2 June 1411. Four years earlier Henry had granted a charter to the Company of Merchant Adventurers of London, an association of the leading overseas merchants of the city trading with the Low Countries, mainly in woollen cloth. Despite the conflicts of king and nobles during this period, the mercantile life of the nation went on and was, in fact, approaching a new era of prosperity.*

Henry V

Henry V's brief reign lasted for nine years and five months, and the king spent half of that time in France. He was England's most successful warrior-king since Henry II, and, like his namesake, he was constantly on the move. His military exploits were famously dramatized by Shakespeare, but they were scarcely less 'heroic' in reality. He made good the English claim to the throne of France and had he lived to cement his military and diplomatic achievements might have linked the crowns permanently.

1413–14

HOLINSHED'S CHRONICLE DESCRIBES Henry as having had a misspent youth and having been a frequenter of bad company but insists that, on his accession, he turned over a new leaf. If he did indulge in a dissolute life during his father's last years it is likely to have been out of frustration with a king who was incapable of wise and measured rule. The prince was impatient to reform the government, and its whole mood changed as soon as he came to power.

Henry V's first objective was to heal the breeches that had caused so much disruption during his father's reign. He had the advantage that Wales and Scotland now posed no serious threat to the peace of the realm. Glyn Dwr's freedom movement had run into the sand, and the continued detention of James I of Scotland

ABOVE **The gilt-bronze tomb effigy of Richard II.** *After Queen Anne died in 1394 Richard contracted a double tomb to be placed in Westminster Abbey, fully intending to be laid to rest beside his wife. This was denied him by Henry IV, but Henry V wanted to close a door on past conflicts and had Richard's remains brought from Kings Langley and respectfully interred at Westminster. The images of king and queen were made by London craftsmen, Nicholas Broker and Godfrey Prest.*

PREVIOUS PAGE **A portrait of Henry V (1387–1422).** *This oil on panel portrait dates from the late 16th century or early 17th century. The profile pose is unusual.*

proved effective in keeping the northern border quiet. Henry could concentrate on reconciling those of his own people who still regarded the 'Lancastrians' (Henry IV and his son) as usurpers. In December 1413 he had the body of Richard II disinterred from its obscure grave at Kings Langley and placed in the impressive tomb that the late king had had prepared for himself in Westminster Abbey. This served the double purpose of demonstrating Henry's respect for Richard's memory and of emphasizing that Richard was definitely dead, for there were still some 'Yorkist' partisans who clung to the belief – or hope – that the old king was hiding in Scotland or some other sanctuary and waiting to reclaim his throne. The king offered pardons – at a price – to those who had been implicated in the recent rebellion, and he began negotiations for the release of Henry Percy, Hotspur's son, who was being held in Scotland. It was necessary to rehabilitate the Percys because they were the only family who could ensure the loyalty of the north.

Such great hope and good expectation was had of this man's fortunate success to follow, that within three days after his father's decease, divers noble men, and honourable personages, did to him homage, and swore to him due obedience, which had not been seen done to any of his predecessors kings of this Realm, till they had been possessed of the Crown.

Holinshed's Chronicles, 1577, IV, p. 1164

But Henry's first problem came from nearer home. Sir John Oldcastle, Baron Cobham, was a seasoned warrior who had fought in Wales and France and was personally known to the king. He was a substantial landowner in Herefordshire and Kent, and he was also a convinced Lollard, one of a small group of shire knights who formed a sort of 'aristocracy' in the largely working-class world of English heresy. Archbishop Arundel and his agents were still enthusiastic about tracking down suspected Lollards, and in the early days of the reign they discovered a cache of heretical tracts belonging to Oldcastle. Arundel, cautious about proceeding against one of the king's associates, informed Henry, who ordered a 'cooling-off period' while he personally tried to reason with the unorthodox knight. Oldcastle refused to budge from his criticism of the papacy and Catholic doctrine, and after several months Henry gave Arundel permission to instigate proceedings in his own court. Oldcastle was lodged, reasonably comfortably, in the Tower of London.

On 23 September the prisoner was taken to St Paul's Cathedral for his trial. The case had provoked enormous interest, and the church was packed with spectators, among whom were several men and women who shared Oldcastle's beliefs. The knight was duly found guilty and handed over to the secular arm. Once again, Henry intervened to allow the prisoner more time for reflection. Plans had probably already been made to rescue him, and on the night of 19 October Oldcastle escaped from the Tower (perhaps with the connivance

own marriage to Charles's youngest daughter, Catherine. And he asked for a huge dowry. Such extravagant demands doubtless were made as the opening gambit in diplomatic bargaining, but Henry had already decided that he would need to back it up with force. He borrowed large sums of money from the bishops and London merchants, including the wealthy mercer Richard Whittington. Yet as late as December 1414 parliament was urging him to reach an accord with Charles VI by peaceful means.

ABOVE **Sir John Oldcastle executed, 1417.** *The treatment of upper-class Lollards always posed a problem to governments. They had no hesitation about burning peasants and artisans at the stake but to execute leaders of society for their beliefs threatened the social order. Oldcastle was punished for both treason and heresy and there is some doubt about the exact details. According to the records he was taken to St Giles's Fields and there 'hung and burned hanging'. Whether Oldcastle was hanged first as a traitor and his body then burned is not clear.*

OPPOSITE **The madness of Charles VI.** *This illustration from the 15th-century* Chroniques d'Enguerrand de Monstrelet *indicates the moment when the French king's mental instability became apparent. He was riding with his entourage when a page dropped a spear. At this Charles went berserk with fear and began attacking his own men. Eventually, he had to be wrestled to the ground. Thereafter, he suffered temporary bouts of insanity that did not warrant the establishment of a permanent regency, but they did encourage rivalry among Charles's relatives for real control.*

RIGHT **Charles VI receiving English envoys** *in an illumination from* Froissart's Chronicles. *Charles and Henry IV had agreed a long extension of the existing Anglo-French truce but Henry V was bent on a more aggressive policy. Difficult negotiations ensued and were made more so by the arrogant behaviour of the dauphin.*

1415–16

AS ANGLO-FRENCH TALKS CONTINUED, the two sides grew further apart. In March 1415 the dauphin, having reached an agreement with the Duke of Burgundy not to support Henry's claims, sent a defiant message. Its insolence may have become exaggerated in the telling and retelling, but according to some sources the king of England was sent a case of tennis balls because playing games was more suited to his youth and inexperience than waging war. What may have stung Henry even more than such a rebuff was the charge that he should not lay claim to the crown of France when he was not even the rightful king of England.

While Henry gathered his army and prepared to cross the Channel there were still signs of disaffection at home. Sir John Oldcastle was still at large in the West Country, where he enjoyed not inconsiderable support, and in March 1415

Dick Whittington

'Turn again Whittington, thrice times Lord Mayor of London.' According to the legend, that was the message Dick Whittington (c.1350–1423) seemed to hear the bells of Bow church telling him when he was leaving the city in despair, having failed to discover that its streets were paved with gold. The story, which has become the basis of countless pantomimes, told how this poor orphan boy left the West Country and acquired a cunning cat, which performed prodigious feats as a ratter and helped his master's rapid rise to fame and fortune, until he did, indeed, become lord mayor three times. Richard Whittington was, certainly, a prominent and important figure in English history, but the facts of his life are more prosaic than the legend.

Whittington was no orphan, but, as a younger son of a minor Gloucestershire landowner, he certainly had a modest start in life. His father managed to get young Dick apprenticed to a London mercer (a merchant dealing in textiles and luxury goods). Thereafter, his rise was the result of a keen business brain and sheer hard work. He established important connections with the royal court, and among his customers were Robert de Vere, Richard II's favourite, John of Gaunt and Henry IV. His wealth enabled him to branch out into money-lending, because rich merchants, especially mercers and goldsmiths, were the first English bankers after the expulsion of the Jews by Edward I. Whittington was careful to keep clear of politics and was one of the leading financiers to the crown throughout three reigns. To Henry V he lent £2,000 in 1413, £1,333 in 1417 and £666 in 1421, and without men like Richard Whittington, Henry's French victories would not have been possible.

Throughout a business life that was, by the standards of the day, exceptionally long, Whittington served the Mercers' Company and the City of London in numerous capacities and funded many charitable causes. He did, indeed, live to be three times Lord Mayor of London – in 1397, 1406 and 1419.

his London associates fixed notices to church doors in the city warning that their revenge for the St Giles's Fields fiasco was imminent. There was some overlap with a Yorkist plot that blew up in the summer of 1415. Richard, Earl of Cambridge, and Sir Thomas Grey devised a plan to reunite all those parties that had been involved in the dynastic challenges of Henry IV's reign. While the king was out of the country they would negotiate Henry Percy's return to England, reactivate the old anti-Lancastrian alliance, stage a military coup and place the Earl of March on the throne. The conspirators were joined, somewhat surprisingly, by Henry, Lord Scrope of Masham, who had served Henry IV as treasurer, taken part in diplomatic missions for Henry V and was engaged to cross to France with the royal army. It is doubtful that the rebellion could have raised sufficient support to succeed even if (as some suspected) it was backed by French money, but it never got off the ground because the Earl of March revealed the details to the king on 31 July in Southampton, where the army was assembling. Cambridge, Grey and Scrope were swiftly tried and executed.

Henry's response to the French taunt

This I say unto you, *that before one year pass, I trust to make the highest crown of your country to stoop and the proudest mitre to kneel down: and say this unto the dauphin your master, that I within three months, will enter into France, not as into his land, but as into mine own true and lawful patrimony ... to conquer it, not with bragging words, flattering orations, or coloured persuasions but with puissance of men ... by the aid of God , in whom is my whole trust and confidence ... Therefore your safe conduct shall be to you delivered, with mine answer, and then you may depart surely and safely I warrant you in to your country, where I trust sooner to visit you, than you shall have cause to salute or bid me welcome.*

HOLINSHED'S CHRONICLES, 1577, IV, P. 1172

On 14 August Henry landed on the French coast near the town of Harfleur, on the north side of the Seine estuary, with some 10,500 troops. His immediate plan was to gain control of the river as a preliminary to capturing Rouen and invading Normandy. This would give him access to Paris and enable him to threaten the capital. Having unloaded all his men and equipment, the king laid siege to Harfleur on 17 August. But the town was well provisioned and Henry did not gain the quick initial victory he had hoped for. Moreover, the marsh estuary was a breeding ground for fever-bearing insects, and English numbers were rapidly diminished by disease, as the *Chronicle of the Grey Friars* recorded: 'there died many of his people, as the Earl of Surrey, the Bishop of Norwich, Sir John Philpot, and

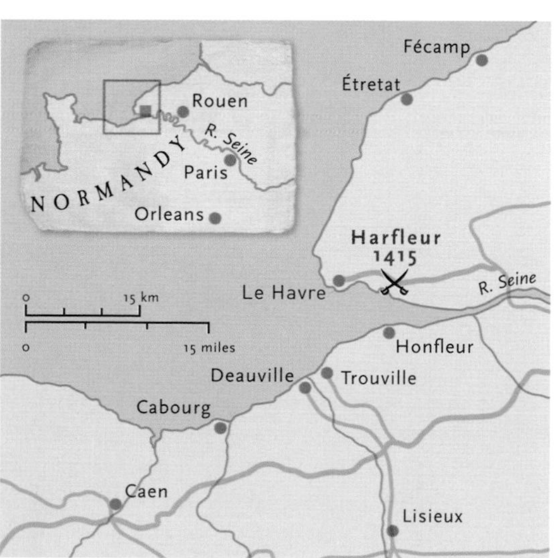

ABOVE **Henry landed near Harfleur** *in August 1415 and laid siege to the town.*

many other knights and squires, and a great many of the common people.'[2] Harfleur did not fall until 22 September.

With time lost and his army much diminished, Henry abandoned the planned ravaging of Normandy and, having sent home the sick and wounded, set out for Calais, where he could rest and provision his men and take stock of the situation. Including recent reinforcements, his army now numbered between 6,500 and 7,000 men. The French had assembled their own army and moved to intercept the invaders. With difficulty Henry got his men across the Somme. Many of them were weak with hunger, fever and long marching, and they did not relish the prospect of the pitched battle that now became inevitable.

On 25 October, the feast-day of Saints Crispin and Crispinian, Henry's small force of Englishmen faced 36,000 of the best knights and foot soldiers in France. The first three hours of daylight saw no action at all, for despite their overwhelming numerical superiority, the French were in no hurry to begin the engagement. They were blocking the road to Calais and were content to let the enemy try to break through. For his part, Henry knew that his only hope of success was fighting a defensive battle on a site of his own choosing. He positioned his main array in a broad defile between woodland close to the villages of Tramecourt and Agincourt, with archers on the flanks and in the front rank to fire into the expected charge of mounted knights as they were forced by the terrain to shorten their lines. The French chronicler Enguerrand de Monstrelet provides a vivid account of the battle. The English, he explained:

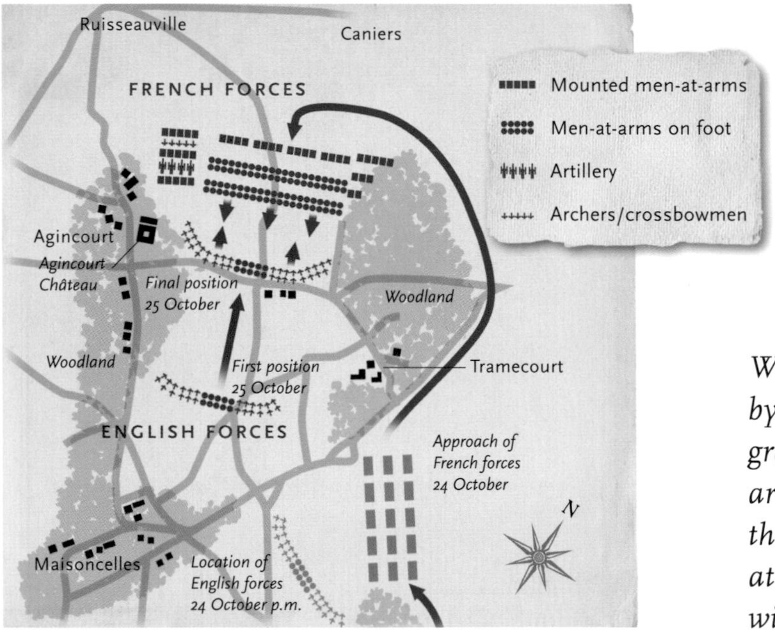

Were shortly after drawn up in battle array by Sir Thomas Erpingham, a knight grown grey with age and honour, who placed the archers in front, and the men-at-arms behind them. He then formed two wings of men-at-arms and archers, and posted the horses with the baggage at the rear ... When all was done to his satisfaction he flung into the air a truncheon ... crying out, 'Nestrocque!' and then dismounted, as the king and others had done. When the English saw Sir Thomas throw up his truncheon, they set up a loud shout, to the great astonishment of the French.[3]

ABOVE **The Battle of Agincourt, 25 October 1415.** *Although this engagement has always been regarded as a great British victory, it might be truer to consider it a spectacular French defeat. The French captains failed to draw the enemy into a position where their superior numbers would count. Though the ground was sodden and difficult and the front on which Henry V had chosen to fight was narrow, the French attack with mounted and foot soldiers was thrown into confusion by a rain of English arrows. When their charge was repulsed they had no room to regroup and manoeuvre.*

ABOVE **Armies advancing at the Battle of Agincourt**. *According to this French, near contemporary source both armies advanced over open ground with their archers in the front ranks. The impression that the bowmen were the most important element in determining victory is correct but the representation of tactics is not. Henry V did place his archers in front in order to repel an expected cavalry charge but, when the enemy failed to advance, moved forward with his archers on the flanks. The French bowmen were to the rear and in no position to play an effective role in the battle.*

RIGHT **The Battle of Agincourt.** *This English account from the 15th-century* St Alban's Chronicle *with Flemish illuminations conveys an impression of the slaughter into which the battle developed. On the right, French horsemen try to turn back but are hampered in the restricted space by fallen men and horses. Henry's knights are able to attack in force and turn the French defeat into a rout.*

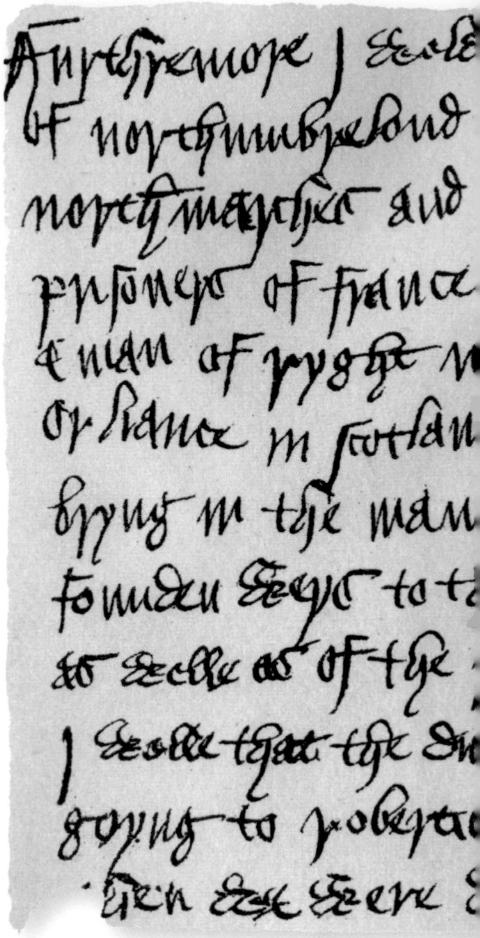

If this was meant to provoke the French knights into a charge, it failed. Henry, therefore, moved his battle line forward to a more exposed position. It is not clear from contemporary accounts exactly how the English bowmen were positioned. What is clear is that their contribution was decisive.

> *The archers who were hidden in the field, re-echoed these shouts, while the English army kept advancing on the French. Their archers ... let off a shower of arrows with all their might, and as high as possible, so as not to lose their effect ... Before ... the general attack commenced, numbers of the French were slain and severely wounded by the English bowmen ... others had their horses so severely handled by the archers that, smarting from pain, they galloped on the van division and threw it into the utmost confusion, breaking the line in many places ... horses and riders were tumbling on the ground, and the whole army was thrown into disorder, and forced back on some lands that had been just sown with corn.*[4]

Heavy overnight rain made things difficult for mounted knights and dismounted men-at-arms in heavy armour. The English soldiers were better dressed for the hand-to-hand fighting that now began: 'They were, for the most part, without any armour, and in jackets, with their hose loose, and hatchets or swords hanging to their girdles. Some, indeed, were barefoot and without hats.'[5] The French came on in divisions too closely packed to wield their weapons to best effect. The English absorbed the first impact, then made progress against the disorganized enemy: 'The English ... kept advancing and slaying without mercy all that opposed them, and thus destroyed the main battalion as they had done the first.'[6] Meanwhile, some 600 French troops circuited to the rear of the English lines and attacked the undefended baggage train.

ABOVE **A letter of Henry V, *c.*1419.** *The king spent much of his time in France and had to conduct English affairs by means of letters to his brother and deputy, John, Duke of Bedford. This one concerns arrangements to be made for royal prisoners. The Duke of Orleans and other French nobles had been captured at the Battle of Agincourt and James I of Scotland had been apprehended at sea in 1406. Reference is also made in the letter to a suspected plot hatched by Orleans and the Duke of Albany, regent in Scotland.*

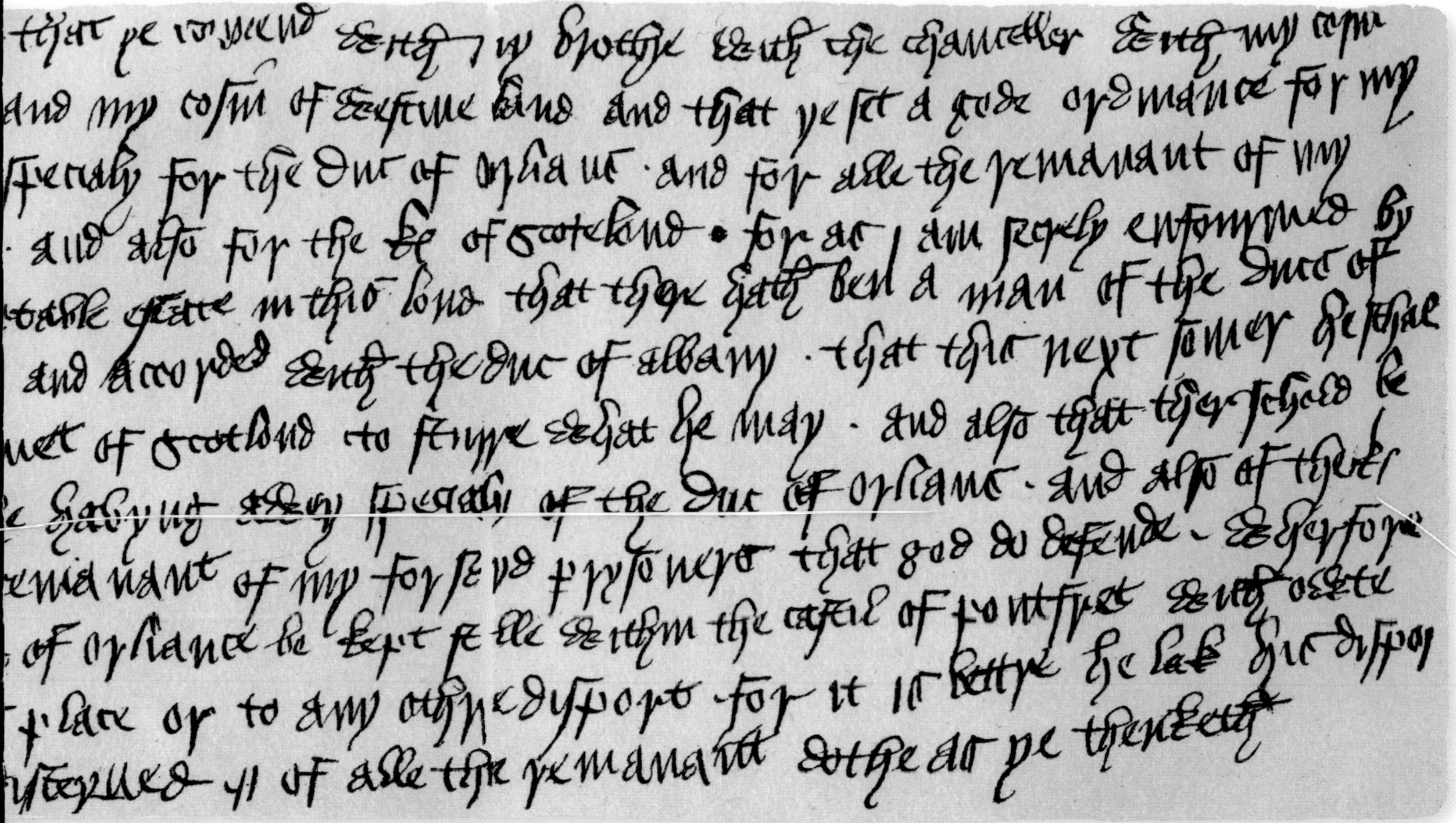

This distressed the king very much, for he saw that, though the enemy had been routed, they were collecting on different parts of the plain in large bodies and he was afraid they would renew the battle. He therefore caused instant proclamation to be made by sound of trumpet that everyone should put his prisoners to death, to prevent them from aiding the enemy, should the combat be renewed. This caused an instantaneous and general massacre of the French prisoners.[7]

The slaughter was not quite as 'instantaneous' as the chronicler intimated. Many captors were reluctant to give up the prospect of collecting ransoms for their prisoners, and the king had to enforce his order with a threat of execution for any who disobeyed. French losses at Agincourt amounted to some 12,000 or 13,000, including three dukes, five counts, more than 90 barons and almost 2,000 knights. The English dead amounted to less than a thousand.

The English army travelled on to Calais from where Henry returned to England. On 23 November he made a triumphal entry to London amid scenes of great rejoicing.

Harfleur gave Henry a new bargaining counter with France and diplomacy was resumed, and this time the king was assisted in the negotiations by the Emperor Sigismund, who paid a long state visit to England in the summer of 1416. Sigismund was acting as the peace-maker of Europe. He was intent on solving the problems of the

a vous entier
a vous entier
a vous entier
a vous entier
a vous entier

divided church and wished to unite all Christian monarchs in this enterprise. However, the French king was mentally incapable, and the dauphin could think of nothing but casting off the humiliation of the recent defeat. As for the Duke of Burgundy, Henry's supposed ally, he was too duplicitous to be trusted.

French land and sea forces blockaded Harfleur and had every expectation of depriving Henry of this prize. In August the king's brother, John, Duke of Bedford, led a fleet to the mouth of the Seine and broke the blockade, and at the same time Henry and Sigismund signed a treaty of mutual defence. In October 1416 Henry, having exhausted all diplomatic means, obtained from parliament a grant of taxation to resume the war.

1417–20

IN AUGUST 1417 Henry was back in France with a new army equipped with cannon to reduce any towns or castles that resisted him. In September he seized Caen and made it the centre of his administration of the province. Other major towns were taken over the

OPPOSITE **John, Duke of Bedford (1389–1435).** *A devotional image of Henry V's brother and deputy. This illumination is from the* Bedford Missal *(1423). It shows the duke praying to his patron saint, St George, a warrior saint who wears armour beneath his cloak and is accompanied by a squire carrying his pennant. The elaborate border carries images of Christian martyrs. Bedford was an important patron of artists and writers and commissioned several superb illuminated books.*

ABOVE **The Emperor Sigismund (1368–1437).** *This painting, c.1600 by Albrecht Dürer, displays his heraldic emblems as Holy Roman Emperor and king of Bohemia, Hungary and Croatia. From his election as emperor in 1411 Sigismund pursued grand ambitions. He sought to end the challenge of Hussite heretics in Bohemia, unite Christendom against the Muslim Turks, raise the moral tone of the church establishment and end the schism in western Christendom. It was his efforts to end the unseemly conflict between rival popes that moved him to seek the support of Henry V and other rulers for his own preferred candidate.*

THE WARS OF THE ROSES

Freres germains
Cousins ou
Second degre
Cousins ou
Tiers degre
Cousins ou
Quint degre
Roy henry

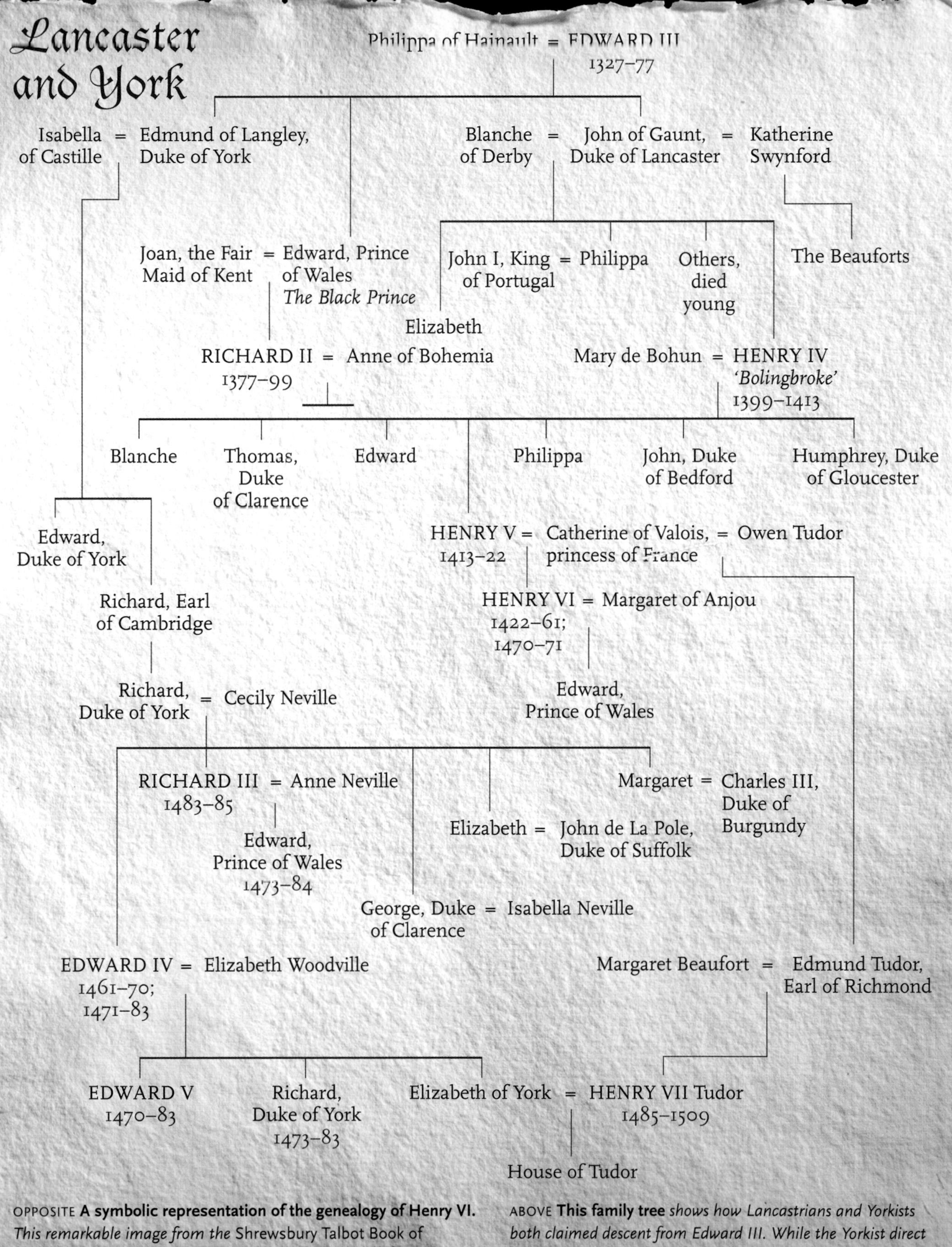

OPPOSITE **A symbolic representation of the genealogy of Henry VI.** *This remarkable image from the* Shrewsbury Talbot Book of Romances *by the Flemish Master of Hoo was presented to Margaret of Anjou on her marriage to Henry in 1445. Henry's descent and right to the two crowns is represented on a large fleur de lys. Margaret's standard supported by an antelope is shown on the right.*

ABOVE **This family tree** *shows how Lancastrians and Yorkists both claimed descent from Edward III. While the Yorkist direct line remained strong, the Lancastrians' descent through the male line ended with the death of Edward, Prince of Wales in 1471. The Tudors could only claim descent through Henry V's widow.*

This year the xxi day of October was the parliament at Westminster. And the xxvi day of November the king was brought in to the Parliament. And the same day the king removed to Waltham, and the parliament was prorogued to the xx day after Christmas.

'A SHORT ENGLISH CHRONICLE: LONDON UNDER HENRY VI (1422–7)', *THREE FIFTEENTH-CENTURY CHRONICLES*, ED. J. GAIRDNER, 1880, P. 58

Gloucester. A third member of the ruling triumvirate was the king's great-uncle, Henry Beaufort, Bishop of Winchester. These three men dominated the royal council that ruled in the king's name during his minority, and despite personality clashes and major differences of opinion among the royal uncles, this system initially worked surprisingly well.

In November 1423 the infant king was taken from his residence at Windsor to Westminster to receive the homage of parliament. Every effort was made to bond the leading families of the realm with the child-king – they were ordered to send their own young sons to the royal court to be brought up in what was, in effect, a noble academy – and at every possible opportunity Henry was shown to his subjects. For example, in April 1425 Henry was taken to St Paul's Cathedral, 'led upon his feet between the Lord Protector and the Duke of Exeter unto the choir, whence he was borne to the high altar'. After the service, he was 'set upon a fair courser and so conveyed through Cheapside and the other streets of the city'.[1]

But there was a different mood abroad the following November when Henry was paraded through London once again. This time he was being used as a pawn in the quarrel between Gloucester and Beaufort. Only days before there had arisen, 'a great dissention between the Duke of Gloucester and the Bishop of Winchester, that was to be Chancellor, for the which all London rose with the Duke against the foresaid bishop'.[2] Beaufort, acting as president of the council during the absence of the king's two uncles, had offended the chief men of the city by not taking action to curtail the privileges enjoyed by foreign merchants. This was such a bone of contention that a mob threatened to duck the bishop in the Thames if they could lay hands on him.

OPPOSITE **Portrait of Henry VI (1421–71).** *This image, after an original by the French artist, François Clouet (c.1510–72), shows the king as a young man. It is not a strong face and by the time Henry had reached his majority it must have been obvious to those close to him that he was not cast in the same heroic martial mould as his father. Contemporaries sometimes described his features as 'childlike' and came to regard him as 'simple' and ineffectual. Henry was bookish and not unintelligent, but he was inconsistent, easily manipulated by stronger characters and more interested in the trappings of royalty than good governance. Before his mental deterioration (which manifested itself in the 1450s) the conviction was growing among many of the king's subjects that he was unfit to rule. During the previous century two kings had been deposed. A precedent had been set for the people to pass judgement on their divinely anointed king.*

When Gloucester returned from France he
his position, and in October 1425 the two men
Bridge, Beaufort with some of his armed retai
armed men drawn from the city and the inns
spilling of blood, but Gloucester claimed a vict
rode through the streets of London days later
to resolve the family feud, and it was he who b
Leicester in February 1426, to preside over the

In France there was political stalemate. Th
allies controlled the country north of the Loire
recognized by his followers as Charles VII, ru
rival king had been crowned at Rheims, which
of influence, and so was not recognized as the
Military action had not changed the situation
1428, Bedford laid siege to Orleans. That was
events in history occurred. A 17-year-old peasa
France gained an audience with Charles at Ch
had been selected by God to lead his armies to
of Arc had an aura about her that inspired Ch
she really did hear angelic voices and might b
was provided with a horse and armour and ac
the siege. The siege of Orleans was successful
victory, Charles broke through English lines to
crowned on 17 July 1429.

This event added urgency to the need for H
at Westminster on 5 November, and plans wer
for his sacred initiation as French king. In Ap
a large army to reinforce the one already there
was captured by the Burgundians. Deserted by
victory, she was examined by the Inquisition o
and in May 1431 was burned at the stake. The
France prevented Henry from being crowned
Beaumont, recently made a cardinal, presided
but at Notre Dame in Paris. Shortly afterwards
changed sides and this initiated the gradual co
In February 1432 Henry's only visit to France

English fortunes in France did not improve
Gloucester and Cardinal Beaufort could not ag
held at Arras in 1435 but broke up in disagreem
and in the same month the alliance of Charles
was formalized.

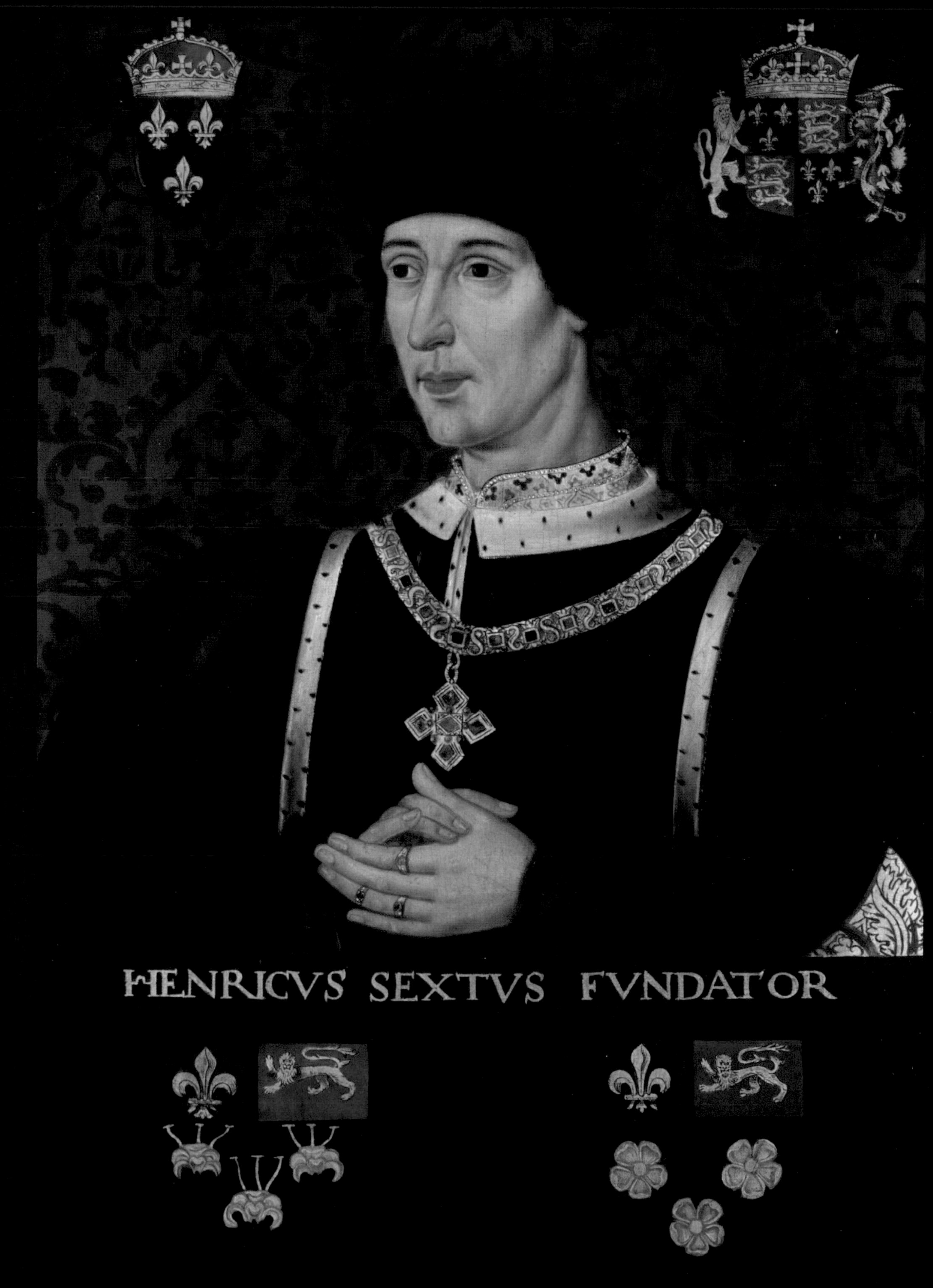

Joan of Arc's ultimatur

King of England *and you Duke of Bedford, callin yourself Regent of France ... Surrender to the Maid sent hither, by God the King of Heaven, the keys of all the good towns you have taken and laid waste in France. She comes in God's name to establish the*

THE WARS OF THE ROSES ✦ *1422–1471*

RIGHT **Henry VI as king of France, 1442.** *In this painting from a contemporary manuscript the king is shown investing John Talbot, Earl of Shrewsbury (c.1388–1453) as Constable of France. Talbot was the most dashing English military commander of the day. Campaigning in France between 1427 and 1453, he led several successful sieges and was twice captured. Unsurprisingly, his promotion was rapid. By 1436 he was Captain of Rouen and Henry's representative in northwest France and by 1439 he was Lieutenant General in France. In 1442 he was created Earl of Shrewsbury and Constable of France; in 1446 he was made Earl of Waterford and Steward of Ireland; and in 1451 he became Lieutenant of Aquitaine. After his death at the Battle of Castillon in 1453 the French generals raised a monument to the commander whose leadership and courage they respected.*

Item des proprietez que doivent avoir gens darmes
et en quoy doivent estre duitz.
Item commence a parler des manieres qui affien
a bon connestable ou chevetain a tenir en son office.

Perpendicular Gothic

John Leland, the 16th-century traveller and antiquary, was impressed with St Mary's Church Nottingham because it was 'uniform in work' and had 'so many fair windows in it that no artificer can imagine to set more there'.[3] He thus identified the most obvious feature of the last stage of Gothic church architecture known as Perpendicular.

Design had continued to develop since the Decorated period, and architects had been particularly interested in grappling with problems of bringing more light into churches and providing larger areas of stained glass to tell the stories of biblical characters and saints. This meant that the spaces between windows had to be narrower and pillars more slender. In order to lessen the load carried by the walls, roofs were often made of timber, rather than stone. With decorative interest now concentrated in the windows, less space was available for paintings and carvings. Interiors were, therefore, simpler and less 'cluttered', hence Leland's approval of the 'uniform' appearance of St Mary's.

The openness of the new style sometimes extended to the roof, where single supporting beams extending the width of the church were replaced by hammer-beams, shorter timbers whose weight was carried to the walls by arched braces. The projecting ends provided fresh decorative opportunities and were frequently provided with carved angels or heraldic devices. The finest example of a hammer-beam roof is that in Westminster Hall, which was refurbished by Richard II in the 1390s. Another spectacular form of roof decoration was the intricate fan vault, made up of interlacing stone ribs.

The emergence of Perpendicular

Perpendicular began to emerge as a distinct style in the second half of the 14th century, and it reached its peak during the Wars of the Roses. This was largely because the increase in mercantile activity created a new breed of capitalists who directed their patronage into building, extending or embellishing their local churches. Because the increase in prosperity was largely associated with the trade in wool and cloth, many Perpendicular churches – particularly in East Anglia, the West Country and Yorkshire – are known as 'wool churches'. Outstanding examples are Sherborne Abbey, Gloucester Abbey and Beverley Minster.

Patrons of church building

Both Henry VI and Edward IV were enthusiastic patrons of church building. Henry took a considerable step forward in the royal patronage of educational and ecclesiastical buildings with the founding of Eton College (1440) and King's College, Cambridge (1441). He was passionately devoted to their development and embarked on these projects as soon as he assumed full control of the government, as the charter of Eton College stated: 'Having now taken into our hands the government of both our kingdoms, [we] have from the very beginning of our riper age carefully revolved in our mind how, or in what manner, or by what royal gift, according to the measure of our devotion and the example of our ancestors we could do fitting honour to that our same Mistress and most holy Mother [the church].'[4] Edward was responsible for the building of St George's Chapel at Windsor Castle. All were fine examples of the Perpendicular style, although completed after the death of the founders. Henry's queen, Margaret of Anjou, founded Queens' College, Cambridge. With the Perpendicular we see the emergence of an English style quite distinct from that prevailing on the continent.

OPPOSITE **St George's Chapel, Windsor Castle**. *This shows the dramatic fan-vault decoration and a ceiling boss with the arms of Edward IV. Building was completed early in the 16th century.*

RIGHT **Westminster Hall.** *This magnificent building dates from the 11th century, though the hammer-beam roof is a later introduction from the 14th century. Westminster Hall is the only remaining part of the original Westminster Palace and is incorporated in the present Houses of Parliament, built between 1840 and 1870.*

Par lenuie du dyable
la mort print entree
ou monde. Et ce le
ensuiuent ceulx qui tiennent sō

Marjorie Jourdemain, the Witch of Eye, to bring about Henry's demise. Henry, particularly sensitive to spiritual influences, both evil and benign, took a close personal interest in the trial of the offenders, which resulted in Eleanor's forced divorce and her lifelong incarceration in a succession of detention centres.

The continuing squabbles between Gloucester and Beaufort undermined their credibility and paved the way for new influences to enter the king's life. The principal beneficiary was William de la Pole, Earl of Suffolk, who had served with distinction in the French war, had been sworn on to the council and was appointed Steward of the Household. He now became Henry's closest adviser and from about 1440 set about achieving a peace settlement with France, backing an alliance involving the marriage of Henry to Margaret of Anjou, the French queen's niece. Arrangements were concluded in 1444, and in the following May the 15-year-old queen was rapturously received in London. With a young royal couple capable of producing an heir on the throne and lasting peace in prospect the people had much to celebrate.

The rejoicing was short-lived. Within months it was learned that, as part of the marriage negotiations, England had forfeited Maine and Anjou. When, despite this sacrifice, war resumed, with Margaret's father, the

Dame Eleanor Cobham … was made to go through London openly bearing a taper in her hand by penance enjoined by the Church and the King, and after her body to perpetual prison. And the clerk was damned to be hanged, drawn and quartered, and the witch was burned in Smithfield for treason.

'A Short English Chronicle: London under Henry VI (1422–7)', p. 63

Lament written by Eleanor in captivity

This is no life, alas, that I do lead;
It is but death as in life's likeness,
Endless sorrow assured out of dread,
Past all despair and out of all gladness.
Thus well, I know, I am remedyless,
For me nothing may comfort nor amend
Till death come forth and make of me an end.

Secular Lyrics of the XIVth and XVth Centuries, ed. R.H. Robbins, 1952, No. 165

OPPOSITE **Witchcraft** *depicted in a page from the* Tractatus Contra Sectam Valdensium *by John Tinctor, c.1470. In an era when, for most people, the world beyond the confines of their village was largely unknown and the vastness of the universe was mostly a mystery, superstition filled the gaps in human knowledge. Spirits and demons were believed to exist beyond the material realm. Sorcerers and witches were believed to have the power to conjure up such beings and to manipulate the unseen world for the benefit of their clients. Tinctor's book was a supposed exposure of the practices of the Waldensians, a heretical Christian sect that existed in southern France and northern Italy from the 12th–16th centuries. Church leaders tried to blacken the reputation of the Waldensians by erroneously accusing them of worshipping Satan in the form of a goat.*

Margaret crowned

The xxix day of May *all the crafts of London with the Mayor and Aldermen met with the queen on horseback in blue gowns embroidered and red hoods, and brought her to the Tower of London; and on the same day was made xlvii knights of the Bath. And on the morrow all the crafts of London in their best array brought her to Westminster, and all the aforesaid knights afore riding. And the xxx day of May ... she was crowned at Westminster. And iii days after open jousting to all that would come.*

'A Short English Chronicle: London under Henry V (1422-7)', I, p. 64

Duke of Anjou, among the leaders of the army that invaded Normandy, the queen's popularity slumped. Nevertheless, she rapidly began to exert influence over her husband and, in concert with Suffolk, turned him decisively against Gloucester. In February 1447, when the duke arrived at Bury St Edmunds to attend parliament, he was arrested. His enemies intended to charge him with treason, but he died, as one chronicler puts it, in sinister circumstances, 'the sickness how God knoweth'. In April Cardinal Beaufort died. It was the end of an era.

1449–54

BY THE TIME PARLIAMENT MET in November 1449 the government was in crisis. The English army in Normandy was being steadily driven back from fortress to fortress. The treasury was empty. There was growing resentment at the suspicious death of Gloucester, for which Suffolk was blamed by the populace. But what lay at the root of the widespread and growing discontent was the personal

ABOVE **Humphrey, Duke of Gloucester** *(1390–1447) in a 16th-century Flemish drawing from the* Recueil d'Arras. *This collection of copies of portraits of 14th–16th-century celebrities was probably made by the French herald, Jacques le Boucq, who used black or red chalks to copy earlier portraits, thus bringing a touch of Renaissance realism to representations that were often icons rather than accurate likenesses. Humphrey was very close to his brother Henry V, who nominated him guardian of the infant Henry VI and designated him as regent in the event of the Duke of Bedford dying before Henry VI achieved his majority. Humphrey, as an effective military leader, was also popular with the people. Margaret of Anjou and her entourage inevitably saw the king's uncle as a threat to their power. Humphrey's death was probably the result of a stroke but conspiracy theories about how he died were soon circulating.*

ineffectiveness of the king. Not only was Henry the first king not to lead his armies in foreign battle, he was also incapable of directing policy. But he seems to have been oblivious of the mounting malaise. He lavished lands, titles and appointments on Suffolk, who was made a duke in 1348, and when the Duke of Somerset, leader of land forces in France, returned after a disastrous and lacklustre campaign, the king publicly expressed complete confidence in him. However, parliament called Suffolk to account and in January 1450 despatched him to the Tower, accusing him of enriching himself at the nation's expense, of misleading the king and of plotting to assassinate him. Henry tried to save his friend and minister by issuing an edict of banishment, but this had two results: it diminished Henry's reputation still further, and it allowed Suffolk to escape. The duke was captured in May as he tried to board a ship, and he was immediately beheaded by a group of sailors.

Suffolk's body was brought ashore at Dover, and within days hundreds of men from Kent and the southeast were marching on London. What the leaders of Cade's Rebellion, as this protest movement was known, were protesting about was a 'lack of governance'. They regarded themselves not as rebels but petitioners. There was general discontent about the collapse of law and order throughout the country, and, as is usual in popular revolts, the spokesmen protested their loyalty, insisting that they only wished to rid the king of his 'evil councillors'. But what fixed the timing of this revolt and gave it its emotional intensity was the loss of Normandy – the final English stronghold fell in July. Not only was this a huge blow to national pride, it also brought great suffering to thousands of English families who had settled in the English cross-Channel dominions and were now forced to flee, leaving their homes, lands and livelihoods behind them. These destitute refugees, smouldering with resentment, were now entering the country through the ports along the southeast coast.

There are similarities between the rebellion of 1450 and that of 1391, but there are also important differences. The leader, Jack Cade, was a smooth-tongued Irishman and an ex-soldier. During the brief insurrection he was guilty of cold-blooded murder and other acts of violence. With a small army at his back he attacked London and, while claiming to be acting in the public interest, accumulated a considerable amount of personal loot. However, his supporters were far from being a vulgar rabble. Included in their number were 74 gentlemen, 500 yeomen and numerous merchants and craftsmen. Important dignitaries included members of parliament, the mayor of Queenborough, the bailiff of Sandwich as well as several constables (manorial officers responsible for keeping the peace) and commissioners of array (officials charged with mustering local levies in the event of threatened invasion). These leaders of rural and urban society were concerned about the state of the country, and they joined Cade's protest march to draw the government's attention to ills that were crying out for

Lawlessness

'God in his mercy give grace that there may be set a good rule and a wise [one] in the country in haste, for I heard never say of so much robbery and manslaughter in this country as is now within a little time.'[5] So wrote the Norfolk gentlewoman Margaret Paston in 1462, describing the disturbed state of affairs in East Anglia, and the situation there was no worse than in most other parts of the kingdom. It was the state of general lawlessness that was both a cause and a result of the Wars of the Roses.

Effective power had always lain in the hands of the major landholders, who used force, threats and bribes to maintain their control, but the intermittent fighting between Yorkist and Lancastrian magnates made matters worse and led to a virtually complete breakdown of law and order in many parts of the country. Leading landowners kept bands of armed retainers for their protection and for the maintenance of their own local standing, and it was such small private armies that the Lancastrian and Yorkist leaders relied on when they were gathering their forces for the next round in the battle for the crown.

Petition sent to the king

The manner in which the principle of 'might is right' filtered down through the social levels came home to the Pastons in 1450. The Lancastrian baron, Lord Moleyns, came with 1,000 men to turn Margaret out of the Paston manor at Gresham. John Paston, her husband, appealed to the sheriff to help him regain possession. This official acknowledged that Paston was in the right but regretted that he dared not intervene because Moleyns was the Duke of Norfolk's protégé.

It was not just unfortunate individuals unable to obtain justice who felt aggrieved. In 1472, parliament sent a petition to the king:

> *In divers parts of this realm great abominable murders, robberies, extortions oppressions and other manifold maintenances, misgovernances, forcible entries ... affrays, assaults be committed and done by such persons as either be of great might, or else favoured under persons of great power, in such wise that their outrageous demerits as yet remain unpunished, insomuch that of late divers persons have been slain, some in Southwark, and here nigh about the City, and some here at Westminster Gate, no consideration taken ... that your high presence is had here at your Palace of Westminster, nor that your high court of Parliament is here sitting, and is in a manner a contumelious contempt of your Highness.*[6]

John Bredhill

Where the great led, lesser men inevitably followed. Private feuding was rife at all levels of society. At Kingswinford, Staffordshire, it was the local vicar, John Bredhill, who was the centre of controversy in the 1430s. The locals accused him of arson, theft, poaching, affray and rape, but they were powerless to oppose him because, as a clergyman, he was

OPPOSITE **A letter of Margaret Paston** *from a remarkable collection of over 1,000 letters written by members of this Norfolk family between 1422 and 1509. They provide a unique glimpse of what was happening to ordinary people not directly involved in the Wars of the Roses. Margaret's husband, John (1421–66), was a Cambridge-educated, upwardly mobile gentleman who divided his time between his East Anglian estate and his legal practice in London. Provincial landowners found it very valuable to maintain contacts in the court and the capital. Society was based on patronage and ordinary families could find themselves up against adversaries who had the backing of powerful nobles like the Duke of Norfolk – as the Pastons discovered.*

answerable only in the ecclesiastical courts where any case was likely to be decided in his favour or where, if found guilty, he would be ordered to perform some simple act of penance, instead of receiving a sentence of imprisonment, branding or death, which would have been the lot of any layman in the same circumstances. Eventually the villagers appealed to Baron Dudley, the lord of the manor. He waited until Bredhill was away and then: [with] 'John Sheldon, John Clerk, Thomas Young and Thomas Bradley ... wrongfully entered into the parsonage ... and there broke up 4 coffers and bore away the goods that were in the same coffers and all other goods that your said suppliant [Bredhill] had. Also they put his servants out of their place.'[7] They then went on to indulge an orgy of destruction, stripping the house and barns, trampling crops, breaking fences, filling ditches and felling trees. When Bredhill came back his response was to carry out similar raids on the property of those he believed to be responsible.

Royal justice had all but broken down by the middle of the century when a chronicler complained in verse:

The law is like unto a Welshman' hose,
To each man's leg that shapen is and mete [fitting];
So maintainers subvert it and transpose,
Through might it is full low laid under feet.[8]

'Maintainers' were henchmen sent into court to uphold their lord's case by whatever means lay to hand. This might involve giving perjured evidence, bribing or threatening jurors, or suborning witnesses. When such activities were the norm rather than the exception, so that ordinary people stood little chance of obtaining justice through the courts, it is not surprising that men like Jack Cade and his followers rose in rebellion.

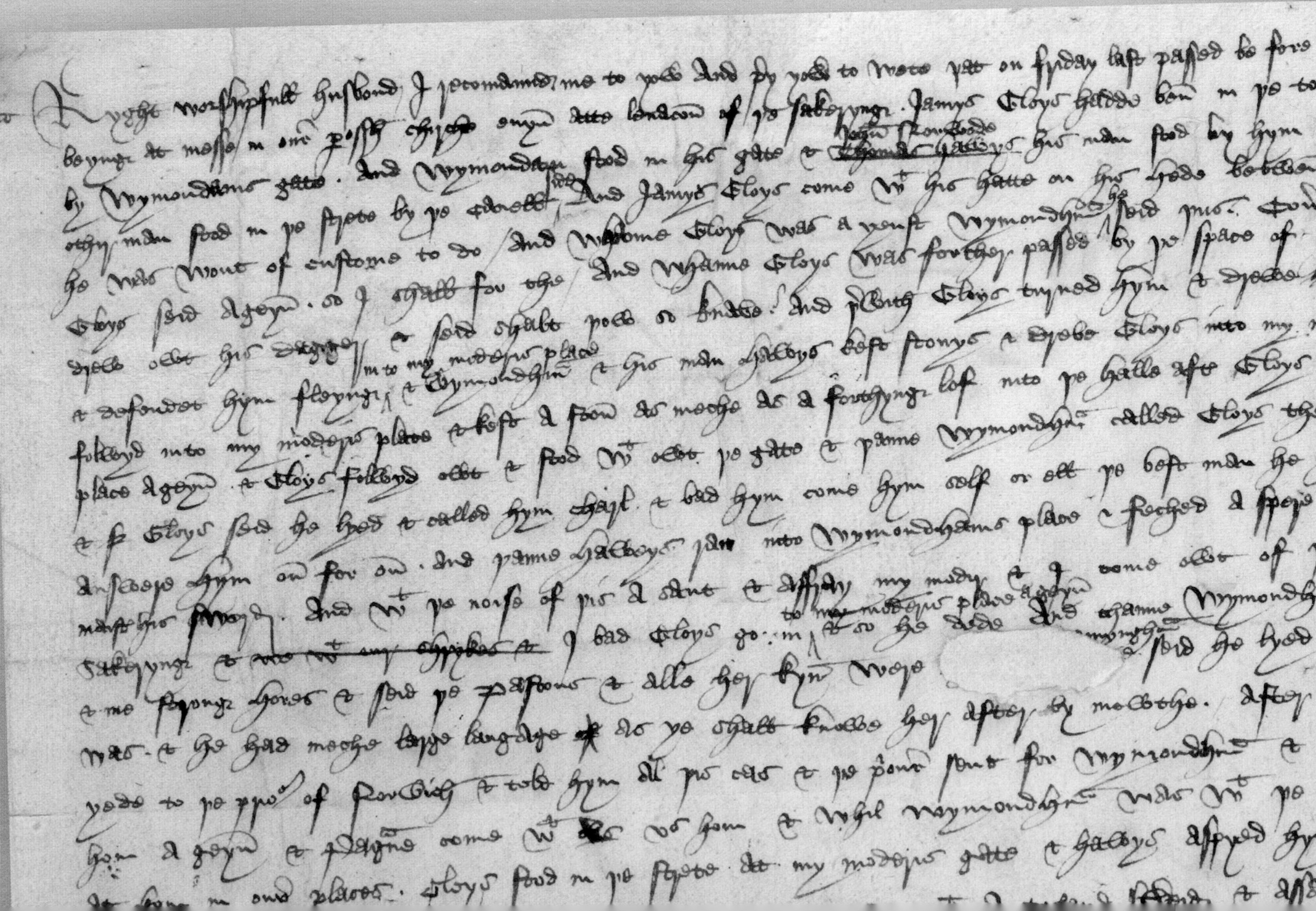

redress. To gull the 'better sort' into following him, Cade called himself 'John Mortimer', a supposed cousin of the Duke of York (the current heir presumptive to the throne; see p. 334).

Cade's host marched to Blackheath and published their demands in placards sent to the king and widely distributed. The list of grievances was a long one but may be summed up in two clauses from the rebels' petition:

> *The law serveth of naught else in these days but for to do wrong, for nothing is sped almost but false matters by colour [under cover] of the law for mede [bribery], drede [fear] and favour, and so no remedy is had in the court of [according to] conscience ...*
>
> *We say our sovereign lord may understand that his false council hath lost his law, his merchandise is lost, his common people is destroyed, the sea is lost [a reference to the French having regained control of the Channel], France is lost, the king himself is so set that he may not pay for his meat nor drink and he oweth more than ever any King of England ought, for daily his traitors about him where anything else should come to him by his laws, anon they ask it from him.*[9]

Henry set out to with an army to meet the rebels, who immediately dispersed because they did not want to be labelled as traitors. However, when the king tried to follow and round up the rebels several of his own captains refused to proceed against their countrymen. Henry, having no confidence that he could command obedience, withdrew, first to Berkhamsted and later to Kenilworth.

RIGHT **A map of Scotland** *by John Hardyng (1378–c.1475). Hardyng was a chronicler who enjoyed the patronage of the Percys. He served under Henry V at Agincourt and later under the Duke of Bedford. His major work was his* Chronicle, *a verse history of England. To this he attached his map of Scotland, a country he knew well. His object seems to have been to persuade the then king, Edward IV, to invade Scotland. He represented the country as a populous land, surrounded by water and containing several fair towns, castles and churches, which are not related to each other in accurate geographical terms.*

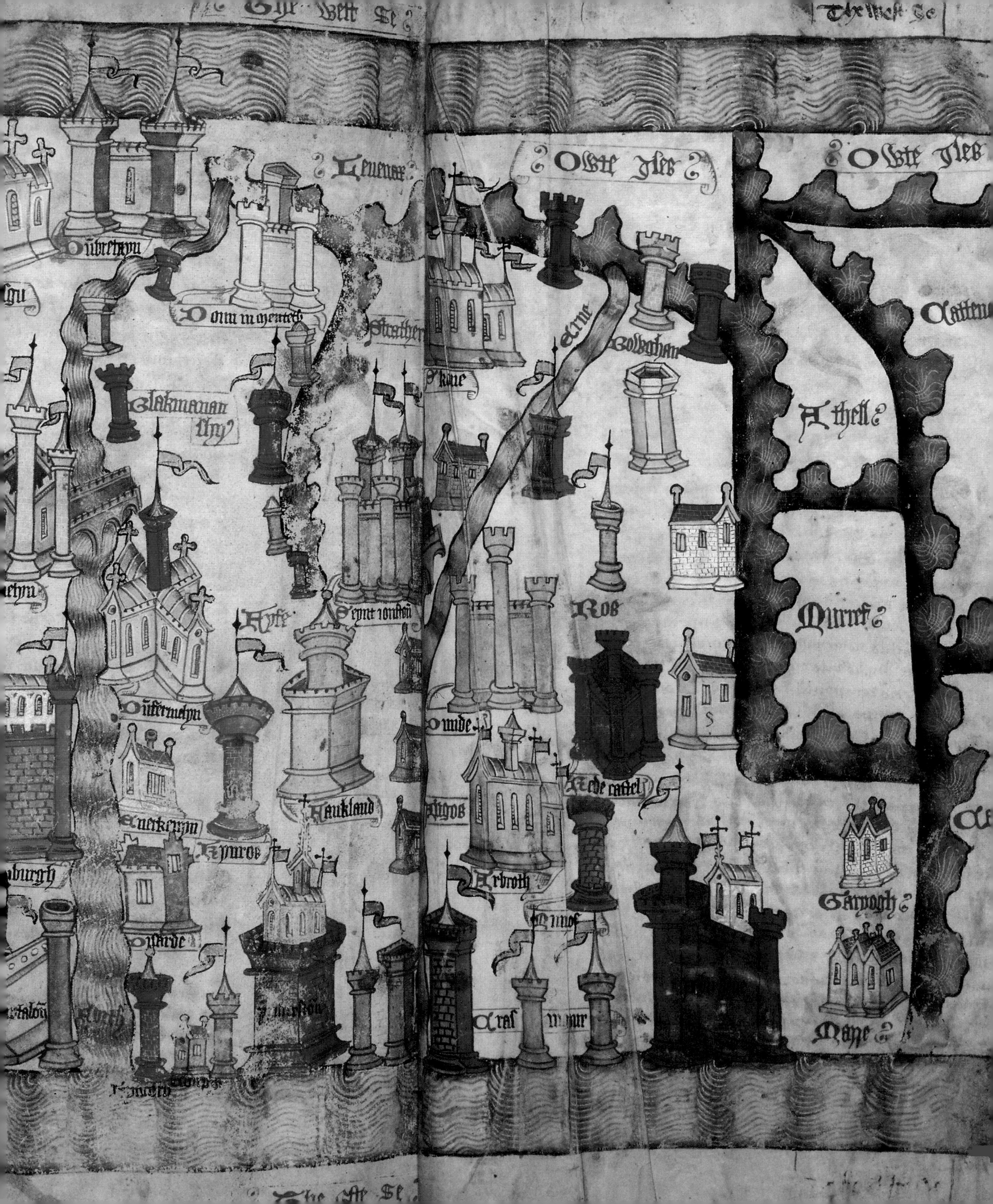
The West Se
Leuenax
Owte Iles
Owte Iles
Strathern
Athell
Murref
Ros
Dunde
Arbroth
Faukland
Dunfermlyn
Kynros
Garvogh
Mane

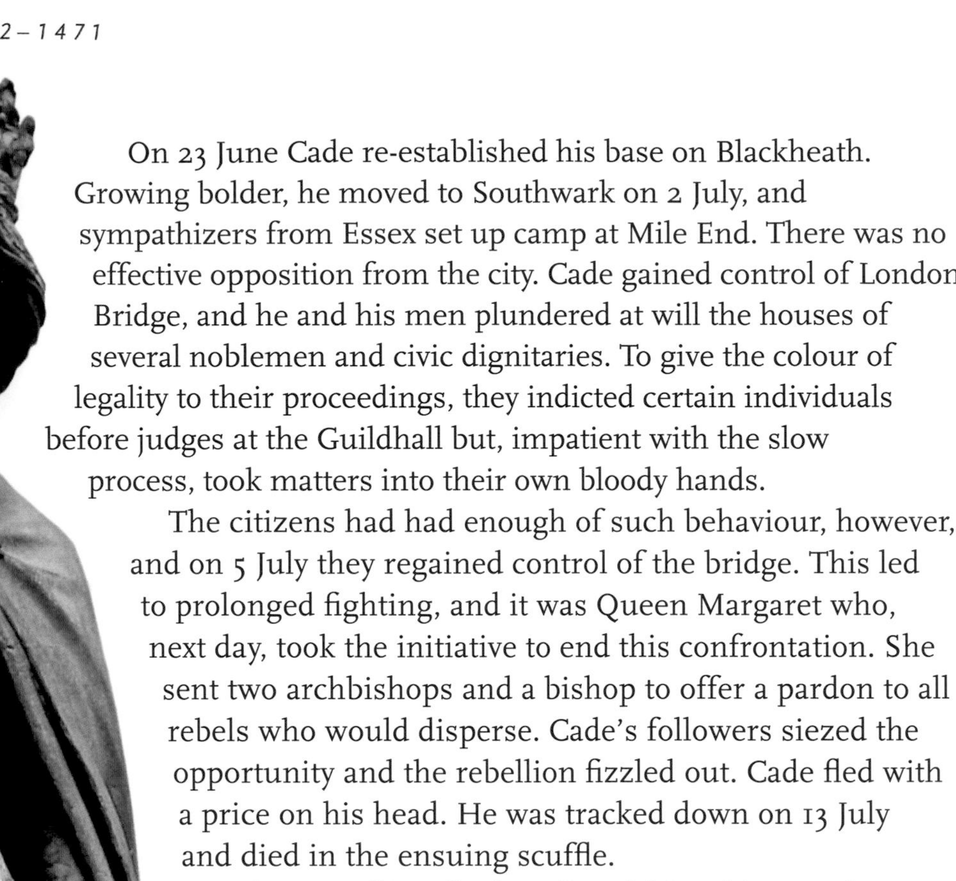

On 23 June Cade re-established his base on Blackheath. Growing bolder, he moved to Southwark on 2 July, and sympathizers from Essex set up camp at Mile End. There was no effective opposition from the city. Cade gained control of London Bridge, and he and his men plundered at will the houses of several noblemen and civic dignitaries. To give the colour of legality to their proceedings, they indicted certain individuals before judges at the Guildhall but, impatient with the slow process, took matters into their own bloody hands.

The citizens had had enough of such behaviour, however, and on 5 July they regained control of the bridge. This led to prolonged fighting, and it was Queen Margaret who, next day, took the initiative to end this confrontation. She sent two archbishops and a bishop to offer a pardon to all rebels who would disperse. Cade's followers siezed the opportunity and the rebellion fizzled out. Cade fled with a price on his head. He was tracked down on 13 July and died in the ensuing scuffle.

This appalling display of weak kingship was the background to the intervention of Richard, Duke of York. In the absence of any son born to Henry and Margaret he was heir presumptive to the throne. On his father's side he was descended from Edward III's fifth son, Edmund, Duke of York, and on his mother's side from Edward III's third son, Lionel, Duke of Clarence. His claim was, therefore, impeccable. In addition, he had acquired great wealth by marrying into the powerful Neville family (his father-in-law was Earl of Westmorland and his brother-in-law was Earl of Salisbury). He had served with some distinction in the French wars and, because of the poverty and incompetence of Henry's government, had funded the army largely out of his own purse. York had been removed from his military position in France in favour of the Duke of Somerset, who had been largely responsible for the loss of England's cross-Channel possessions. Unsurprisingly, York and Somerset loathed each other, but Somerset had the advantage of enjoying the king's favour. In 1447 York was appointed the king's lieutenant in Ireland, to get him out of the way, but the more the king and his council lost credibility, the more people looked to York to restore morale and efficient government.

In September 1450 York returned from Ireland without permission. His motives were probably a mixture of a desire to assert his own right to a place on the council and a response to pleas that he should break the power of the Somerset clique. His appearance certainly alarmed the Lancastrian leadership, and efforts were made to arrest him. Nevertheless, he reached London and established himself on the king's council. During the next two years the rival factions vied with each other for power, but Somerset continued to enjoy royal support.

In July 1453 England suffered the final humiliation of the loss of Gascony, and of all the continental lands that Henry VI had inherited only Calais now remained. It may have been this disastrous news that broke the king's health, and he had a complete mental breakdown. The implications for the country and the dynasty were dire. Ironically, it was at this time that Queen Margaret was delivered on 13 October of the long-awaited heir, christened Edward, but the king's incapacity made it imperative to make arrangements for a regency. Margaret, who now began to emerge as the real power behind the throne, staked her claim, but the following spring parliament appointed York as protector and defender of the king and realm, and he wasted no time in having Somerset and his other opponents arrested.

In December Henry recovered as suddenly as he had fallen ill, and the roundabout of power turned again. Somerset, released from the Tower, was determined on a showdown with his rival, and both sides gathered their forces for a possible military confrontation.

Beheaded

[Cade, the captain] *caused Sir James Fines, Lord Say and Treasurer of England, to be brought to the Guildhall, and there to be arraigned; who ... desired to be tried by his peers, for the longer delay of his life. The captain perceiving his dilatory plea, by force took him from the officers, and brought him to the standard in Cheapside, and there (before his confession ended) caused his head to be stricken off, and pitched it upon an high pole ... [He] went to Mile End, and there apprehended Sir James Cromer, then Sheriff of Kent, and son-in-law to the said Lord Say; causing him likewise (without confession or excuse heard) to be beheaded, and his head to be fixed on a pole; and with these two heads this bloody wretch entered into the city again, and as it were in a spite caused them in every street to kiss together, to the great detestation of all beholders.*

Holinshed's Chronicle, ed. 1808, III. p. 632

OPPOSITE **Margaret of Anjou (1430–82)**. *The ex-queen of England died in 1482 in the cathedral of her native town of Angers. She is commemorated in this statue in the Place de l'Academie near the castle and the cathedral in a monument featuring several kings and queens of Anjou. This sensitive monument shows Margaret in a defensive role, protecting her young son, Prince Edward. She fought like a tigress to preserve Edward's right to the English crown and his death after the Battle of Tewkesbury (1471) made Margaret a political non-person and she spent most of her remaining years in quiet retirement.*

Major events of the Wars of the Roses, 1450–71

1450 SEPTEMBER *Return from Ireland of Richard, Duke of York*

1453 AUGUST *Henry VI's first bout of mental illness*
13 OCTOBER *Birth of Prince Edward*

1454 APRIL *Start of York's first protectorate*
DECEMBER *Recovery of Henry VI*

1455 FEBRUARY *End of York's first protectorate*
22 MAY *First Battle of St Albans (Yorkist victory)*
NOVEMBER *Start of York's second protectorate*

1456 22 FEBRUARY *End of York's second protectorate*

1459 23 SEPTEMBER *Battle of Blore Heath (Yorkist victory)*
12 OCTOBER *Battle of Ludford Bridge (Lancastrian victory)*

1460 *Henry VI's final slide into mental illness*
10 JULY *Battle of Northampton (Yorkist victory)*
30 DECEMBER *Battle of Wakefield (Lancastrian victory); death of Richard of York*

1461 2 FEBRUARY *Battle of Mortimer's Cross (Yorkist victory)*
17 FEBRUARY *Second Battle of St Albans (Lancastrian victory)*
29 MARCH *deposition of Henry VI and accession of Edward IV; Battle of Towton (Yorkist victory)*

1464 25 APRIL *Battle of Hedgeley Moor (Yorkist victory)*
15 MAY *Battle of Hexham (Yorkist victory)*

1469 26 JULY *Battle of Edgecote Moor (Lancastrian Victory)*

1470 12 MARCH *Battle of Losecote Field (Yorkist victory); Henry VI restored to the throne*

1471 14 APRIL *Battle of Barnet (Yorkist victory)*
4 MAY *Battle of Tewkesbury (Yorkist victory); death of Prince Edward*
21 MAY *Death of Henry VI*

ABOVE **Major events of the Wars of the Roses.** *This long civil war brought intermittent military conflict to many parts of the country but the map and the list of events may give a false impression. Throughout these two decades the amount of time taken up with military campaigning amounted to no more than a few weeks. For most people, like the Pastons, it was the political dislocation arising from weak and contested government that most affected them.*

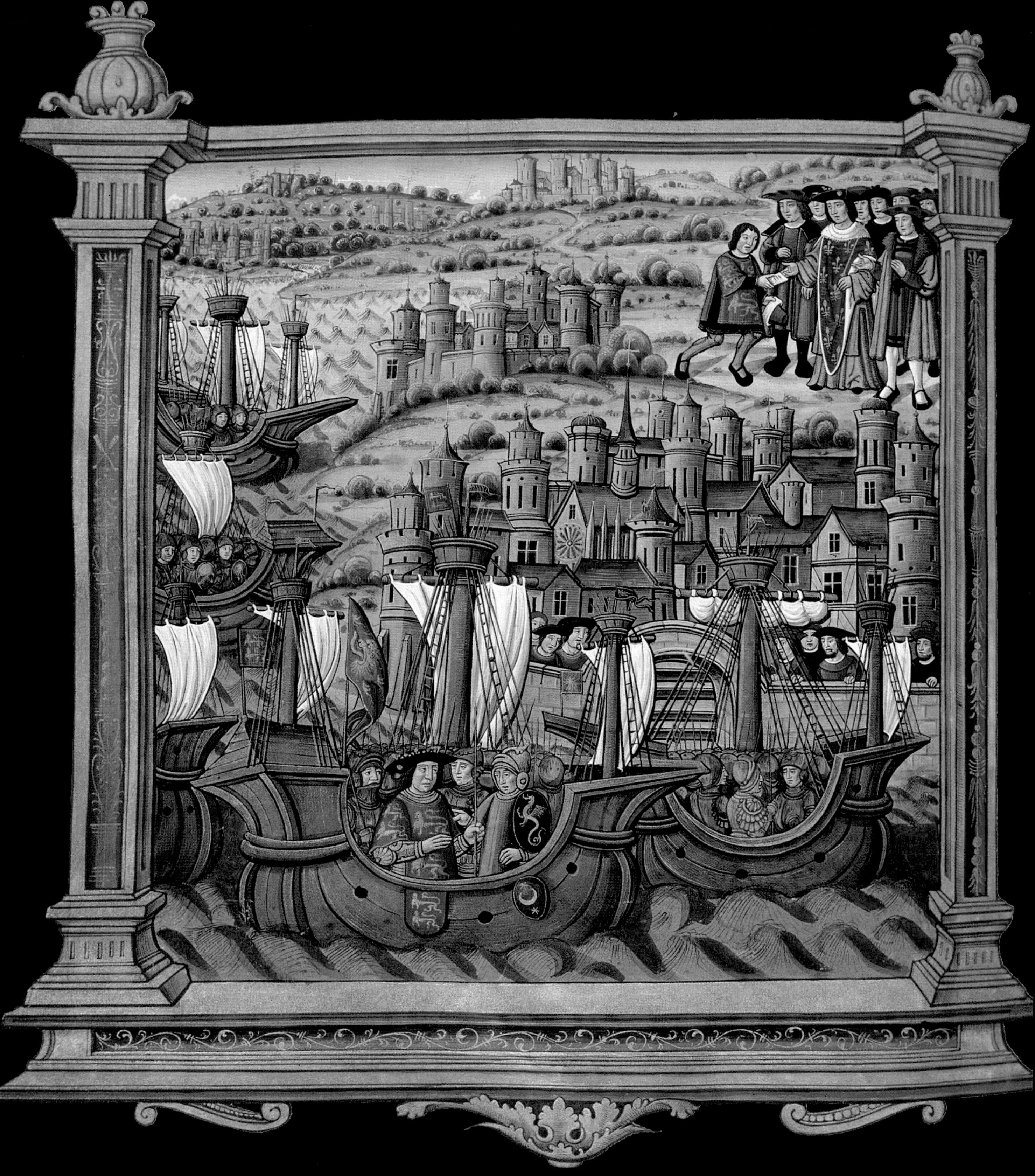

ABOVE **Edward, Earl of March (later Edward IV), disembarking at Calais, 1459.** *On 12 October Richard of York and his followers were confronted by a larger Lancastrian army at Ludford Bridge. When some of their own supporters defected to Henry VI, the Yorkist leaders deserted their men and fled. Edward, Richard's eldest son, made his way via Devon and the Channel Isles to Calais. This early 16th-century illustration from the* Mémoires de Philippe de Commynes *shows him disembarking and seeking the aid of Charles VII of France.*

1455-71

IN MARCH 1455 SUMMONSES WENT OUT for a parliament at Westminster to which the Duke of York and his allies were not invited. They responded by marching from the north at the head of an army to claim their right, and at St Albans in Hertfordshire on 22 May 1455 they met the king's force. The resulting First Battle of St Albans was little more than a skirmish, but it was important for two reasons: the Duke of Somerset was killed, and it was the first battle of the Wars of the Roses.

The events of the following years were complex. The civil war involved not only rivalry for the crown between the supporters of the white rose and the red, but also private feuds between noble families and clashes of territorial ambition, often involving the participants changing sides in order to secure personal advantage. There were three main phases to the war.

For most of the period from May 1455 to December 1460 the government was hampered by rivalries that did not break out into open hostility but that prevented the reforms that were necessary. York remained the major influence in the council, while Margaret, with the king and the infant prince in tow, spent much of the time on royal estates in the Midlands, where she felt secure. When parliament was summoned to meet at Coventry the Yorkists usually absented themselves. When it met in London Lancastrian attendance was light. Henry drifted in and out of sanity. York assumed the protectorate again for three months from November 1455, but with Margaret dominating her husband his position was meaningless. The political and dynastic position was a mess, and neither side was ready to take the drastic action necessary to create stable and effective government. In late 1459 a parliament at Coventry laid charges against the Yorkist leadership, and this precipitated another slide into armed conflict. Henry had, by now, become nothing but a cipher, and his mental disintegration in 1460 was permanent. In his name Margaret instituted what amounted to a reign of terror, using spies, informers and inquisitorial methods to force the obedience of a populace who had no respect for their sovereign. In a battle at Northampton on 10 July 1460 the king was

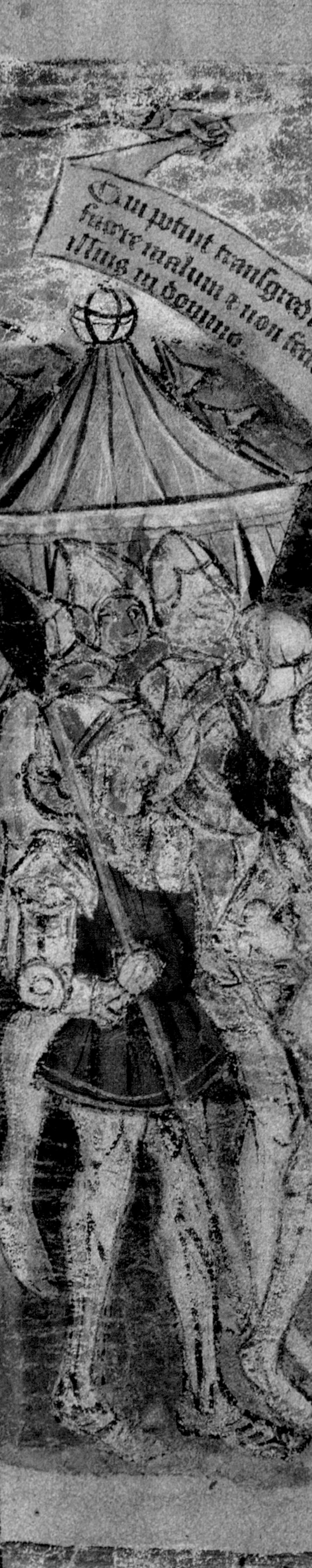

RIGHT **Henry VI captured at the Battle of Northampton, 10 July 1460.** *The Yorkist army of 20,000 confronted the king's force of 12,000 in a field outside the town. Henry's superior artillery dissuaded the Yorkists from attacking and the Earl of Warwick attempted to arrange a parley. However, when a sudden squall dampened the powder of the king's guns, Warwick ordered a cavalry charge. The Lancastrians were overwhelmed with great losses in the space of half an hour. Henry VI was captured by a common soldier, but Queen Margaret was still at large and commanded considerable support. In December, at the Battle of Wakefield, Margaret turned the tables and defeated the Yorkists. The illustration is from the mid 15th-century* Life of Edward IV.

Sic edwardus henricum : northamptone comprehenso .

Edwardus cathcam : ductus est p trauualam ,

nostre souverain
seigneur Edward
par la grace de dieu roy den
gleterre et de france, et seigneur
dirlande, departist du pais de zellande et

captured and taken to London, and on 30 October he accepted a constitutional settlement decreeing that, after his death, the Duke of York would inherit the crown. York's triumph was short-lived, however: on 30 December he was killed at the Battle of Wakefield, and his army scattered.

The second phase lasted from February 1461 to April 1464. Margaret marched south, defeated a Yorkist army at the Second Battle of St Albans and rescued her husband from the Yorkist camp. She expected then to take possession of London, but the citizens refused to open the gates to her, fearing the looting of her ill-disciplined troops. Meanwhile, York's son, Edward, Earl of March, had defeated Margaret's allies in Wales and the border at the Battle of Mortimer's Cross. The queen headed north to gather her supporters there and to do a deal with the Scots. Edward marched into the capital, which welcomed him. He declared Henry unfit to rule and had himself crowned as Edward IV. He then set out to encounter the Lancastrian army, and his decisive victory at Towton, Yorkshire, confirmed his hold on the crown. Margaret and her family took refuge with their Scottish allies.

During the third phase, which lasted from May 1464 to March 1470, Margaret, who was determined to regain the throne for her husband and her son, negotiated with the Scottish regent, Mary of Gueldres, and her French relative, Louis XI. She was prepared to barter away Berwick and Calais. However, Edward outmanoeuvred her by agreeing truces with both countries, and Henry VI was forced to take refuge in Northumberland. The new regime gradually extended its authority northwards. The Battle of Hexham in May 1464, at which several Lancastrian lords and knights were slain, was a major disaster for Henry's cause. He was captured in July 1465 and taken to the Tower of London, where he was held in comfortable captivity.

That would probably have been an end of the war had there not now been a rift within the Yorkist ranks. Edward had relied heavily on the support of Richard Neville, Earl of Warwick, a wealthy, energetic and charismatic nobleman who enjoyed considerable influence, but, once ensconced, the new king was determined not to be dominated by the earl. The two men disagreed over foreign policy and over Edward's choice of bride. While Warwick was negotiating a French marriage for the king, Edward secretly married the Lancastrian widow, Elizabeth Woodville, Lady Ferrers, and began to bestow honours on members of her family.

OPPOSITE **The Battle of Barnet, 14 April 1471.** *Depicted here in an image from a contemporary Flemish manuscript, this battle must go down as one of the 'what ifs' of English history. Its outcome was decided by an unfortunate twist of fate. After helping Edward IV to the throne, the Earl of Warwick was disgusted by his friend's ingratitude, drove Edward into exile and placed Henry VI back on the throne as his puppet. Edward returned with a mercenary army and confronted Warwick at Gladmore Heath, near Barnet. The early part of the engagement, fought in thick fog, went Warwick's way and some of Edward's men were pursued towards the town. When the pursuing troops returned to the main battle they mistook the heraldic device of one of Warwick's commanders for Edward's device. They, therefore, charged part of their own army, which fled in confusion. Warwick was killed. The Battle of Barnet was the prelude to the final Yorkist victory.*

ABOVE **Elizabeth Woodville** *(c.1437–92) in a contemporary portrait. Elizabeth, as a beautiful young woman, was unfortunate to become embroiled in the dynastic conflicts of her day. She was widowed in 1461 when her husband, Sir John Grey, was killed at the Second Battle of St Albans. In May 1464 she appealed to King Edward for help in her distressed situation. Instead, Edward married her in secret (the first time an English king had married one of his own subjects). This, and the honours subsequently bestowed on the queen's family, provoked considerable jealousy and anger from Edward's brothers and advisers. After Edward's death, Elizabeth and her children were at the mercy of their enemies. Elizabeth's fall was swift and complete.*

ABOVE **Edward IV** *(1442–83) in a painting c.1540, by an unknown artist. Edward was an imposing figure, handsome, well built and over 6 feet in height. He was licentious and self-indulgent and had a string of mistresses. He was easy-going and too readily gave his trust to others. But in battle he was valiant and in politics determined. He did much to improve the running of royal government. After the weak rule of Henry VI, the tyrannous behaviour of Margaret of Anjou and the dislocation caused by dynastic friction, Edward emerged as a popular monarch.*

Warwick plotted with Edward's brother, George, Duke of Clarence, defeated the king at the Battle of Edgecote Moor (26 July 1469) and took him prisoner. But by now the country was in such turmoil that the imposition of a third king was out of the question. Warwick transferred his allegiance to the Lancastrians and planned a fresh campaign with Margaret in France. In October 1470, while Edward was busy suppressing a Lancastrian rising in the north, Warwick gained control of London, freed Henry VI and proclaimed his rule to be resumed (this was known as the 'Readeption' of Henry VI). Edward fled to Burgundy, where he gained the support of Duke Charles. He landed in Yorkshire in March 1471 at the head of an Anglo-Dutch army and faced Warwick at Barnet in a battle that was decided by confusion caused by heavy fog. Warwick was killed trying to escape (14 April).

Margaret and Prince Edward had, meanwhile, landed in the west and were busy rallying support in Wales and Gloucestershire when Edward confronted them at Tewkesbury (4 May). Here the Lancastrian force was annihilated. Prince Edward was killed, and most of Margaret's noble supporters either died in battle or were executed immediately afterwards. Ten days later, Henry VI was murdered in the Tower of London to prevent any further outbreaks of Lancastrian support.

t doncques ceste battaille
ainsy achevee le roy se tray
en la ville de tewkesburi
en laquelle lui la venue
le vj jour dudit mois de may fist decoller

OPPOSITE **A letter of Edward IV to Francis II,** *Duke of Brittany, 9 January 1471. The previous October Edward had been forced to flee from his enemies and had sought refuge in the court of Charles, Duke of Burgundy, the husband of his sister, Margaret. From there he wrote to Francis begging for help in the recovery of the English crown. It was with the support of troops supplied by his foreign allies that Edward was able to return to England in March and defeat the Earl of Warwick at the Battle of Barnet.*

LEFT **The execution of the Duke of Somerset, 6 May 1471.** *Beaufort was not an enthusiastic supporter of Margaret of Anjou but he fought with the Lancastrians at Tewkesbury on 4 May 1471. After the defeat he took refuge in Tewkesbury Abbey but was dragged out two days later and summarily executed. Shown in this image from a 15th-century Flemish manuscript, his death ended the direct male Beaufort descent from John of Gaunt. Somerset's only surviving relative was Margaret Beaufort, the mother of the future Henry VII.*

EDWARD IV, EDWARD V AND RICHARD III

After half a century of governmental breakdown, baronial strife and dynastic uncertainty the country needed internal and external peace and a firm hand on the tiller, and Edward IV certainly settled things down for a dozen years. However, following his death at the age of 41 his family managed to tear itself apart, provoke fresh conflicts and pave the way for a challenge from a minor branch of the Lancastrian dynasty, which had up to that moment seemed inconceivable.

Beyond central politics profound changes were taking place in these years. Commerce – especially the trade in woollen cloth – flourished, and a wealthy capitalist, mercantile class emerged. Renaissance influences from the continent began to affect cultural life and provoke new patterns of thought. But most revolutionary of all was the appearance of cheap books from the new print shops, which brought the world of ideas within the reach of many more people.

1471–8

THE DEATH OF HENRY VI and several of the leading Lancastrian magnates persuaded many of the late king's supporters to abandon their cause and offer their loyalty to Edward. Margaret of Anjou was kept in confinement in London until 1476, when, as part of a treaty with Louis XI, she was ransomed for 50,000 crowns and allowed to retire to France. Among the few Lancastrians not reconciled to the regime were John de Vere, Earl of Oxford, and the Tudor brothers, Edmund and Jasper, the sons of Owen Tudor resulting from his scandalous marriage to Henry V's widow, Catherine of Valois. Henry VI had decreed Edmund's marriage to the 12-year-old Margaret Beaufort, daughter of

OPPOSITE **Louis XI of France (1423–83).** *This magnificent illumination from the 16th-century* Mémoires de Philippe de Commynes *represents a monarch known as the Spider King, because of his mastery of European intrigue. One aspect of his machinations concerned his relationship with Edward IV. By supporting the Lancastrians Louis angered Edward, who invaded France in 1475. But Edward was more interested in money than in claiming his traditional rights. Louis bought him off in return for Edward's resignation of all his claims in France, except Calais. Louis boasted that he had ended the Hundred Years War by fêting Edward with pâté, venison and good wine.*

PREVIOUS PAGE **Portrait of Richard III** *(1452–85), oil on panel by an anonymous 16th-century artist. During the reign of his brother, Edward IV, Richard, then Duke of Gloucester, was appointed Governor of the North, Constable of England, Chief Steward and Chamberlain of Wales, Great Chamberlain of England and Lord High Admiral of England. He served faithfully in these capacities and enjoyed wealth and status that was all but royal. On Edward's death he was made regent for the young Edward V but was not prepared to see the crown go to a child, especially a child of the hated Elizabeth Woodville.*

Monsieur larceuesque
de Vienne pour sa
tisfaire a la requeste
quil vous a pleu
me faire de vous escrire et met
tre par memoire ce que Jay
sceu et congneu des faictz du
Roy loys unziesme a qui dieu
face pardon / nre maistre et
bienfaicteur / Et prince digne
de tresexcellente memoire / Je
lay faict le plus pres de la ve 351
rite que Jay peu et sceu auoir
souuenance / Du temps de sa
Jeunesse ne scauroye parler
sinon par ce que ie luy en ay

Our moost goode and graciouse. Queue Elisabeth
Soster unto this oure ffraternite: Of oure blessed
lady. And moder of mercy. Saint Mary Virgyn the
moder of God

from Burgundy. However, the presence of an English army in his kingdom did persuade Louis XI to pay Edward to take it away. By the terms of an agreement reached at Picquigny in August 1475 Edward scooped a pension of £10,000 a year and a down payment of £15,000. Taken together with his other profitable enterprises, this enabled the king to live without parliamentary taxation until 1482.

Trouble between the brothers flared up again in 1477 when, following the death of Clarence's wife, the king vetoed his ambitious remarriage plans. Matters came to a head in May 1477, when one of Clarence's retainers was executed for imagining the king's death by necromancy. The duke took this as a personal affront and had the man's protestation of innocence read to the council. The king was furious at this questioning of royal justice and had Clarence arrested, although it is more than likely that Woodville antipathy was behind this attempt to remove a vociferous opponent of their supremacy. The following January the Duke of Clarence was tried by a parliament summoned for the purpose. It had been packed with the king's supporters but, even so, Edward found it difficult to obtain the desired result.

ABOVE **Dyers produce red cloth** *by soaking it in a heated barrel of dye in this image from* Des Proprietez des Choses *of Barthélémy l'Anglais (late 15th century). Trade flourished during Edward's reign thanks to the return of peace and stability and the king's direct interest in commerce.*

OPPOSITE **Elizabeth Woodville,** *Queen of Edward IV and mother of Elizabeth of York, who married Henry VII, in an image from a 15th-century illuminated manuscript.*

Anne

Richard, Duke of Gloucester, *sought the said Anne in marriage. This, however, did not suit the views of his brother ... who had previously married the eldest daughter of the same earl. Such being the case he caused the damsel to be concealed, in order that it might nor be known by his brother where she was; as he was afraid of a division of the earl's property, which he wished to come to himself alone in right of his wife and not to be obliged to share it with any other person ... the craftiness of the Duke of Gloucester so far prevailed that he discovered the young lady in the city of London disguised in the habit of a cookmaid, upon which he had her removed to the sanctuary of St Martin's.*

THE CROYLAND CHRONICLE, PART VI, THE THIRD CONTINUATION

Clarence's execution

The circumstances that happened in the ensuing Parliament my mind quite shudders to enlarge upon ... For not a single person uttered a word against the duke, except the king, and not one individual made answer to the king except the duke. Some parties were introduced, however, as to whom it was greatly doubted by many whether they filled the office of accusers or ... of witnesses. The duke met all the charges made against him with a denial ... Parliament being of the opinion that the informations they had heard were established, passed sentence upon him of condemnation ... In consequence of this, in a few days after, the execution, whatever its nature may have been, took place (and would that it had ended these troubles!) in the Tower of London.

THE CROYLAND CHRONICLE, PART VI, THE THIRD CONTINUATION

Exactly what form Clarence's secret execution took has never been established beyond doubt. However, the rumour that he was drowned in a barrel of Malmsey wine was in circulation at a very early date.

1479–83

IN 1480 EDWARD, irritated by Scottish cross-border raids, prepared for a major campaign. Richard of Gloucester, who was heavily involved in restoring law and order in the north, made a sally into Scotland in 1481 (intended as the precursor of a full-scale invasion the following year) to set upon the Scottish throne the Duke of Albany, the discontented brother of King James III. By an agreement made at Fotheringhay in June Albany agreed to restore Berwick and to do homage to Edward as his overlord. Edward was too unwell to undertake the campaign himself, and it was Richard who invaded the Lowlands and occupied Edinburgh. However, by this time, the Scottish brothers had made up their differences, and at the same time, Edward's continental diplomacy came unstuck when Louis XI and the Duke of Burgundy signed the Treaty of Arras (March 1482).

All that Edward's diplomacy and threats of war had achieved was a temporary improvement in the finances of the crown. This had been valuable in the work of restoring stability in England, but it left the international situation much as he had found it in 1471. That stability was now threatened again. In the spring of 1483 the king fell ill, possibly as a result of over-indulgence, and he died on 9 April, bequeathing the crown to his 12-year-old son. Once again England faced the prospect of rule by a minor.

OPPOSITE **Edward IV and Jean de Wavrin.** *Jean de Wavrin (c.1398–c.1474) was a French chronicler and diplomat. The book that he is here shown presenting to King Edward is* Recueil des chroniques et anchiennes istories de la Grant Bretaigne, *which related the history of England from early times to 1471. Edward appears enthroned wearing the collar of the Order of the Golden Fleece. The figure on the left wearing the Order of the Garter is thought to be Richard, Duke of Gloucester. Jean de Wavrin relied heavily on the chronicles of both Froissart and Monstrelet, but his knowledge of the period 1444–71 was first-hand and provides valuable details concerning the political life of the period.*

Prologue de lacteur sur la totalle recollation des sept volumes des anchiennes et nouuelles croniques dangleterre a la totale loenge du noble roy Edouard de ... IIIIe de ce nom. Actā.

Edouard par la grace de dieu Roy de france et dangleterre seigneur dirlande. Pour ce que au commencement de toutes choses contendans a bonne fin. Selong la sentence des philozophes anchiens doit estre grace requise a celluy dont

1483–5

THE KING'S SUDDEN DEATH set a power struggle in motion. Edward IV died at Westminster with his wife and her close relatives around him, but his heir, Edward V, was at Ludlow with his uncle, Earl Rivers. Richard of Gloucester was at Middleham in the Yorkshire Dales. Both parties immediately set out for London for both needed to secure the person of the young king. Richard intended to take up the role of protector, which he believed was his by right, but the Woodvilles planned to establish a regency council of which Gloucester would be only one member. It was in their interests to have the young Edward crowned as quickly as possible so that they could begin to issue instructions in his name. This Richard was determined to prevent, and on 28 April he intercepted Earl Rivers and his charge. The earl was sent north to Pontefract Castle and was discreetly executed. Richard took control in the capital and lodged the king in the Tower, where he was joined in June by his younger brother.

The rival groups spent the next weeks building up their support, but Richard was quicker, more efficient, more thorough and more ruthless. He carried out a purge of the council, claiming that his victims had plotted against him and the king, and on 22 June his own accession was publicly proclaimed, on the grounds that Edward's sons were bastards. On 6 July he was crowned as Richard III. His motives were probably a mixture of ambition, contempt for the Woodvilles and concern for the good government of the country. Handing power to a child in the control of an upstart clique who lacked the support of England's political elite seemed a certain way to return the country to the situation that had existed during the worst days of Henry VI's reign. Richard could justify his usurpation to himself, if not to everyone else.

Richard's callously efficient seizure of power was probably his undoing, especially when the rumour spread that he had had his young nephews murdered in the Tower (There was no word of their being seen after mid-July.) In the autumn one of his own allies, the Duke of Buckingham, rose against him, calling for people to rise in the name of Henry Tudor, Earl of Richmond (a fact that may indicate that he believed the 'Princes in the Tower' were now dead). This revolt quickly fizzled

OPPOSITE **Edward IV and Earl Rivers, *c*.1477.** *This painting on vellum is interesting for at least two reasons. First, it shows King Edward IV with a family group. Behind him stands his wife, Elizabeth, and beside him his son, Edward. On the king's right (in blue) is Richard, Duke of Gloucester. The man kneeling is Anthony Woodville, Earl Rivers. Secondly, the book Rivers is presenting is probably the first English book to come from the printing press of William Caxton. Rivers was a cultured man and quite a scholar. He translated from the French* Dictes and Sayings of the Philosophers, *which he is shown presenting to the king. This volume was a compendium of quotations from the great philosophers of history since ancient times.*

out, but it was precursor to more widespread opposition to the new regime.

Destiny seemed to be closing in on Richard. In April 1484 his only son died, and his wife survived this tragedy by less than a year. His attempt to have Henry Tudor apprehended in Brittany failed, and Henry was able to escape to France where he was supported by King Charles VIII. He steadily gained credibility as a potential rival, and several influential figures crossed the Channel to join him. Richard, meanwhile, gathered as much support as he could and even sought a rapprochement with the Woodvilles. However, in September 1484 he reluctantly agreed a truce with the Scots in order to leave himself free to face the expected challenge from Henry Tudor.

Henry landed in south Wales on 7 August 1485 and began his march eastwards, picking up fresh adherents along the way. The king summoned his nobles to join him with their armed retainers and was able to gather an army of

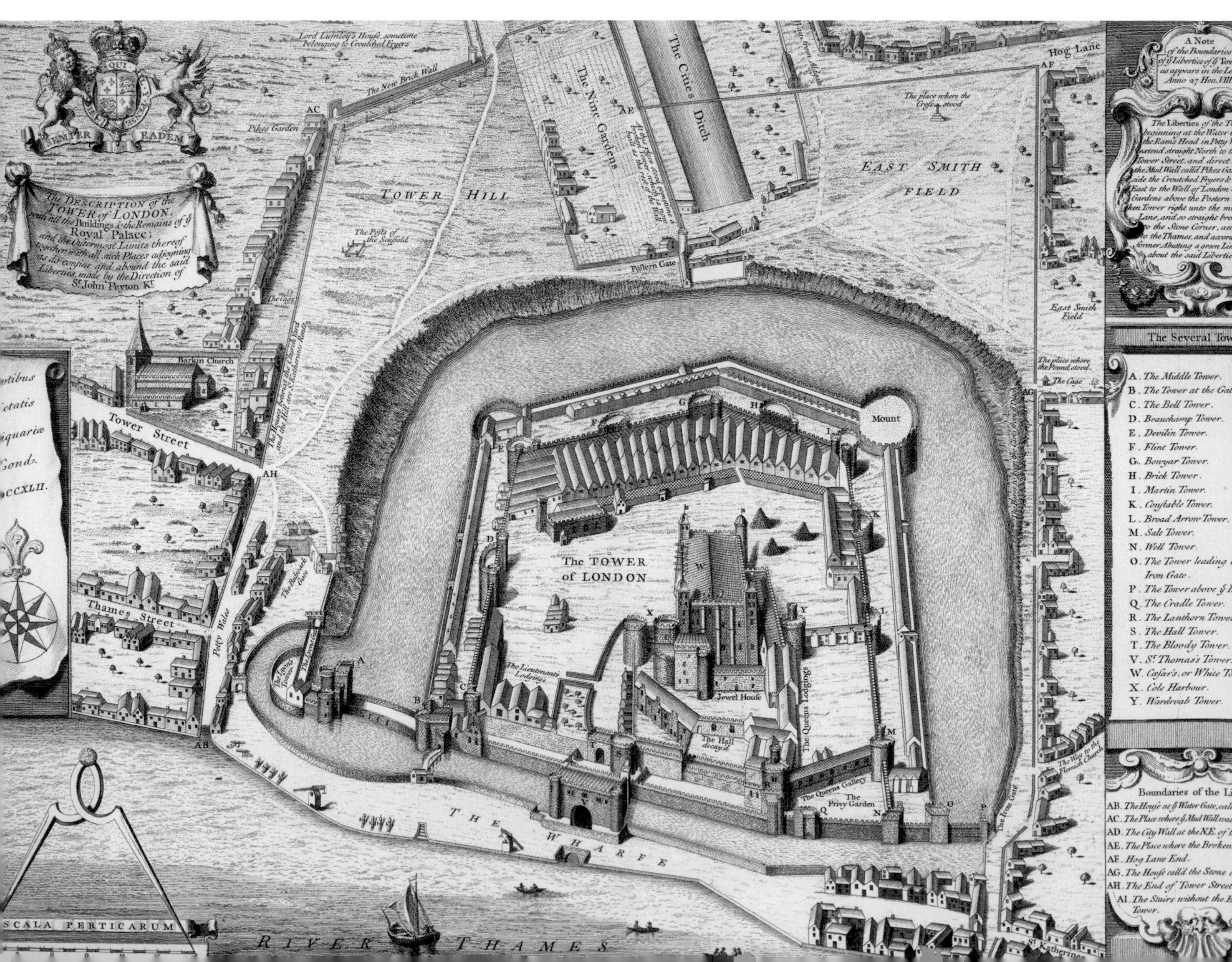

more than 10,000 men with which to confront the rebel force of some 5,000 at Market Bosworth in Leicestershire on 22 August. The overwhelming odds should have ensured victory for Richard, but he could not rely on some of his captains, such as the Earl of Northumberland, who waited to see how the battle would turn out before committing themselves. There is no clear account of the Battle of Bosworth, and existing reports contain conflicting details but three facts are beyond dispute: Northumberland refused to commit his troops; Lord Stanley, after keeping his men at a distance, went over to Henry's side; and Richard III met his end in a death-or-glory charge upon the standard of his opposite number. According to one colourful account by a Spanish servant in Richard's entourage, the death of the last Plantagenet occurred in this manner:

> *Now when Salazar ... who was there in King Richard's service, saw the treason of the king's people, he went up to him and said, 'Sire, take steps to put your person in safety, without expecting to have the victory in today's battle, owing to the manifest treason in your following'. But the king replied, 'Salazar, God forbid I yield one step. This day I will die as king or win.' Then he placed over his head-armour the crown royal, which they declare be worth 120,000 crowns, and having donned his coat of arms, began to fight with much vigour, putting heart into those that remained loyal, so that by his sole effort he upheld the battle for a long time. But in the end the king's army was beaten and he himself was killed ... After winning this victory Earl Henry was at once acclaimed by all parties. He ordered the dead king to be placed in a little hermitage near the place of battle, and had him covered from the waist downward with a black rag of poor quality, ordering his top be exposed there for three days to the universal gaze.*[1]

Opposition

The people *of the southern and western parts of the kingdom began to murmur greatly, and to form meetings and confederacies. It soon became known that many things were going on in secret, and some in the face of the world ... There was also a report that it had been recommended ... that some of the king's [Edward IV's] daughters should leave Westminster, and go in disguise to the parts beyond the seas, in order that, if any fatal mishap should befall the ... male children of the late king in the Tower, the kingdom might still in consequence of the safety of his daughters, some day fall into the hands of the rightful heirs.*

The Croyland Chronicles, part VI, The Third Continuation

OPPOSITE **The Tower of London, 1597.** *This drawing commissioned by Elizabeth I's Constable of the Tower shows the fortress as it was by the late 16th century. However, there had been little change over the preceding hundred years, so that the buildings were much as the last Plantagenets would have known them. Richard III used it as his base in the weeks following Edward IV's death. Richard summoned a council meeting in the Tower on 13 June 1483 and promptly had four of its members arrested. One of them, William Hastings, the Lord Chamberlain, was immediately taken onto Tower Green and beheaded. It was here that Richard had Edward's two sons brought and it was here that they were last seen alive in July.*

ABOVE **Henry VII** *(1457–1509) in an anonymous 16th-century oil on panel portrait. Henry was the grandson of Owen Tudor, a Welsh Lancastrian knight who had married Catherine of Valois, Henry V's widow. Since Owen's two sons represented the only viable Lancastrian heirs to the throne in the event of his dying childless, Henry VI conveyed titles upon them. Edmund was created Earl of Richmond. He died in 1456 but had already sired a son, Henry. Young Henry, as the only hope of Lancastrian revival, was forced to spend several perilous years in France and Brittany evading all Yorkist attempts to capture him.*

ABOVE **Charles VIII** *(1470–98), king of France. Charles became king in 1483 at the age of 13. His health was never robust and his strong-willed sister, Anne, was appointed a regent. When Henry, Earl of Richmond, approached the French court for support he was given a cautious welcome. However, the protection granted by the king (or in his name) was vital to Henry. In 1485 Charles provided Henry with money and cannon for his attempt to claim the throne. With the French funds he was able to recruit a very small force (probably no more than 2,000) and convey them across the Channel.*

Postscript

So ended three turbulent centuries of rule by Henry II and his Plantagenet successors. They were years of almost unremitting warfare as kings contended with foreign monarchs and with their feudal barons, whose power in their own regions was greater than the king's. The Plantagenet rulers gained and lost a sizeable continental empire and gained control of Wales, but failed to conquer Scotland or to extend effective rule over the whole of Ireland.

Although we use the term 'England' to describe the heartland of Plantagenet territory, this land was far from being a recognizable, independent entity. Not only was the country divided into petty princedoms held in fee from the crown, but also, for much of the period, the magnates who held sway in their localities had more in common with their counterparts on the other side of the Channel, and their fortunes were intertwined with those of French dukedoms such as those of Normandy, Brittany, Anjou and Maine. The English had no common language, regional dialects varying widely from each other. Norman French was spoken at court and was the language of diplomacy. Churchmen, scholars, lawyers and the scribes who drew up official documents used Latin, the language that united England with the rest of western Christendom. Only gradually did the language of London and the southern counties emerge as a common vernacular and this process was only completed in the 16th century thanks to the greatest invention that the Plantagenet age bequeathed to its followers – the printing press.

OPPOSITE **This manuscript depicts in a single tableau three events of 1226 – the siege of Avignon, the death of Louis VIII and the coronation of Louis IX.** *Avignon had tried unsuccessfully to assert independence from the French crown. Kingship and war – these seemed to be the dominating concerns of their ancestors as viewed by writers and artists of the late 15th century. The illustration is by Jean Fouquet (1420–81), an artist who worked for many years for the French court. He brought the craft of medieval book illumination to a peak of perfection with his exquisite miniature illustrations for books of hours. But Fouquet also stands on the threshold of a new age, for he spent some years in Renaissance Italy perfecting his craft and taking it in new directions. This illustration is from a copy of the* Grandes Chroniques de France, *which he decorated for an unknown patron.*

PREVIOUS PAGE **Henry VII (1457–1509).** *A portrait in oil on panel c.1505 by an unknown artist. Renaissance influences clearly appear in this painting.*

William Caxton

'...I have practised and learned at my great charge and dispense to ordain this said book in print after the manner and form as ye may here see, and is not written with pen and ink as other books [have] been, to the end that every man may have them at once, for all the books of this story named the recule [collection] of the histories of Troy thus imprinted as ye here see were begun in one day, and also finished in one day.'[1]

So wrote the merchant turned printer, William Caxton (*c.*1422–91), in the preface to the first book to be printed in the English language. His *Recuyell of the Histories of Troy* began a revolution. The invention of the printed book was the biggest single development in communication before the invention of the telephone. Caxton was a successful member of the London Mercers' Company who, by about 1450, settled in Bruges and enjoyed the patronage of Margaret, Duchess of Burgundy, Edward IV's sister. There he developed a commercial interest in the latest craze sweeping Europe – cheap books.

ABOVE **A monk writing, *c.*1200.** *from* Topographica Hibernica *by Giraldus Cambrensis (c.1146–c.1223). Throughout the centuries when the Plantagenets ruled England the pace of life was slow. One reason lay in the problem of disseminating knowledge. Books could only be laboriously copied by hand. Printing was the technological revolution that ushered in a new age.*

Gutenberg's legacy

Johannes Gutenberg had developed in Mainz an apparatus that combined movable type, oil-based ink and a wooden screw press. The result was a machine for mass-producing books, pamphlets, posters and official documents. The printing press caught on rapidly and by 1475 there was scarcely a town or city of any size in continental Europe that did not have at least one printworks. The cheap book was an idea whose time had come. The gradual spread of education created a demand for the written word. The 'Clerk of Oxford' in Chaucer's *Canterbury Tales* was shabbily dressed because he spent all his money on books:

For he would rather have at his bed's head.
Twenty books, bound in black and red
Of Aristotle and his philosophy,
Than rich robes or a fiddle or a psaltery.[2]

OPPOSITE **The Gutenberg Bible, *c.*1450–56.** *Johannes Gutenberg (c.1398–1468) set up the first printing press using movable type about 1439. His invention led to the main production of books and the easier interchange of information and ideas. The splendid Gutenberg Bible was printed in 1455 and 180 copies were run off. It symbolized a new age in which religion could be studied by an ever-widening circle of lay people.*

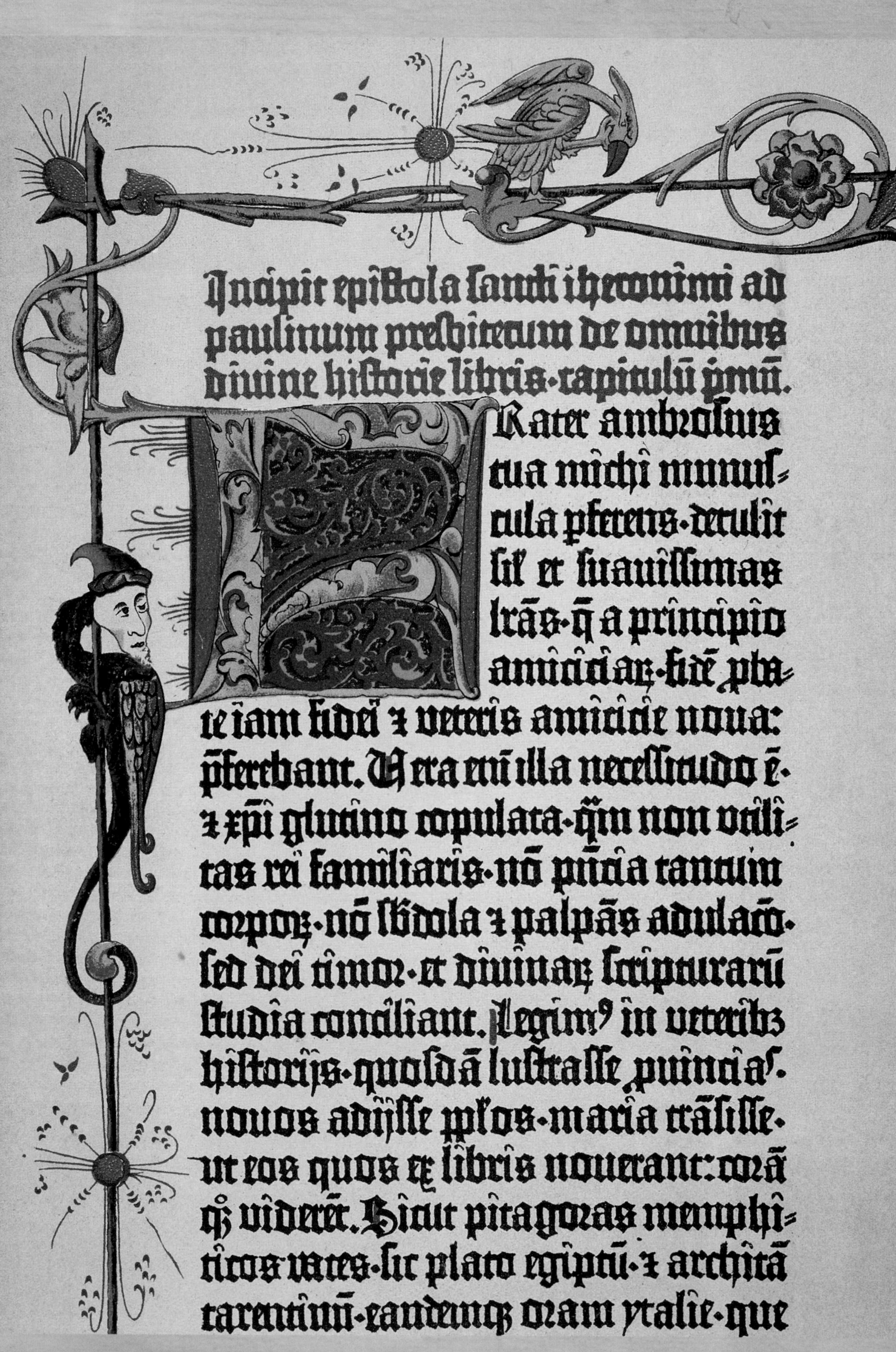

Incipit epistola sancti iheronimi ad
paulinum presbiterum de omnibus
diuine historie libris. capitulum primum.

FRater ambrosius
tua michi munus-
cula perferens. detulit
sil et suauissimas
litteras. que a principio
amiciciarum. fidem proba-
te iam fidei et veteris amicicie noua:
preferebant. Uera enim illa necessitudo est.
et christi glutino copulata. quam non utili-
tas rei familiaris. non presencia tantum
corporum. non subdola et palpans adulacio.
sed dei timor. et diuinarum scripturarum
studia conciliant. Legimus in veteribus
historiis. quosdam lustrasse prouincias.
nouos adiisse populos. maria transisse.
ut eos quos ex libris nouerant: coram
quoque viderent. Sicut pitagoras memphi-
ticos vates. sic plato egiptum. et architam
tarentinum. eandemque oram ytalie. que

Books were expensive because they were laboriously hand made and took days or weeks of work to complete. Originally they were produced by monks labouring in the scriptoria of monasteries. This was because most books were intended for religious use – bibles, psalters and devotional works. Many were labours of love whose pages were embellished with beautiful coloured decoration. But there was also a secular trade in volumes of stories, technical manuals and songsheets. By the 13th century many commercial scriptoria had come into being employing teams of scribes who worked long hours to meet the growing demand. But this was still a luxury industry whose products could only be acquired by the relatively well-to-do. An efficiently run printworks was, therefore, a potential gold mine. Caxton returned to England and set up his press in Westminster in 1476.

The impact of books

The impact of the printed book was incalculable. Just as a literate clientele had created the demand, so the growing volume of books encouraged more people to become literate. Writers were able to spread their ideas more rapidly and widely than had ever been conceivable. This was not always welcomed by the authorities. We have seen how the church clamped a ban on the circulation of Lollard bibles and tracts. The spread of 'heretical', unorthodox or 'seditious' books created fresh problems for ecclesiastical and government censors. From time to time they staged public burnings of 'undesirable' books. But there was no effective way to stop people reading. As the 15th century came to a close books were bringing a whole new dimension to the lives of many people.

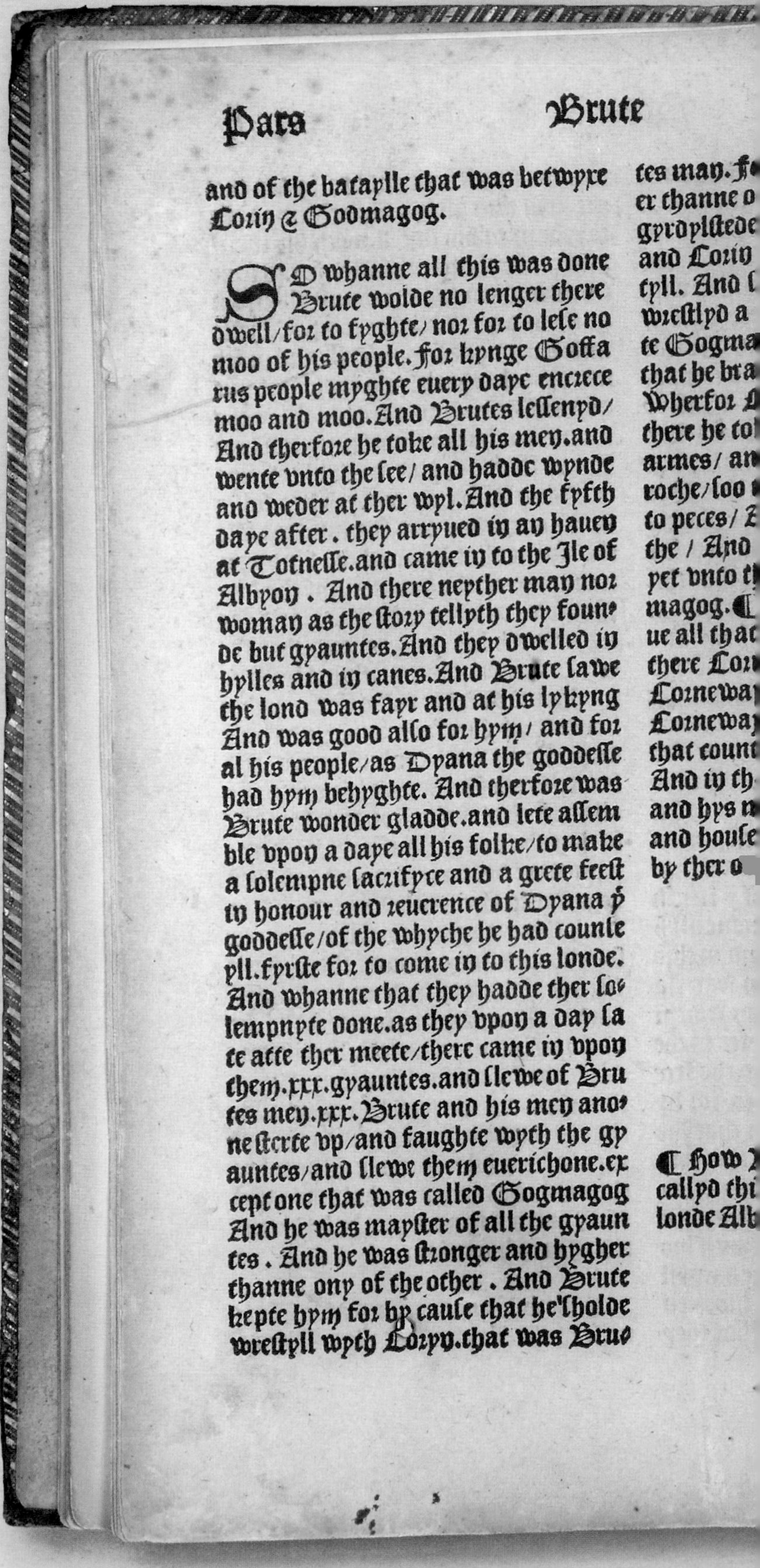

RIGHT ***The Chronicles of England.*** *In 1480 William Caxton issued this account of the history of England from the earliest times to 1471. This later edition (c.1491) was from the press of another pioneer printer, Wynkyn de Worde (d.1534), who took over Caxton's workshop. By this time England was a new land and the Plantagenets were history.*

Pars Brute

and of the bataylle that was betwyxe Coryn & Godmagog.

So whanne all this was done Brute wolde no lenger there dwell/for to fyghte/nor for to lese no moo of his people. For kynge Goffarus people myghte euery daye encrece moo and moo. And Brutes lessenyd/ And therfore he toke all his men. and wente vnto the see/ and hadde wynde and weder at ther wyl. And the fyfth daye after. they arryued in an hauen at Totnesse. and came in to the Jle of Albyon. And there neyther man nor woman as the story tellyth they founde but gyauntes. And they dwelled in hylles and in caues. And Brute sawe the lond was fayr and at his lykyng And was good also for hym/ and for al his people/as Dyana the goddesse had hym behyghte. And therfore was Brute wonder gladde. and lete assemble vpon a daye all his folke/to make a solempne sacrifyce and a grete feest in honour and reuerence of Dyana þ goddesse/of the whyche he had counseyll. fyrste for to come in to this londe. And whanne that they hadde ther solempnyte done. as they vpon a day sate atte ther meete/there came in vpon them. xxx. gyauntes. and slewe of Brutes men. xxx. Brute and his men anone sterte vp/and faughte wyth the gyauntes/and slewe them euerichone. except one that was called Gogmagog And he was mayster of all the gyauntes. And he was stronger and hygher thanne ony of the other. And Brute kepte hym for by cause that he sholde wrestyll wyth Coryn. that was Bru ij

he was greter aud hygh
of Brutes men from ẏ
pwarde. ¶Gogmagog
ndertoke ther for to wrel
togyders they went/and
nge tyme. But at the las
g helde Corin soo faste.
two rybbes of his syde/
in was sore angry. And
Gogmagog betwyx his
caste hym downe vpon a
at Gogmagog brake all
so he deyed an euyll de
erfore the place is callyd
s daye. the saut of Gog
nd thenne after Brute pa
untree vnto Corin. And
callyd it after hys name.
. And his men ben called
es. and soo sholde men of
e be called for euermore/
countreye dwelled Corin
. And they made townes
and enhabyted the londe
wyll.

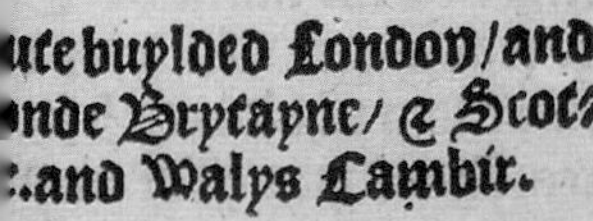
uite buylded London/and
nde Brytayne/ & Scot
. and Walys Cambir.

Pars Brute K Lotrin .ij.

¶London

Brute & his men wente forth/& sawe aboute in dyuers places. where that they myghte. fynde a gode place & couenable/ that they myghte make a cyte/ for hym & for his folke/ So at the last they came by a fayr ryuer. that is called Tamys: and there Brute began a fayr cyte/& lete call it newe Troy/in mynde & remembraũce of the grete Troy/ from the whyche place al ther lygnage was comen. And this Brute lete fell downe woodes/& lete ere & sowe londes/ and lete mawe downe medowes. for sustenaũce of hym & of his people. And he departed the londe to them/so that eueryche had a parte/& certen place for to dwelle in. And thenne Brute lete call all this londe Brytayne after his owne name/& his folke he lete call Brytons. And this Brute had gote on his wyf Gennogen thre sones/that were worthy of dedes. The fyrste was callid Lotrin. the seconde Albanak. & the thyrd Cambar. And Brute bare crowne in the cyte of Troy. xx. yere after ẏ tyme that the cyte was made. And there he made the lawes ẏ the Brytones holde. And this Brute was wonderly wel beloued among al men. And Brutes sones also loued wonderly wel togyder. And whan Brute had soughte all the londe in length. & also in brede he fonde a londe that Joyned to Brytayne/that was in the northe. & that londe Brute yaue to Albanak his sone. And lete calle it Albanie after hys name/ ẏ now is callyd Scotlonde. & Brute fonde a nother cõutree towarde the weste/ & yaaf that to Cambar his other sone/ & lete calle it Cambar after his name. & now is callyd Walys. And whan Brute had regned. xx. yere/as before is sayd: thenne he deyed in the cyte of newe Troy. ij

¶How Lotrin that was Brutes sone entred wyth moche honour. & gouerned the londe well & worthyly.

After Brute regned Lotrin his sonne/ that was the seconde kynge in Brytayne. The whyche beganne to regne the second yere of Samuell. / And thys Lotrin was crowned kynge wyth moche solempnyte & glory of al ẏ londe of Brytayne. And after whañe he was crowned kynge /

c

But the printed word was far from being the only positive contribution of the Plantagenet centuries to posterity. Political and constitutional conflict produced a bicameral parliament. Thanks to the honing of technical and entrepreneurial skills England emerged as the producer of Europe's finest woollen cloths. The church's long struggle with Lollard heresy indicates that there existed a vigorous intellectual life struggling for independence from control by ecclesiastical and political hierarchies, which produced, *en passant*, the universities of Oxford and Cambridge where many of the acutest English minds were trained and have continued to be trained throughout ensuing centuries. When we think of 'medieval England' the image that comes most readily to mind is of soaring Gothic cathedrals and parish churches filled with masterpieces of the carvers' and glaziers' art. But, if we were to seek the 'biggest' contribution to national

life made during the period 1154–1485, a case could very well be made for the growth of the British legal system. From manorial and market courts, through regional assizes and episcopal courts right up to parliament and the king's council there developed a complex but functional system whereby – theoretically at least – the ordinary subject might obtain justice. The system did not always work well; there were times and places when and where it did not work at all. But Magna Carta, the Constitutions of Clarendon, the Peasants' Revolt and the numerous adjustments to the workings of the judiciary displayed a deeply felt concern for the right relationships between the king and all his subjects, high and low, under a written code, impartially administered.

It was the refusal of ordinary people to submit to baronial terrorism and royal tyranny that built up a body of statute law, established the inns of court as

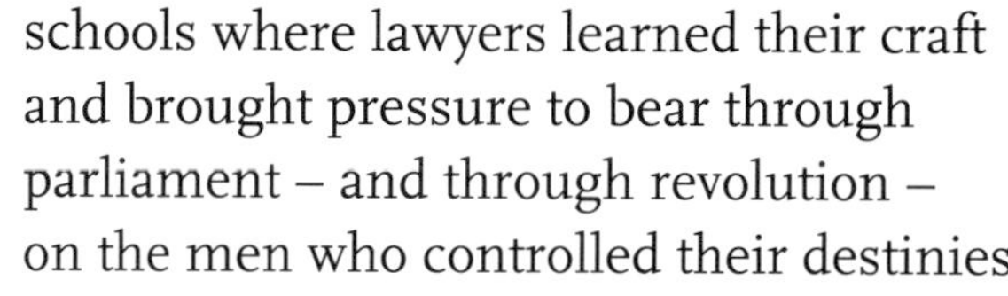

schools where lawyers learned their craft and brought pressure to bear through parliament – and through revolution – on the men who controlled their destinies.

Ultimately, it was the sort of people who joined Jack Cade's rebellion who shaped England as much as – perhaps more than – all the kings and councillors of the Plantagenet years.

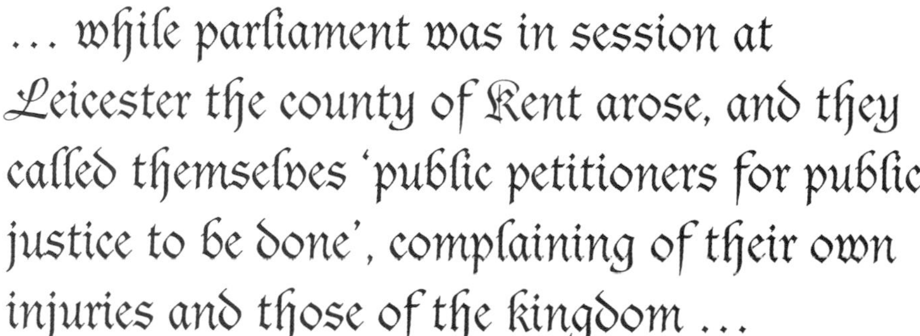

... while parliament was in session at Leicester the county of Kent arose, and they called themselves 'public petitioners for public justice to be done', complaining of their own injuries and those of the kingdom ...

LOCI E LIBRO VERITATUM: PASSAGES SELECTED FROM GASCOIGNE'S THEOLOGICAL DICTIONARY ILLUSTRATING THE CONDITION OF CHURCH AND STATE 1403–1458, ED. J.E.T. ROGERS, OXFORD, 1881, P. 189

LEFT **Battle on the bridge.** *So ended three centuries in which violence and warfare played prominent roles. This skirmish from an illustration in* Chroniques de France ou de St Denis *was fought by English and French forces for possession of a bridge over the Seine during the Hundred Years War.*

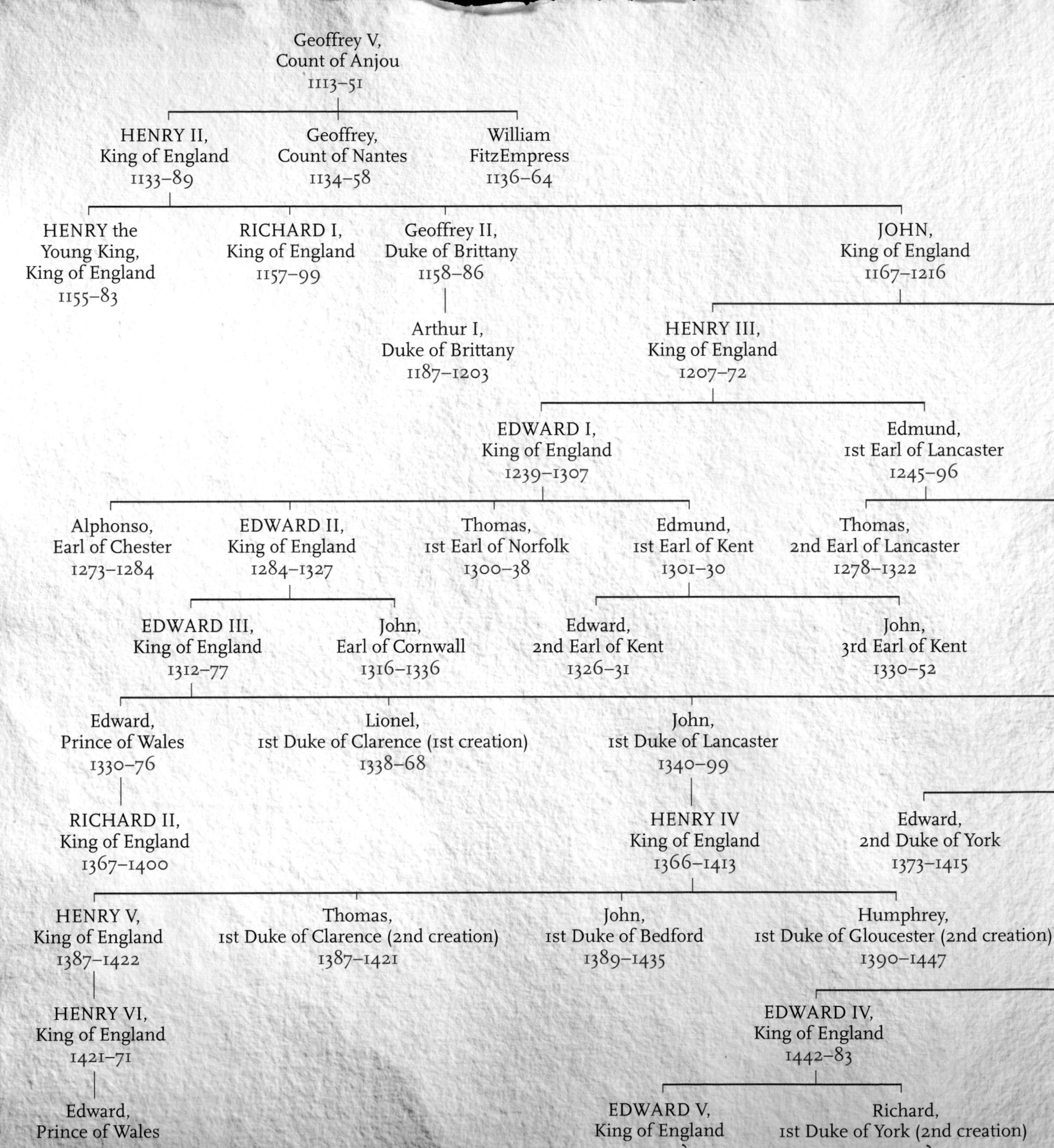
Geoffrey V, Count of Anjou 1113–51
HENRY II, King of England 1133–89
Geoffrey, Count of Nantes 1134–58
William FitzEmpress 1136–64
HENRY the Young King, King of England 1155–83
RICHARD I, King of England 1157–99
Geoffrey II, Duke of Brittany 1158–86
JOHN, King of England 1167–1216
Arthur I, Duke of Brittany 1187–1203
HENRY III, King of England 1207–72
EDWARD I, King of England 1239–1307
Edmund, 1st Earl of Lancaster 1245–96
Alphonso, Earl of Chester 1273–1284
EDWARD II, King of England 1284–1327
Thomas, 1st Earl of Norfolk 1300–38
Edmund, 1st Earl of Kent 1301–30
Thomas, 2nd Earl of Lancaster 1278–1322
EDWARD III, King of England 1312–77
John, Earl of Cornwall 1316–1336
Edward, 2nd Earl of Kent 1326–31
John, 3rd Earl of Kent 1330–52
Edward, Prince of Wales 1330–76
Lionel, 1st Duke of Clarence (1st creation) 1338–68
John, 1st Duke of Lancaster 1340–99
RICHARD II, King of England 1367–1400
HENRY IV King of England 1366–1413
Edward, 2nd Duke of York 1373–1415
HENRY V, King of England 1387–1422
Thomas, 1st Duke of Clarence (2nd creation) 1387–1421
John, 1st Duke of Bedford 1389–1435
Humphrey, 1st Duke of Gloucester (2nd creation) 1390–1447
HENRY VI, King of England 1421–71
EDWARD IV, King of England 1442–83
Edward, Prince of Wales 1453–71
EDWARD V, King of England 1470–?
Richard, 1st Duke of York (2nd creation) 1473–?

The Plantagenet Succession

This family tree shows the Plantagenet line of succession and the principal claimants.

Richard,
King of Germany
1209–72

Henry of Almain
1235–71

Edmund,
2nd Earl of Cornwall
1249–1300

Henry,
3rd Earl of Lancaster
1281–1345

Henry,
1st Duke of Lancaster
1310–61

Edmund,
1st Duke of York (1st creation)
1341–1402

Thomas,
1st Duke of Gloucester (1st creation)
1355–1397

Richard,
3rd Earl of Cambridge
1375–1415

Humphrey,
2nd Earl of Buckingham
1381–99

Richard,
3rd Duke of York
1411–60

Edmund,
Earl of Rutland
1443–60

George,
1st Duke of Clarence
(3rd creation) 1449–78

RICHARD III,
King of England
1452–85

Edward,
17th Earl of Warwick
1475–99

Edward,
Prince of Wales
1473–84

ABOVE **Edward, Prince of Wales, son of Richard III** (c. *1473–84). In this image from the 15th-century Rous Roll, Edward is shown holding a sceptre and is standing on his father's badge, the White Boar. The royal arms of England are depicted above.*

REFERENCES

NOTE: Place of publication is London, unless otherwise stated.

CHAPTER 1

1 William of Newburgh, *Historia Rerum Anglicarum*, ed. H.C. Hamilton, 1856, I, pp. 105–6.
2 *Materials for the History of Thomas Becket*, eds. J.C. Robertson and J.B. Sheppard, VII, pp. 572–3.
3 W. Stubbs, *Select Charters and other Illustrations of English Constitutional History*, 1921, pp. 175–6.
4 Roger of Howden, *Gesta Regis Henrici Secundi*, ed. W. Stubbs, 1867, I, pp. 191–4
5 *Giraldi Cambrensis Opera*, eds. J.S. Brewer, J.F. Dimock and G.F. Warner, 1861–91, VIII, pp.178–9.
6 *Gesta Regis Henrici Secundi*, p. 337.
7 *The Historical Works of Gervase of Canterbury*, ed. W. Stubbs, 1879–80, I, p. 436.

CHAPTER 2

1 William of Newburgh, *Historia Rerum Anglicarum*, ed. H.C. Hamilton, 1856, II, p.105.
2 *Poésies complètes de Bertran de Born*, ed. A. Thomas, New York, 1971, p. 97.
3 *The Rare and Excellent History of Saladin by Baha' al-din ibn Shaddad*, ed. D.S. Richards, Farnham, 2002, p. 173.
4 *Poésies complètes de Bertran de Born*, p. 103.
5 *Ibid.*, p. 190.
6 T. Rymer, *Foedera*, 1704–35, I, pp. 353–4.

CHAPTER 3

1 Matthew Paris, *Chronica Majora*, ed. H.R. Luard, 1872–81, III, p. 324.
2 *Matthew Paris's English History: From the Year 1235 to 1273*, tr. J.A. Giles, 1852–4, I, pp. 315–6.
3 *Ibid.*, p. 240.
4 *The Song of Lewes*, ed. C.L. Kingsford, Oxford, 1890, p. 33.

CHAPTER 5

1 *Vita Edwardi Secundi*, ed. W.R. Childs, 2005, pp. 68–9.
2 *Chronicles of the Reigns of Edward I and Edward II*, ed. W. Stubbs, Rolls series, 1882–3, II, p. 167.
3 Quoted in S. Phillips, *Edward II*, New Haven, 2010, p. 175.
4 *Vita Edwardi Secundi*, pp. 30–31.
5 *Ibid.*, pp. 96–7.
6 *Ibid.*, p. 136.
7 *Ibid.*, No.10, p. 136.

CHAPTER 6

1 *Froissart's Chronicles*, ed. J. Jolliffe, 1967, p. 35.
2 'The Anonimalle Chronicle, 1307–1334', ed. W.R. Childs and J. Taylor, in *Yorkshire Archaeological Society*, No. 147, 1987, pp. 58–9.
3 *English Historical Documents 1327–1485*, ed. A.R. Myers, 1969, VI, p. 60.
4 *Froissart's Chronicles*, p. 134.
5 B.W. Tuchman, *A Distant Mirror: The Calamitous Fourteenth Century*, 1978, pp. 87–8.
6 *Froissart's Chronicles*, p. 172.
7 *Ibid.*, p. 213.

CHAPTER 7

1 William Caxton, *The Chronicles of England*, 1520, ccxxxix, p. 264.
2 *Rotuli Parliamentorum*, ed. J. Strachey *et al.*, 1767–77, III, p. 90.
3 *Froissart's Chronicles*, ed. J. Jolliffe, 1967, pp. 314–15.
4 *Oeuvres Complètes de Eustace Deschamps*, ed. De Queux de Saint-Hilaire and G. Raymond, Paris, 1878–1903, I, pp. 156–7.
5 *Chronicon Henrici Knighton vel Cnitthon, monachi Leycestrensis*, ed. J.R. Lumby, Rolls Series 92, 1889–95, II, p. 295.
6 University College, Oxford MS (Coxe) 97, fo.124v; cited in K.B. McFarlane, *Lancastrian Kings and Lollard Knights*, Oxford, 1972, pp. 205–6.
7 *Froissart's Chronicles*, p. 387.
8 *Chronica Monasterii S. Albani, Thomae Walsingham ... Historia Anglicana*, ed. H.T. Riley, I, p. 230.

CHAPTER 8

1 *Chronicon Adae de Usk*, ed. E.M. Thompson, 1904, p. 29.
2 *Statutes of the Realm*, 2:12S–28: 2 Henry IV.
3 *Piers Plowman by William Langland*, ed. D. Pearsall, 1967, Passus V/Prologue, II.156–162 [tr. by author].
4 *The Complete Works of Geoffrey Chaucer*, ed. W.W. Skeat, Oxford, 1920, II.390–399, p. 557.
5 A.W. Pollard, *Records of the English Bible*, Oxford, 1911, p. 79.

CHAPTER 9

1 *Chronicles of London*, ed. C.L. Kingsford, Oxford, 1905, p. 69.
2 *Chronicle of the Grey Friars of London*, ed. J.G. Nichols, 1852, p. 12.
3 *Chronique de France*, Enguerrand de Monstrelet, *c*.1450, in www.deremilitari.org/resources/sources/Agincourt.
4 *Ibid.*
5 *Ibid.*
6 *Ibid.*
7 *Ibid.*

CHAPTER 10

1 *Robert Fabyan's Concordance of Histories*, ed. H. Ellis, 1811, p. 594.
2 'A Short English Chronicle: London under Henry VI (1422–7)', *Three Fifteenth-Century Chronicles: With historical memoranda by John Stowe*, ed. J. Gairdner, 1880, p. 59.
3 *Leland's Itinerary in England and Wales*, ed. L. Toulmin Smith, 1964, I, p. 94.
4 *See* M.R. James, *Etoniana*, April 1920, p. 387.
5 *Paston Letters*, ed. J. Gairdner, 1872–5, No. 435.
6 *Rotuli Parliamentorum*, ed. J.Strachey *et al.*, 1767–77, VI, p. 8.
7 *See* D.R. Guttery, 'The Two Johns: Patron and Parson', in *County Borough of Dudley Library, Museums and Arts Dept., Transcript No. 13*, 1969, p. 4.
8 *Hardyng's Chronicle*, 1457 *see* C.L. Kingsford, 'Extracts from the First Version of the Hardying's Chronicle', *English Historical Review*, October 1912, p. 749.
9 'Historical Memoranda of John Stowe: On Cade's Rebellion (1450)', *Three Fifteenth-Century Chronicles* pp. 94–5.
10 *J. de Waurin: Anchiennes Chronicques d'Engleterre*, ed. E. Dupont, 1863, III, p. 184.

CHAPTER 11

1 'A Spanish account of the battle of Bosworth', ed. E.M. Nokes and G. Wheeler, *The Ricardian*, No. 36, 1972.

POSTSCRIPT

1 William Caxton, *The Recuyell of the Histories of Troy*, Bruges, 1475.
2 *The Complete Works of Geoffrey Chaucer*, ed. W.W. Skcat, Oxford, 1920, p. 422.

INDEX

Figures in *italics* refer to captions.

D

E